Love that Rescues

Love that Rescues

*God's Fatherly Love
in the Practice of Church Discipline*

ERIC J. BARGERHUFF

WIPF & STOCK · Eugene, Oregon

LOVE THAT RESCUES
God's Fatherly Love in the Practice of Church Discipline

Wipf & Stock
An Imprint of Wipf and Stock Publishers
199 W. 8th Ave., Suite 3
Eugene, OR 97401
www.wipfandstock.com

ISBN 13: 978-1-60608-561-5

Manufactured in the U.S.A.

In memory of my father, Jerry J. Bargerhuff,
whose fatherly love and discipline were a source of affirmation
and encouragement to me and a genuine reflection of the love
I have discovered in my Heavenly Father.

Contents

Acknowledgments

THIS STUDY ORIGINATED AS a doctoral dissertation for my PhD in systematic theology from Trinity Evangelical Divinity School in Deerfield, Illinois. It was completed and successfully defended in the winter of 2004–5 and has been revised and updated for this publication. I am deeply indebted to the professors, pastors, and colleagues who helped shape my mind and heart during those years of intense study at Trinity. I now look back on those years as some of the most enjoyable and formative years of my life and ministry.

It was during these years of study that God began to do a fresh work in my heart. Following the completion of a master of divinity degree, it was my intention to remain in the church as a pastor for a number of years, complete an advanced doctoral degree, and return to the academy to teach. But as the Proverb so aptly reminds us, "Many are the plans in a man's heart, but it is the LORD's purpose that prevails" (Prov 19:21, NIV).

It was during the final year of my doctoral degree while writing a dissertation that I received a phone call requesting that I consider serving as an interim pastor of a church on the North Shore in the northern suburbs of Chicago. Hesitant to put my continued progress on hold or to slow it down, I originally dismissed the idea of serving. But the Spirit had different intentions, and through regular times in the word, private prayer, and conversations with my wife (places where I often hear the Spirit speak), it became increasingly clear that God was calling me to consider this need in his church. Therefore, with a clear sense of calling in my soul, I accepted the role of serving as the interim senior pastor of the Winnetka Bible Church in Winnetka, Illinois, in the summer of 2003. My period of service lasted for fifteen months, and it was life changing. It was through that experience that God grabbed hold of my heart and gave me an even deeper love for the church. To be more specific, I fell in love once again with the preaching and teaching of the word of God and the joys of shepherding God's flock. Further, the experience served to highlight, refine, and cultivate my pastoral gifts.

At the end of my term of service there, I knew that God had called me to continue the ministry of the pulpit and to the shepherding of his flock. What I soon discovered was that this was what was in my heart all along, for even my dissertation was written as a theological reflection geared toward the church. Indeed, the providence of God was written all over those years of study, and upon completion of the degree, I once again returned to pastoral ministry with a renewed sense of purpose and calling.

I owe so much gratitude to my beautiful wife, Gina, who worked hard as the director of student accounting at Trinity during those years of study. Her faithful love, sacrifice, godly counsel and intuition, and unconditional support were amazing, and she continues to play that role even today now as a pastor's wife and mother of two vibrant young boys.

To the leadership and fellow pilgrims at Winnetka Bible Church, I owe you a great deal of thanks for your understanding, unconditional love, and support in helping this project come to fruition. You encouraged me, believed in what I was studying and writing about, and accommodated my schedule needs to make it a reality. I owe much more to you than you possibly know, as God used you all in my life in helping me discern the Lord's will. I am eternally grateful.

I am deeply indebted to my program mentor and teacher, Dr. Wayne Grudem, who truly embodies a pastor's heart as a scholar and teacher. Dr. Grudem impressed upon me the importance of sound biblical scholarship coupled with a love for the church that expresses itself in simple and understandable terms. I had the privilege of serving under him while he was doing some of the final edits for the ESV Bible translation, and it was a humble privilege and pure joy to watch him work. Thank you, my friend.

To my dissertation mentor, Dr. Kevin Vanhoozer, I wish to express my deepest appreciation. His wise counsel, encouraging words, gentle redirections, and incredible knowledge helped fuel my passion for theological reflection and doctrinal precision. He was also one of those who reaffirmed to me the high calling that is pastoral ministry. To the others on my dissertation committee, Drs. Willem VanGemeren and Steve Roy, I thank you for your challenging questions, affirmation, and relational support.

I further wish to thank the leadership of Crossroads Church in Grayslake, Illinois, led by Senior Pastor Steve Farish, who was a source of spiritual nourishment and encouragement to Gina and me during my years of study. It was there that I saw church discipline practiced with love and fidelity and that is no doubt one of the many reasons God has his hand of blessing on that church.

To my friends and brothers in the Lord, Tim Stoner and Tom Schiefer, you both have been my accountability and support in the ministry, and I love you as if you were my own flesh and blood. I further wish my to thank my friend and fellow graduate Dr. Scott Swain, whose conversations about fatherly discipline were extremely beneficial in shaping my view of the subject.

There are countless others who have shaped my life, theological understanding, and love for the church. There are too many to mention. I would like to further dedicate this book to my two sons, Joshua and Andrew Bargerhuff. May I reflect the same kind of love to you that God has shown to me, so that if and when you two become fathers someday, you may bring him glory and praise by the way you love and train your own children.

Preface

I HAVE BEEN IN pastoral ministry in a variety of contexts since my calling
to ministry in 1990 and subsequent entrance to seminary in 1993. It just
so happened that in the fall of the latter year, I lost my earthly father to
congestive heart failure, a loss that leaves a void in my life even to this day.
I truly loved him. Though I rejoiced in my father's promotion to glory as a
man who knew and loved Christ, it was through that grief that I was drawn
into a deeper hunger to know just what it means to say that God is my
Heavenly Father. I therefore began to search through the Scriptures, discov-
ering timeless truths about God that the Spirit began to impress upon my
heart. It was during this private study and conversations with friends that I
began to understand at a much deeper level the love, affirmation, and grace
that is given me through the "fatherly discipline" of God.

There is much to be said about a child hearing the voice of love and
affirmation from his or her father. Such was seemingly the case even for
our Lord. When God the Father audibly spoke and affirmed the Son at
Jesus' baptism, there is no doubt that this had everything to do with sub-
stantiating his life, ministry, authority, and unique relationship to God
the Father to all those who were there that day. Yet at a human level, I
can't help but wonder if the thirty-year-old man who no longer had an
earthly father found that heavenly voice as a comfort and timely word of
affirmation before his entrance into the ministry.

This is where fatherly discipline plays a significant role as a voice of
affirmation, a way of legitimizing our true adoption as God's people (Heb
12:8), while at the same time training us for the greater good that is the
increasingly holy and God-glorifying life of a true disciple (Heb 12:5–11).
My journey of understanding fatherly discipline naturally began to merge
with my experiences in pastoral ministry. I observed that there was a significant lapse in teaching on the subject of discipline, both formative and
corrective. Yet if this was one of God's chosen means to affirm, nurture,
and train disciples and the church's ministry is a ministry of reconciliation

and discipleship, then choosing to teach about it and enact it is a matter of faithfulness. It is a necessary component of any church that claims to be a herald of the gospel message.

There are many and varied reasons as to why the evangelical church of today is noticeably weak in areas. That, in and of itself, is a subject for other books. But this book seeks to inform us of one noticeably glaring omission in the ministry of the church—the practice of biblical church discipline. To be sure, the subject may make one immediately recoil, since the word "discipline" carries no shortage of emotional baggage and negative connotations. But this work aims to correct all of that so that we can rightly understand the intentions of a loving God who has chosen to use church discipline in dynamic ways in accordance with his redemptive purposes. In the individualistic and relativistic culture the church ministers to and finds itself in, it is all the more important to rediscover the corporate identity and accountability that comes from being a people "set apart" for God. The gospel of God's glory and grace is the message we proclaim; it is a message of salvation through repentance and faith. And if this is to be faithfully proclaimed as a message of life to a sinful world, then that very same message of repentance and faith must also be embraced as a way of life for the redeemed of God. It is my contention that church discipline, rightly understood, practiced, and appropriated, is key in that endeavor.

Introduction: Living Theologically in the Church

A PRIMARY CRITICISM DIRECTED toward Christian academia and scholarship is that it often produces material that only reaches and engages the theological elite. The layperson who seeks to understand and encounter God in his or her daily life and ongoing place of worship is said to be often overlooked. If true, this would seemingly perpetuate a despairing gap between the academy and the church.

Yet the opposite critique has also been voiced as well. Some think that the evangelical church of today is guilty of focusing primarily on the attainment of an "experience" with God devoid of any profound theological reflection, dialogue, or foundation. Further, the critics asserts that the average Christian on the street rarely reflects upon the doctrines of God or his attributes, names, and nature, as well the ways in which we acquire that knowledge. The result is that we have pragmatism (an emphasis on "what works" in today's culture) coming at the expense of theological fidelity. John Armstrong asserts that the church for way too long has been preoccupied "with everything from revivalism to church growth" and that this focus "has almost sterilized our schools and churches to serious doctrinal reflection, especially in written form."[1]

In spite of (or maybe *because of*) these criticisms from both sides, a newfound dialogue is surfacing today. It is becoming evident that the academy is seeking to engage the church in an attempt to bridge this perceived gap. The hopeful result is that the mind, the heart, and the daily walk can be connected in a more holistic manner within the community of faith. John Feinberg notes:

> As Paul wrote to Timothy, God has given divine revelation for
> many purposes, including ones that necessitate doing theology,

1. Armstrong, "The Trinity: What and Why?," 9.

but the ultimate reason for giving divine revelation and for theologians doing theology is that the people of God may be fitted for every good work (2 Tim 3:16–17).[2]

The doctrine of God has to be understood as more than a mere assent to cognitive truth claims. The truths *about God* have implications *on us* both in an individual and corporate sense. Paul consistently weaved together the knowledge with everyday living all the time, and this can easily be seen in many of his pastoral prayers for the church (i.e., Col 1:9–12). So there cannot be a separation between them. Theology must take root and reveal itself in church life, especially in its worship and concrete, biblical practices. This is one of the primary arguments and basic assumptions that serve as the foundation for a recent series of essays edited by James J. Buckley and David S. Yeago found in *Knowing the Triune God: The Work of the Spirit in the Practices of the Church*. In these essays, the authors aim to bring theology and practice together, arguing that biblically speaking, there is no such thing as head knowledge of the truth that is divorced from the "faith, worship, and godly life of all who are incorporated into Christ as members of His body."[3]

Therefore, one of the primary goals of the formal discipline known as "systematic theology" should be to do this very task—to bring a deeper theological understanding of God into the practical life and ministry of the church. Our theology, daily walks, and church practices must inform, interact, and shape one another.[4] This, according to Millard Erickson, must be an inseparable and ongoing reality, for "our theological beliefs affect the nature of our relationship with the Lord."[5] Indeed, we are to think biblically and theologically so that we, by God's grace, may live faithfully and obediently as the children of God in a foreign world.

2. Feinberg, *No One Like Him*, xxiii.

3. Torrance, *The Trinitarian Faith*, 33; quoted in Buckley and Yeago, *Knowing the Triune God*, 9.

4. As evangelicals, our biblical theology must be derived from a sound literal, grammatical, historical exegesis of the text. Bernard Ramm has pointed out the significance of theology for the Christian life when he writes, "To the evangelical, *theology is a matter of life and death, vindication or judgment, to be in the love of God or under the wrath of God.* Theology must then be built on the most absolute foundation possible—the revelation of God in Scripture. And that revelation can only be known by the evangelical's becoming an expert in the exegesis of Scripture and a master of its contents" (emphasis mine). Ramm, *The Evangelical Heritage*, 154.

5. Erickson, *Where Is Theology Going?*, 12.

APPREHENDING THE TRIUNE GOD
IN THE LIFE OF THE CHURCH

For the Christian, experiencing and knowing God in one sense means that one acknowledges the implicit testimony of Scripture that God is triune and exists in three persons as the Father, Son, and Holy Spirit. Through faith in the person and work of the Son, we have access to the Father, who brings us into union with Christ by the power and work of the Holy Spirit, who sustains and carries on to completion the work of God within us. Although all evangelicals would acknowledge these truths, we have paid very little attention to them.[6] The full ramifications of worshiping and living in covenant relationship with a God who makes himself known in Triune fashion has escaped serious contemplation in many evangelical circles. For those who are steeped in the self-serving pursuit of pragmatism and cultural relevancy, it may seem to serve no practical purpose. However, this neglect of theological reflection on the Triune nature of God and its practical relevance for our lives is without a doubt a crucial error in our understanding of the nature of the Christian life. It is important for us to consider not only how we *understand* but also *how we experience* God as the Father, Son, and Holy Spirit so that *our actions* are to be intimately tied to the fullest biblical expression of the *nature and purposes* of God.[7] This, after all, is what it means to reflect him on earth.

For example, as we show love, it is to be a reflection of the love that we ourselves receive from God (1 John 4:7–12). If we receive comfort and compassion from him, we are to manifest this in relation to others (2 Cor 1:3–7). In doing so, we are reflecting the reality of our participation in the divine nature of which the Apostle Peter spoke (2 Pet 1:3, 4). Christ is in us, and we are in him. This is the spiritual union that will naturally bear

---

6. For an interesting discussion and lament of the apparent lack of evangelical reflection on the Trinity, see Bray, "Evangelicals Losing Their Way," in Armstrong, *The Compromised Church*, 53–65.

7. The Apostle Paul reminded us of our union with and experience of the Triune God in his farewell to the church in Corinth, where he says, "May the grace of the Lord Jesus Christ, and the love of God, and the fellowship of the Holy Spirit be with you all" (2 Cor 13:14, NIV). Unfortunately, many Christians may view God somewhat modalistically, seeing the Father as the God of the Old Testament, the Son as the God of the New Testament and Church Age, and the Holy Spirit as simply God's "presence" in a mystical way.

fruit as we travel the road of progressive sanctification and become more like him in ever-increasing glory (2 Cor 3:18).

In sum, the Bible states that our relationship to and experience of God is intimately connected with who we are (our identity) and what we do (our works). If this is not the case, then our faith is null and void (Jas 2:17, 18). And further, we should understand that participating in the divine nature as we live the Christian life is no less than a participation in the spiritual union we have with a *Triune God*, a God who has chosen to announce and enact His redemptive purposes *through us* as we faithfully live and proclaim the gospel. Today he chooses to tangibly express and communicate the reconciling love of Christ through his Spirit-embodied church. In fact, Paul called us "Christ's ambassadors in the ministry of reconciliation" (2 Cor 5:18–20).

PURPOSE OF THIS STUDY AND THESIS STATEMENT

As we turn our attention to this "divine life" lived out in the church, we have stated that due to our spiritual union with God and each other, we become part of the means through which God has chosen to work out his redemptive plan on the earth. This gives added emphasis on making sure that what we do in the church is in keeping with the truth about God and his ways as prescribed from Scripture. We should therefore reflect upon everything we do (or are not doing) to make sure it is in keeping with the truth revealed to us. It is from this idea that the purpose of this work emerges.

There is one essential biblical practice of the church that is in desperate need of practical and *theological* reflection. Currently, there is a void within evangelicalism with respect to the biblical practice of church discipline, as well as its relationship to the doctrine and purposes of God, who, as our heavenly Father, longs to see his adopted children live in faithful obedience to his will. George B. Davis provides an initial definition of church discipline when he writes:

> Church discipline, properly defined, refers the faithful application
> of biblical principles and procedures within a local congregation
> to preserve doctrinal purity, holiness of life, and useful efficiency
> among its membership.[8]

8. Davis, "Whatever Happened to Church Discipline?," 345. Davis further notes that a "logical progression exists in the matter of discipline: (1) parental discipline, (2) self-discipline, (3) corporate or church discipline, and (4) divine discipline. A breakdown in any one of the first three will result in a demonstration of the fourth." Ibid., 359.

We will define what these "principles and procedures" are in this book, but our initial observation is this: *few churches actually practice church discipline properly, if at all, and this has caused the church to lapse into moral decay and relativism, a mirror image of the culture we live in.*

R. Albert Mohler Jr., president of Southern Seminary in Louisville, Kentucky, has remarked that "the decline of church discipline is perhaps the most visible failure of the contemporary church."[9] What was once a "mark of the church," according to many Reformation theologians, is now simply something that is misunderstood and ignored altogether in many contemporary Christian circles.[10] One author argues that our current socio-political situation may have something to do with it. Maurice Martin remarks:

> The factor which probably creates the greatest dissonance is the preponderant individualism of our society which militates against effective covenantal relationships in the congregation. Our historic faith is informed out of the first century biblical world and the sixteenth century European society, both pre-democratic societies. The covenantal view of the church falls on rockier soil in our contemporary democratic and increasingly individualistic society. Hence part of the burden is the difficulty of translating the vision into current practice.[11]

There is a consumer mentality in many churchgoers today, which reveals itself in a lack of commitment to a specific faith community (local church). Couple this with increasing biblical illiteracy, doctrinal confusion, individualism, rampant moral decay, and relativism, and there is no surprise that the idea of church discipline seems strange and utterly

9. Mohler, "Church Discipline: The Missing Mark," 16.

10. Davis asks, "Can a local church conscientiously claim to be following a NT pattern if it knowingly ignores the biblical mandate for church discipline?" Davis, "Whatever Happened to Church Discipline?," 345. Mark Dever builds off of the Reformation concept of the "marks" of the church as he expounds on what makes a sound, healthy, and biblical church today. The proper use of church discipline is one of the marks he lists in a recent text. See his Nine Marks of a Healthy Church, 153–79. Further, it is significant to note that within the introduction to the aforementioned work of Buckley and Yeago, there is no mention of church discipline in their list of practices covered among their contributors, which may be a reflection of the current trends of neglecting to think theologically about discipline as a Spirit-embodied practice in the church. To their credit, however, they state that they "have not aimed to agree on a comprehensive list of practices, or a theory thereof." Buckley and Yeago, Knowing the Triune God, 12.

11. Martin, "The Pure Church: The Burden of Anabaptism," 31.

ridiculous in certain circles. For some postmodern Christians, church discipline may be out of the question if a church wants to "grow" or be "successful" according to today's secular standards.[12]

Unfortunately, this is not a new train of thought. Maria Pascuzzi argues that similar cultural forces were at work in New Testament Corinth, which added to that church's apathy toward sin and lack of action to enact church discipline on the immoral brother of 1 Corinthians 5.[13] Further, Pascuzzi asserts that Paul's correctives speak loudly to us today.

> Some of the key implications emerging from [the] message of 1 Cor5 [sic] with regard to Christian moral living stand as challenges to three symptoms of the exercise of freedom skewed by radical individualism that are discernable today: *moral relativism, the denial of the social significance of individual acts and the abdication of responsibility on the part of the communities* (emphasis mine).[14]

Biblical church discipline involves the difficult task of discernment, often leads to uncomfortable conflict and confrontation, and carries with it a level of accountability to which few are willing to commit. In a pluralistic, non-judgmental culture where sin in many ways has been redefined, few see this as an expression of brotherly love, or for that matter, even the love of God. This is because God's love has been misconstrued in today's culture. According to D. A. Carson, the love of God is seemingly becoming more detached and less identifiable with the biblical witness and testimony about God. In his powerful book, *The Difficult Doctrine of the Love of God,* where he briefly summarizes the differing ways that the Bible speaks of the God's love, he writes:

> I do not think that what the Bible says about the love of God can long survive at the forefront of our thinking if it is abstracted from

12. Davis further argues that the neglect of church discipline is due to "a denial of the biblical mandate, the demand for perfection [in its implementation, which few churches think they could achieve], the wrong interpretation of some passages of scripture [sic], the abuse of church discipline in the past, the appearance of a non-loving spirit, the lack of 'models,' and the difficulty of the task." Davis, "Whatever Happened to Church Discipline?," 346.

13. Pascuzzi argues that Paul's challenge to and battle with the Corinthians over their lack of discipline of the immoral brother was due in large part to the church's tolerance of moral relativism that stemmed from their "*ethos* and ethics of radical individualism within which the Corinthians community operated." Pascuzzi, *Ethics, Ecclesiology and Church Discipline,* 197.

14. Ibid., 198.

the sovereignty of God, the holiness of God, the wrath of God, the providence of God, or the personhood of God—to mention only a few nonnegotiable elements of basic Christianity.[15]

All of these attributes and actions of God must be held together, lest we distort his nature and character and misunderstand his saving activity. In the same way, if church discipline is not rightly seen as an expression of God's love, then it will inevitably be erroneously construed as an oppressive, intolerant, divisive, and harsh expression of human power.[16] It will be viewed as a presumptuous and arrogant practice whereby it is wrong to sit in *any* form of judgment upon someone else. A skepticism of authority and the desire for moral autonomy lie behind this type of thinking. "Judge not, lest you be judged," is the verbal objection given, which is often taken out of biblical context and misapplied.[17] The responsibility to judge, it is reasoned, is given to God alone, who is the only one who has the authority to exercise discipline or judgment.

Herein lies the problem, for the objection assumes that the church practice commanded in the New Testament is completely separated from the Triune God's saving activity and specifically the presence of the indwelling Holy Spirit, whose task, among others, is to lead and guide the Christian into all truth. This truth is not merely a cognitive assent to propositional facts but an embodied way of personal and communal life encompassing morality and doctrine.[18] Church discipline, in many ways,

15. Carson, *The Difficult Doctrine of the Love of God,* 11. Tony Lane, in a recent essay, addresses today's popular postmodern and problematic view of love and how it is irreconcilable with other biblical concepts that need to be kept in balance and maintained, such as God's wrath. His essay presents some helpful correctives with respect to the nature of God's love that assist us in our development of a theology of discipline. See Lane, "The Wrath of God as an Aspect of the Love of God," in *Nothing Greater, Nothing Better,* 138–67. For instance, Lane asserts that "God's role in judgment is not merely passive." Ibid., 158.

16. The French philosopher Michel Foucault argues that the church uses and abuses power in order to get people to conform. For him, this is the source of the modern disciplinary society. Cf. Foucault, *Discipline and Punish.*

17. This citation from Matthew 7:1 is perhaps one of the most common objections to the idea of church discipline among today's Christians. We will look at this passage in more detail in chapter 6. Mark Dever, in commenting on the misuse of this passage, states, "Could it be that, in our day, a misunderstanding of Matthew 7:1 has been a shield for sin and has worked to prevent the kind of congregational life that was known by the churches of an earlier day, and could be known by us again?" Dever, "Biblical Church Discipline," 39.

18. The goal of this leading of the Holy Spirit is to direct us into a right relationship with God, each other, and his creation. We must understand that at the root of the Christian life is the necessity to make judgments and practice discernment on a day-to-

is about the ability of Christianity to make "truth claims." As John Roth
has argued:

> Religiously-oriented people in the United States and Canada are
> embracing a kind of generic Christianity cut free from historical
> traditions, doctrinal claims, or clearly defined ethical norms.[19]

The postmodern epistemological "crisis," if you will, that challenges
anyone who may attempt make a universal truth claim is connected to the
current mindset that rejects the church's authority to "stake a claim" about
God or individual morality. But the church, as "the pillar and foundation
of the truth" (1 Tim 3:15), inevitably has to be able to make truth claims
that will affect the way Christians are called to behave and believe in the
community of faith.[20]

In summarizing the ecclesiology and thought of the Martin Luther,
Reinhard Hütter describes how specific church practices (of which church
discipline is a part) are to be uniquely linked with the knowledge and
saving work of God.[21] He emphasizes the role of the Spirit in Luther's
ecclesiology (doctrine of life in the church) and writes:

---

day basis. It is hypocritical judging that Jesus is addressing in his rebuke of the Pharisees
(Matt 7:1–6). As believers, we are emphatically called to make judgments between right
and wrong, who is caught in sin and is in need of salvation, and how we are to treat
moral and doctrinal issues with respect to individuals in the church. The Apostle Paul
exclaimed, "I say this to shame you. Is it possible that there is nobody among you wise
enough to judge a dispute between believers?" (1 Cor 6:5, NIV). Thus we must exercise
discernment and the wisdom of Christ daily.

19. Roth, "The Church 'Without Spot or Wrinkle' in Anabaptist Experience," in Koop
and Schertz, *Without Spot or Wrinkle*, 22.

20. Yet this is not arbitrary, for "a theological truth claim will ultimately be about *the
Word of God* and the difference it makes to human being" (emphasis mine). Vanhoozer,
"The Trials of Truth: Mission, Martyrdom, and the Epistemology of the Cross," in Kirk
and Vanhoozer, *To Stake a Claim*, 124.

21. Luther identified seven marks of the church: the proclamation of God's word and
its reception in faith, confession, and deed; baptism; the Lord's Supper; office of the keys;
ordination/offices; prayer/doxology/catechesis; and the way of the cross/discipleship.
Hütter calls these the "core practices" of the church and says that they can be warranted
christologically and are "normed by the proclamation and teaching of the gospel as it is
specified in doctrine." This may need further exploration and clarification, but the point
he seeks to make is clear, that the ecclesial life as set forth by the New Testament is not
devoid of the embodiment or work of the Spirit. As found in Hütter, "The Church, The
Knowledge of the Triune God: Practices, Doctrine, Theology," in Buckley and Yeago,
Knowing the Triune God, 34–35. It is the "office of the keys" that Luther identifies that
denotes the "core practice" of church discipline. See Hütter, ibid., 34, n. 36. For the au-

Luther opens the avenue toward a *pneumatological ecclesiology:* the church is to be understood as a web of core practices which at the same time mark and constitute the church. These practices are the Spirit's works through which the Holy Spirit enacts his sanctifying mission in the triune economy of salvation.[22]

It is a major contention of this book that the practice of church discipline is an extension of the Triune God's saving work along the path of authentic discipleship. This discipline is informed by the parameters of Scripture and is a means by which God, in his covenant love, maintains ethical and doctrinal purity in his church, while expressing his forgiveness, restoration, and reconciling love toward the children of God. The following thesis statement will be our working hypothesis: *The church, as an embodiment of Christ empowered by the Holy Spirit, is authorized and obliged to exercise discipline as an expression of God's "fatherly" love toward the company of his redeemed children. When the church fails to do so, it is withholding one of God's prescribed actions for the church whereby he embodies his forgiveness, grace, and love.*

Within this book the parameters and controls of church discipline that are specified and established in Scripture are set forth, as well as church discipline's function as a means that God uses to transform our lives. A necessary distinction between judgment, discipline, and punishment is made, as well as a discussion as to what extent church discipline can be connected to the forgiveness and discipline of God. Discipline indeed can be qualified as God's "fatherly" love displayed through the church's actions. Historical considerations, exegesis, theological integration and reflection, and practical application shape the argument of the thesis. Our goal will be to take a redemptive historical approach to the matter of divine discipline so that we might see how God uses discipline in the process of working out his plan for his people.

---

thority to practice "binding and loosing" in matters of discipline and forgiveness given to Peter and the church is given by Jesus (Matt 16:18–19; Matt 18:15–18). We will look at this further in our biblical theology of church discipline in chapter 6.

22. Ibid., 35. Martin Jeschke, in his text on church discipline, argues that church discipline is none other than a "renewed presentation of the gospel message to the impenitent persons in that it confronts them with the truth." Jeschke, *Discipling in the Church*, 88. Therefore, it has soteriological concerns.

CHAPTER OUTLINES

Chapter 2 officially opens the study through historical investigations. Our goal in this chapter is to take a cursory look at how the church has understood the nature and purpose of church discipline at various points in its history. We will see that there are distinguishable positions regarding how discipline is to be carried out, as well as differing positions on the severity of the action. One classic argument for the church to practice discipline as an expression of God's love is found in St. Augustine's treatise *On the Correction of the Donatists*. Here Augustine sets forth his case for the use of force to Count Boniface, who upon the order of the emperor was enforcing imperial laws against the Donatists, a schismatic sect.[23] Augustine argued that enforced behavior had the power to humble, to educate, and to bring spiritual reconciliation, and that the enforcement of the imperial laws (church and state were united at this time) was no less than an extension of God's mercy. We will discover that Augustine frequently talked about church discipline's nature and purpose and note how his position gradually changed from the use of rhetoric, writing, and decree to the endorsement of state-sponsored force. An evaluation and critique of Augustine's view of church discipline concludes this section.

Several church traditions have a history of understanding of divine discipline and its applicability to the church. We take a look at a few of the main advocates who are especially noteworthy due to their understanding of the nature and authority of the church and how discipline is a crucial element in the believer's relationship to God.[24] A significant tradition that is worthy of investigation is that of the radical reformers of the Protestant reformation known as the Anabaptists. In light of their view of the cultural and ecclesial situation and corruption at the time of the Reformation, church discipline became a key biblical issue and a litmus test for faithfulness within this tradition. The theme of church discipline permeates the writings of many of the leaders of the movement, especially Menno Simons, leader of the Mennonites. For them it was an essential mark of

---

23. Tilley, "Anti-Donatist Works," in Fitzgerald, *Augustine through the Ages*, 36.

24. To be sure, there are several other traditions that would make contributions to our study, but I have selectively chosen only a few due to their unique history with church discipline, as we show in our study. As John D. Roth has stated with respect to the Anabaptists, "To stand with the Anabaptist-Mennonite tradition virtually demands that one engage the question of church discipline." Roth, "The Church 'Without Spot or Wrinkle' in Anabaptist Experience," 15.

the church, with the intention of restoring a "wayward member to a fuller understanding of faith, discipleship, and relations within the fellowship of believers."[25] The Anabaptists provide a crucial historical contribution to our thesis due to their convictions that *knowing Christ and his love* is so intimately connected to life and discipline in the church.

John Calvin, a significant Reformer, differs on the matter of church discipline with Menno Simons as to its degree and kind and even states that the magistrate and the church should complement one another in discipline. He was critical of the hyper-zealousness that he perceived among the Anabaptists with regard to discipline. However, this did not stop Calvin from being a strong advocate of it, and though he did not officially regard it as a "mark" of the church, he does link it strongly to the ordinances (word and sacrament) that are an essential and mandatory part of ecclesial life.

Finally, our chapter concludes with a brief look at someone from the liberal church tradition, Friedrich Schleiermacher. We take a look at how discipline is understood in the context of a tradition that views religious experience as possessing more authority than Scripture.

Our exegetical study of discipline will commence in our third chapter as we begin our redemptive historical look at divine discipline. In this chapter we seek to gain an understanding of the complexity of divine discipline as seen in the Old Testament. We survey the roles of corporate discipline, as well as individual discipline, and how both anticipate a resolution found in the cross. Further, we will give special attention to the discipline of Israel as a nation, King David and his royal line, as well as certain individuals who felt the chastening hand of God. We will discover that we can learn much from their respective experiences about the complexities, nature, and purposes of divine discipline.[26] It is apparent that discipline can have more than one purpose or multiple senses (e.g., instruction, testing, or punishment) depending on context, but is undoubtedly a way in which God expresses his covenant love to his children. Special attention is given to relevant passages to our thesis, such as Deuteronomy 8, Proverbs 3, and 2 Samuel 7, to name a few. We will fur-

25. Roth, "The Church 'Without Spot or Wrinkle' in Anabaptist Experience," 13.

26. Our goal is to develop and assess the viability of a biblical theology of discipline without collapsing or importing the individual nuances that are found in each context, in order to avoid what linguists call "illegitimate totality transfer."

ther distinguish the difference between the discipline that believers incur and the judgment of God that falls upon the unbelieving and wicked.

Chapter 4 introduces a discussion of a significant theological issue that is discovered when one takes a close look at divine discipline in Scripture—and this is the idea of discipline being designated as a "fatherly discipline." The metaphor of God disciplining as a father is found in multiple texts (Deut 8:5; 2 Sam 7:14; Ps 89; Prov 3:11–12; Heb 12:4–11) and would suggest that discipline is closely linked to and based on our relationship with God and how we are to see him. Yet this is problematic for many, especially feminists, who object to such a "patriarchal" metaphor. Therefore, we answer some of those objections by noting what this metaphor does and does not communicate about God in specific contexts, building off of the works of Janet Soskice and Christopher Seitz. We will see that the idea of God as a "father" is not overtly used in the Old Testament. But when it is used, it is seemingly very purposeful.

In a constructive sense, we explore the extent to which divine discipline is necessarily "fatherly," as this makes a significant difference as to how we are to view and accept the discipline that comes from God, who is "treating us as sons" (Heb 12:7). Furthermore, it would seem that the "fatherhood" of God helps to form a conceptual bridge that crosses redemption history that assists us in understanding the nature of our relationship to our Redeemer and his purposes for us in discipline as his adopted children. For as Marianne Meye Thompson has argued, to speak of God as father

> . . . is to speak of how God has acted and continues to act with respect to humankind, and to do so concretely in terms, images, and actions appropriate to the relationship of a father and child in the historical contexts in which the scriptures were written. With respect to the world of the scriptures, to speak of God as father is to evoke a narrative of birth, care, and provision, love and mercy, and of promise and redemption.[27]

The fifth chapter deals with the culmination and resolution of divine discipline, as we look at the significance of the cross of Christ on our understanding of discipline (now practiced in the church) in this new era

27. Thompson, *The Promise of the Father*, 166. Later in chapter 6, we will see how these ideas of love, mercy, and reconciliation are embodied in New Testament church discipline, which will help substantiate the connection of the doctrine of God with the practices of the church.

of redemption history. Specifically, we will see that there is no longer any room for the punitive (or retributive) sense of discipline for God's people in light of the penal substitutionary atonement for believers achieved by Christ on the cross.[28] Therefore, this substantiates our claim that church discipline, as a practice of the forgiven and redeemed community, cannot be seen as punishment, since the judicial retribution for sin has already been atoned for. To be sure, we argue that church discipline is a practice of the church that embodies and proclaims God's forgiveness. It is an expression of God's forgiveness in communicative action.

In our sixth and final constructive chapter, we seek to develop a constructive biblical theology of church discipline that builds on all that we have discovered from our previous chapters. Knowing that discipline is a way in which God expresses his reconciling love to his children as our heavenly Father, and that the cross of Christ serves as the ground of forgiveness due to its penal substitutionary atonement, divine discipline as manifested through the church becomes a reconciliatory and restorative action and a means that the heavenly Father uses to express his covenant love. As God has now chosen to work his redemptive purposes (saving activity) through the Spirit-embodied community of faith, the practice of church discipline is uniquely linked with those purposes in keeping with the message of the gospel and a life of discipleship.

This chapter also surveys the teaching of Jesus in Matthew 18, along with the Pauline application in 1 Corinthians 5, as the essential building blocks of developing a biblical theology of church discipline.[29] Through exegesis and theological reflection, we will discover the nature, purpose, and end goals of church discipline, along with its parameters as outlined from Scripture. The authority and mandate to carry out this reconciliatory practice is given by Christ himself to the church as the "power of the keys." Further, when the community refuses to act in keeping with its charge to discipline, the removal of God's blessings and in extreme cases, the affliction of divine judgment may ensue.

---

28. Should this view of atonement be abandoned, as is happening in some evangelical circles, it may necessitate seeing church discipline as retributive in nature (since retributive justice would not have been met on the cross). However, this does not seem compatible with the New Testament texts concerning church discipline. We will provide a brief defense of PSA as a viable biblical model and critique some of the arguments of its critics.

29. To be sure, we survey all that the New Testament says regarding church discipline.

Our conclusion to this study will summarize our findings and succinctly reiterate the primary argument that our thesis asserts. Additionally, we will take a look at some examples of church discipline and suggest some possible theological and practical ramifications of our study. If our thesis is correct, then a fundamental understanding of church discipline as a practice intimately linked to the doctrine of God and his redemptive purposes is in order, and this ought to profoundly call the church to theological reflection, action, and faithfulness on this oft-misunderstood church practice.

2

Historical Considerations of the Nature
of Divine Discipline as Practiced in the Church

A S WE BEGIN OUR study, it is necessary that we ask the following question: how has the church understood divine discipline and its role within the church throughout the history of the faith? To be sure, it is beyond the scope of this work to do complete justice to this question, yet it is necessary that we look at significant historical figures and traditions who have expressed their views regarding the *nature* of divine discipline as manifested in the church, for we are surrounded by a great cloud of witnesses who have gone before us. We will select a few traditions that have tended to place emphasis on church discipline as an expression of the grace and mercy of God as well as an essential element in the believer's relationship with the Lord.

AUGUSTINE AND CHURCH DISCIPLINE

Perhaps one of the most significant theologians who dealt with this issue firsthand was St. Augustine, the fourth-century bishop of Hippo who spent much of his time combating a heretical sect known as the Donatists. The Donatist controversy has its roots in periods long before Augustine broke on the scene, but he was thrust into the middle of the controversy and became the preeminent spokesperson for the church in North Africa and confronted Donatism at all levels.

Briefly, the Donatists were a sect that broke off from of the North African branch of the church and claimed legitimacy as the only *true church* of Jesus Christ. These Donatist "Christians" originated in the early part of the fourth century after the persecution of Christians under the emperor Diocletian. The following recounts their story.

When the violent persecution had subsided, many Christians were at odds as to what to do with those who had committed the heinous sin of "turning over" the sacred Scriptures, which were subsequently burned by the Roman authorities. Those who handed over the Scriptures gained the reputation of being "apostate," and their sinful actions were known in Latin as *traditio*, which means to "hand over or surrender." To be sure, many had *refused* to hand over the Scriptures and commit this "sin," and this cost them their very lives. Others, however, succumbed to the persecution and renounced the faith and handed over the Scriptures in order to be spared death. Unfortunately, many of these who succumbed were bishops, priests, and laity in the North African region of Numidia.

As a result, those who succumbed were essentially seen as traitors by the Donatists, and they opposed them and anything connected with them. They objected to readmitting these "lapsed" Christians back into the church unless they were willing to be rebaptized, a rather graceless posture.[1]

The informal division became more formal in the church when a controversial incident took place. A man named Caecilian, a deacon in the church in Carthage, was ordained as the new bishop of that church sometime between 308 and 311. The "Donatists" (who were not yet labeled that at the time) objected that he was illegitimately consecrated by bishops who had committed the heinous sin of *traditio*. Therefore a rival bishop named Majorinus was elected as bishop, of whom Donatus (whom the movement was later named after) became the successor. Now, with two rival bishops in Carthage, the church was in a formal schism. There were the Catholics (this is pre-Reformation) and their rivals, the "Donatists," a designation rejected by the dissidents, who would have preferred to simply be called Christians, since in their minds they were the only true church.[2]

1. This custom was common and debated in the African church for years dating back to the time of St. Cyprian of Carthage in the middle of the third century, who dealt with the issue after the Decian persecution. The zeal for church purity is admirable, but it must not forget or deny the actual state of believers on the "already not yet" road of sanctification or the presence of the Spirit in the life of the church. For a helpful historical and theological summary of the ideas and events leading up and pertaining to the Donatist schism, see Keleher, *Saint Augustine's Notion of Schism in the Donatist Controversy*, 11–26; Markus, "Donatus, Donatism," in Fitzgerald, *Augustine Through the Ages*, 284–7; Frend, *The Donatist Church*, 1–24; and Corcoran, *Augustinas Contra Donatistas*, 15–50. Peter Brown's biography also gives a detailed sketch of the attitudes of the North African church that helped fuel the schism of Donatism. See his *Augustine of Hippo*, 207–21.

2. Markus, "Donatus, Donatism," 285. Indeed, the nature of the church was a primary

Throughout the region of Numidia in North Africa and the entire Roman Empire, the Donatists grew in great numbers. However, an appeal by the Donatists to the Emperor to recognize their legitimacy backfired as a council convened at Arles in 314 declared Donatism an official schismatic sect and condemned any required rebaptism. The council declared in effect:

> The spiritual standing of the one who ministered the sacraments does not in any way render the sacrament valid or invalid.[3]

Therefore, with the doctrine of God's grace upheld, the Donatists suffered a formal, legal blow to their cause.[4] This, however, did not quiet them, and Donatism began not only to have religious but political activists as well.[5] Some extreme branches of the Donatists known as *Circumcelliones* may rightly be called terrorists. They were a radical group who would go to great lengths, using violence and warfare to destroy Catholic influence and churches, and even beat or murder priests.[6] A few would go as far as

---

issue in the debate with the Donatists, who felt that Christ's true church was restricted to North Africa. Further, their denial of the doctrine of God's grace to those who repented after committing *traditio* was a central point of contention in this controversy. Augustine comments with disgust over their attitude when he states, "The clouds roll with thunder, that the House of the Lord shall be built throughout the earth: and these frogs sit in their marsh and croak—We are the only Christians!" As found in Brown, *Biography*, 217.

3. Marshall, *The Restless Heart*, 117. For more on the Donatists' position on sin in the priesthood and Augustine's response, see Crespin, *Ministère et Sainteté*, 207–80.

4. One can assert that God's grace has been upheld in that Scripture declares that we believers possess the treasure of the Gospel in "jars of clay" (2 Cor 4:7) so that it can be seen that its power comes from God and not sinful humanity. It is only by God's grace that he uses human beings to accomplish his purposes, whether this is through acts of service or administering the ordinances. Augustine often argued against the Donatists, who were claiming the absolute necessity of the purity of the priest, as noted earlier (i.e., that the priest cannot be tainted by sin, especially that of *traditio*). Augustine claimed that all of us were sinners saved by grace, and he countered the Donatists by using the words of 1 John 1:8, where in writing to the church the apostle claimed that the one who claims to be without sin is self-deceived. See his "Answer to Letters of Petilian, Bishop of Cirta, Ch.106.241," in Schaff, *Nicene and Post-Nicene Fathers of the Christian Church*, 593.

5. Marshall, *The Restless Heart*, 117.

6. Marshall recalls a horrifying incident done by the *Circumcelliones* to the bishop of Bagai, who had left the Donatists and converted to Catholicism. The bishop was captured, forced to watch his cathedral burned, and then stabbed and thrown off the church tower, falling in a heap of dung (which ironically saved his life). The bishop would eventually recover to testify against the Donatists. For other examples of such violence by the *Circumcelliones* and Donatists, see Merdinger, *Rome and the African Church in the*

suicide, with the desire to seek a type of "martyrdom" rather than submit to the imperial laws. Their resistance to Catholic and imperial persuasion (the church and the state were united at this time) made the schism an ugly scene, and their violence would eventually lead Augustine, the Catholic bishop of Hippo, to speak in favor of the harsh discipline of the state that was employed against the radical sect. Coercion was often used in order to suppress the schism and condemn their heresy, and though Donatism long survived Augustine, it was no longer to be found on the North African map by the sixth century, thanks in part to Augustine's efforts.[7]

Augustine's attitude toward the Donatists and the nature of discipline is a worthwhile focus in our historical understanding of divine discipline. This is because the bishop of Hippo wrote several treatises against Donatist leaders and many letters to Imperial officials discussing the nature of church discipline.[8] Though his was a unique situation in that church and state were united during this time, Augustine nonetheless deals with the theology of discipline, and he spells out why discipline is an act of grace and love toward those who have fallen away from the faith or into sin.

Augustine's writings span many different years and contexts. Yet one of the more telling pieces of literature he wrote on the discipline of the Donatists is found in what is known as "Epistle 185," also entitled *The Correction of the Donatists*, written by Augustine to Count Boniface, the tribune and later the count of Africa in 417.[9] Boniface was in charge of enforcing the imperial laws against the Donatists and inquired of Augustine about the nature of Donatism. The result of his inquiry was a fully stated case by Augustine against the schismatic sect, a recounting of

---

Time of Augustine, 102. It is beyond the scope of this work to trace the entire history of the schism, its major events, theological issues, and primary players, for our focus is now to be turned toward Augustine's attitude with respect to the discipline of this sect. But understanding some of the history of the sect and its actions is vital in understanding how Augustine developed his thought on the topic of divine and church discipline.

7. Markus, "Donatus, Donatism," 285.

8. Frend notes that "the energy with which he pursued them is remarkable. From his first discussions with the local Donatist clergy during his presbyterate until his final exchanges with Gaudentius of Thamugadi, not a year passes without some anti-Donatist tract or sermon." Frend, *The Donatist Church*, 228.

9. Our survey will also include other letters and writings of Saint Augustine (especially "Letter 93") that will help us piece together his theology of discipline, though "Epistle 185" will be our primary focus due to its significant ability to contribute to the task at hand.

their violence, and the nature and purpose of the discipline that, according Augustine, had providentially been imposed upon them.

Early on in his battle against the Donatists, Augustine sought to use reason alone with the schismatic Donatists in an attempt to bring them "back to orthodoxy through persuasive speeches and debates."[10] He was hesitant to call upon the state for help in solving the issue.

> For my opinion was that no one should be forced to the unity of Christ, but that we should act with words, fight with arguments, and conquer by reason. Otherwise we might have as false Catholics those whom we had known to be obvious heretics.[11]

Augustine's fear was that many Donatists would not have a change of heart with regard to their error but that they would simply join the church out of fear of civil punishment. Yet as the Donatists persisted in their obstinate thinking, opposition, and even violence, Augustine gradually began to lean toward the use of coercion to compel the renegades to recognize the truth and the gravity of their error. He even used the parable of wedding banquet in Luke 14 where the guests were "compelled to come in" as justification for the right of the church to use persecution. He was also unafraid to use the examples of God's discipline on the people of Israel in the Old Testament (where God brought calamity when the religious nation was astray) as further evidence that this type of action was justified. Brown paraphrases Augustine's thoughts.

> The persecution of the Donatists was another "controlled catastrophe" imposed by God, mediated, on this occasion, by the laws of Christian Emperors.[12]

Romans 13 further states that the state does not possess the sword for nothing and that it seeks to punish the evildoer and reward the righteous.

---

10. Merdinger, *Rome and the African Church*, 102. This was, after all, how Augustine himself came to the faith through the challenge to his heart and mind, arguably through the ministry of Saint Ambrose of Milan. See Willis, *Saint Augustine and the Donatist Controversy*, 127–28.

11. Augustine, "Letter 93.5.17," to Vincent, Rogatist bishop of Cartenna, as found in Rotelle, *The Works of Saint Augustine*, 387. Also quoted by Frend, *The Donatist Church*, 239. The official declaration of "heretics" upon the Donatists came with the "Edict of Unity" offered by the Emperor Honorius posted in June 405. This edict officially disbanded the Donatist Church from a legal standpoint. See Brown, *Biography*, 230; and Frend, *The Donatist Church*, 263–65.

12. Brown, *Biography*, 233.

Augustine saw this as grounds for using coercion since both church and state were providentially united at this time. For in his view, Christ was building his church "to the ends of the earth."[13] He saw this providential union as a divine gift, and in his reasoning, he states:

> By fearing what he does not want to suffer, he abandons the stubbornness that holds him back or is compelled to recognize the truth he had not known. Thus out of fear he either rejects the error for which he was fighting or seeks the truth he did not know, and he now willingly holds what he did not want to hold.[14]

This was for Augustine simply a "temporal chastisement," able to save one from the eternal consequences of his error, specifically the sin of schism. He compared the coercion of the state to the restraining of a madman in order to keep him from injuring himself.[15] Augustine was quick to cite testimony from a few Donatists who had "come to their senses" and

13. The bishop directly addresses the Donatists' concern in using this type of argumentation. "'But,' you claim, 'it is not permitted that Christians persecute even bad people.' Granted: it should not be permitted. But is it right to raise this as an objection to the authorities that were established precisely for this purpose? Or shall we do away with the Apostle? Or do your books lack those lines that I quoted [Rom. 13:2–4]?" Augustine, "Letter 87.8," to Emeritus, Donatist bishop of Caesarea in *Works*, 348. Also, in his letter to Vincent, he proclaims, "I think that it is not useless that they [Donatists] be held in check and corrected by the authorities established by God." Augustine, "Letter 93.1.1," in *Works*, 377. More on Augustine's view of church and state can be found in Willis, *Donatist Controversy*, 127–43.

14. Augustine, "Letter 93.5.16," 387. Augustine also was willing to cite the experience of the Apostle Paul (formerly Saul) in this letter as further evidence of God forcing one "to come to know and to hold onto the truth by the great violence of Christ who compelled him." See Augustine, "Letter 93.2.5," in *Works*, 380. Further, he also uses the illustration of Hagar and Sarah where Sarah righteously punished the slave girl. Augustine claims that Sarah "did not cruelly hate her since she had previously made her a mother by her own generosity; rather, she was subduing pride in her in a way conducive to her salvation." Augustine, "Letter 93.2.6," in *Works*, 380.

15. Augustine's legitimizing of coercion has drawn much criticism as a precursor to other abuses later to be seen in the Catholic church (i.e., the Inquisition of the Middle Ages). One scholar has remarked, "It was under these circumstances, and by such questionable methods of argumentation, that he developed his theory, as far reaching in its historical consequences as it is incompatible with modern ideas of religious toleration, that the state, under the guidance of the church, the divinely appointed teacher of revealed truth, must perform a pedagogical and disciplinary function that involves the use of civil power for the conversion of heretics and schismatics or for their adequate punishment if they obstinately persist in their errors . . ." Loetscher, "St. Augustine's Conception of the State," in Ferguson, *Studies in Early Christianity*, 409. The essay is the published form of an address given by Loetscher on December 27, 1934.

were now rejoicing after having been compelled to comply by the state. His experience of their recovery was even more reason to find coercion as a beneficial action.

> Hence, they were shown a great mercy when they were first rescued against their will, even by those of the laws of emperors, from that sect in which they learned these evil practices through the teaching of lying demons so that later they might be healed in the Catholic church, once they had become accustomed to her good commandments and morals. *For many of them, whose pious and fervent faith and love we now admire in the unity of Christ, give thanks to God with great joy that they are free from the error in which they thought those evil practices were good.* And they would not now offer thanks willingly if they had not earlier also left that wicked community unwillingly (emphasis mine).[16]

What then can we say about how Augustine viewed the nature of the discipline he so readily advocated against the Donatists? Here is where the aforementioned "Letter 185" can give us valuable insight. We have already made several references to the way he describes discipline. But we will now see that Augustine viewed them as acts of mercy, correction, instruction, and love.

First we note that Augustine recognized the laws of discipline imposed on the Donatists as none other than *mercy*. Specifically, he names it the "mercy of Christ."

> But by the mercy of Christ these laws, which seem to be against them, are rather in their favor since many Donatists have been corrected by them and are being corrected each day, and they give thanks that they have been corrected and set free from that mad destruction.[17]

He elsewhere calls it a "most merciful discipline,"[18] that which is "beneficial and merciful,"[19] "the art of medicine,"[20] "a great mercy,"[21] and "a work of mercy."[22]

16. Augustine, "Letter 185.3.13, The Correction of the Donatists," as found in Rotelle, *The Works of Saint Augustine*, 187.

17. Augustine, "Letter 185.2.7." in *Works*, 183.

18. Augustine, "Letter 89.2" in *Works*, 360.

19. Augustine, "Letter 93.2" in *Works*, 378.

20. Augustine, "Letter 93.3" in *Works*, 379.

21. Augustine, "Letter 185.3.13" in *Works*, 187.

22. Augustine, "Letter 185.8.34" in *Works*, 198.

It is also easily recognizable that Augustine viewed this not as mere punishment (though he does use this term often), but primarily as *correction* or *correptio* in Latin.[23] In commenting to Boniface, Augustine characterizes the count's duty.

> The Lord will grant you understanding so that you may have answers for those who need to be corrected and healed, for our mother, the Church, commends them to you as a faithful son in order that you may correct and heal them where you can and however you can, whether by speaking to them and replying to them or by bringing them to the teachers of the Church.[24]

Further, Augustine believed that temporal suffering of the Donatists was also for "remedial"[25] purposes, in order that they may be *instructed*. The imperial orders were to "help" and to "rescue" those who had been trapped into the evil thinking and actions of the schismatic sect.[26] And it was the church's responsibility to act, as it would be "excessive cruelty"[27] and "heartless"[28] not to do so. The persecution and enforcement of the imperial laws, then, were enacted by the emperor and sanctioned by the Catholic church.

Above all, Augustine desired that the discipline of the Donatists be seen as nothing less than genuine *love*, even if the actions seemed harsh. For he said, "It is better to love with severity than to deceive with leniency."[29] In his commentary of 1 John, he remarks:

> Human acts should be judged by their basis in love. Many things have a surface appearance of good, but are not based on love–like blossoms on a thorn plant. Other things look hard, look forbidding, but they instill a discipline informed by love. Once again, to

23. The thought that New Testament church discipline is a retributive "punishment" is an idea that I will refute. But it would seem that Augustine's use of it is tainted by the union of church and state, where the state would have the right to punish. Brown notes, "The power of *correptio*, of admonition, which Augustine exercised as bishop, preoccupied him deeply. Even in his early works as a priest, Augustine will constantly attempt to define the uneasy boundary between severity and aggression." Brown, *Biography*, 204.

24. Augustine, "Letter 185.10.51" in *Works*, 206.

25. Augustine, "Letter 185.7.26" in *Works*, 194.

26. Augustine, "Letter 185.3.13" in *Works*, 187.

27. Augustine, "Letter 185.8.32" in *Works*, 198.

28. Augustine, "Letter 185.8.33" in *Works* 198.

29. Augustine, "Letter 93.2.4" in *Works*, 379. Augustine stated that the church seeks to heal with her "maternal love." Ibid., "Letter 93.13.53" in *Works*, 407.

put it simply: act as you desire, so long as you act with love. If you are silent, be silent from love. If you accuse, accuse from love. If you correct, correct from love. If you spare, spare from love. Let love be deep rooted in you, and only good can grow from it.[30]

In his letter to Vincent, the Rogatist bishop (a branch of the Donatists), Augustine rebuked those who enforced discipline for any other reason than corrective love.

Whoever persecutes you as the result of the opportunity provided by this imperial law, not out of a desire to correct you, but out of a hatred for you like enemies, does not have our approval.[31]

However, on the surface of things, there is one area that seems a bit troubling. For as difficult as it sounds to the modern ear, Augustine advocated that the church "persecute" the Donatists. To be sure, this must be understood in context, but the word brings forth negative connotations today. Augustine defended it by asserting that the *nature* or the *spirit* of this persecution was much different than the persecutions of the wicked Emperors of the past or of the Donatists themselves. No, this "persecution," he would adamantly state, was only to be performed *in love*. Augustine defended the difference between a healthy and unhealthy persecution.

If good and holy people never persecute anyone but only suffer persecution, whose words do they think are found in the psalm where we read, "I shall persecute my enemies and seize them, and I shall not turn back until they collapse" (Ps 18:37) . . . the Church persecutes by loving; they persecute by raging. The Church persecutes in order to correct; they persecute in order to destroy. The Church persecutes in order to call back from error; they persecute in order to cast down into error. The Church, finally, persecutes and lays hold of enemies until they collapse in their vanity so that they may grow in the truth . . . the love of the Church labors to set them free from that perdition . . .[32]

Therefore we see that Augustine's notion of the church's "persecution" was that it was to be done as an obligation of charity, a special duty and

30. Augustine, "Interpreting John's Parthian Letter 7.8" as translated and cited in Wills, *Saint Augustine*, 112–13.

31. Augustine, "Letter 93.12.50" in *Works*, 406. Elsewhere he remarks, "So by all means enforce discipline, but rid your heart of anger." Augustine, "Sermon 114A.5" in Rotelle, *The Works of Saint Augustine*, 196.

32. Augustine, "Letter 185.2.11" in *Works*, 185–86.

calling of leadership in the church, all for the cause of Christ.[33] It was to be done with different motives and in moderation, and Augustine would reject outright the use of the death penalty except for extreme cases. In fact, as a clergyman called to pastoral ministry, he felt it was the duty of the bishop to intercede for sinners condemned to death, in order to allow for repentance. Augustine stated that the use of moderation in discipline and the rejection of the death penalty was to "maintain Christian gentleness even toward those unworthy of it."[34] It must be remembered that Augustine was hesitant to endorse state coercion in the first place, and he was very concerned that the discipline enforced had the reputation of being carried out in love instead of hatred. "We do not hate them," he said. "In fact, we embrace them, desire them, exhort them . . . it is not their possessions but themselves that we seek."[35]

As stated earlier, the key for Augustine was motives. He desired to keep a clean conscience in his motives.[36]

> The exhortations to use moderation in correcting others, or even to refrain from correcting if such were not possible, were the result of an intense zeal to see that this form of reaction to sin should flow from love.[37]

The challenge of the Donatist controversy was emotionally difficult for Augustine, and his shepherd's heart was often seen in his writings. He was convinced, however, that it was the call of God on his life to admonish, correct, and advocate the "punishment" of the Donatists. For him it was the right thing to do, and he sought to strike a balance between the idea of being gentle yet firm.

> What a deep and dark question it is what the limit in punishing should be, not only in terms of the quality and quantity of the sins,

33. van Bavel, "Discipline," in Fitzgerald, *Augustine Through the Ages*, 274–75.

34. Augustine, "Letter 185.7.26" in *Works*, 195.

35. Ibid., "Letter 185.9.46" in *Works*, 204.

36. Augustine would remark, "Since the good and the evil do the same things and suffer the same things, they must be distinguished, not by their actions and punishments, but by their motives." Augustine, "Letter 93.2.5" in *Works*, 380. He appeals to Paul's handing over of certain people to Satan (1 Tim 1:20). "Did he repay evil with evil, or did he rather judge that it was a good deed to correct the evil, even by means of an evil?" Ibid., "Letter 93.2.7" in *Works*, 381.

37. Keating, *The Moral Problems of Fraternal, Paternal, and Judicial Correction According to Saint Augustine*, 124.

but also in terms of the particular strength of minds-what anyone might endure and what he might refuse—for fear not only that he might not make progress, but also that he might give up . . . and even when it seems that one should judge, what a great worry and fear there is as to the extent one should judge . . . what grounds for fear there are in all these areas.[38]

He knew in his heart that the discipline was beneficial at all levels, for it had benefits for the sinner, for the one who did the correcting, and for others who saw the discipline enacted.[39] Further, he felt the very nature of the church as a forgiven and unified community was at stake. He refused to consider the thought of the church being divided, and he insisted that we are all sinners saved by grace who ought not to establish a "church on an island" (e.g., only in North Africa) but remain in fellowship with others in the Catholic church. Church unity was essential, and to break from it was sinful. Further, the effectual nature of the sacraments, according to Augustine, did not depend on man's fidelity or on the spiritual status of the one distributing the sacraments but on God's grace alone. These are the reasons why Augustine wrote with such conviction, as he himself feared God. This ultimate fear of the final judgment of God was deep within his conscience and was also the backbone of his authority as bishop in an African culture where God was viewed as the awe-inspiring Judge.[40]

AN EVALUATION OF AUGUSTINE
ON DISCIPLINE

So what are we to make of this? This great theologian and shepherd of the church, Augustine, is a giant within church history, and his actions on this issue warrant some conclusions.

We have noted that he viewed the discipline of the Donatists as an act of temporal chastisement, a mercy of Christ manifested in the actions of the church. The discipline of the church was not to proceed from hatred but from genuine love, a point to be lauded. Its primary purpose was remedial, a correction of the schism that threatened the nature of the church, the understanding of the grace of God, and church unity itself. These are note-

---

38. Augustine, "Letter 95.1.3" in *Works*, 417. This is a letter written to Augustine's friends Paulinus and Therasia some time around 408 or 409 A.D.

39. See Keating, *Moral Problems*, 15–22.

40. Brown, *Biography*, 191.

worthy and positive aspects of his understanding of discipline, applicable even today. This was a test for the church, as Augustine notes.

> It was predicted, after all, that there would be heresies and scandals so that we might develop our minds in the midst of our enemies and that in that way our faith and love might be more tested—our faith, of course, in order that they may not deceive us, but our love in order that we may also work for their correction as much as we can, not merely striving so that they may not harm the weak and so that they may be set free from their wicked error, but also praying for them so that the Lord may open their minds and they may understand the scriptures.[41]

Augustine saw the church as having been providentially united to the state, which, in his mind, legitimized coercion to bring back the Lord's sheep.[42] To his credit, he often stated that it should fall short of the death penalty, lest the sinner not have an opportunity for repentance. Regardless of this fact, however, this union of church and state poses many problems with regard to church discipline.[43] What Romans 13 describes as actions reserved for the state (the right to punish) are now mingled and muddled in with the official actions of the *church*. This was never seen before and was not a reality of the world of the apostles and the early church when the New Testament was written. To be sure, the Apostle Paul appealed to

41. Augustine, "Letter 185.1.2" in *Works*, 180–81.

42. A very peculiar point, as the bishop felt that this was a significant period in church history. He stated, "The Church earlier waited without forcing anyone until the message of the prophets was fulfilled concerning the faith of kings and of the nations." Augustine, "Letter 185.6.23" in *Works*, 193. This was a reference to Psalm 72:11. Later in the next paragraph, Augustine proclaims that the "power" that the church received by being united to the state was "God's gift through the religion and faith of rulers . . ." Ibid., "Letter 185.6.24" in *Works*, 194. The trouble here is that Augustine does not have apostolic authority to declare the fulfillment of prophecy and perhaps even that he sees the church in complete continuity with Israel in the Old Testament, whereby the mandate to use force against her enemies was restricted to that previous covenant as directly commanded from God. The New Testament church could not lay hold to such a command in ushering in the kingdom of God, for it was not to be characterized by violence, but by compassion, kindness, humility, gentleness, and patience, bearing each other's grievances and forgiving one another in love, as members of one body called to peace (Col 3:12–15, paraphrase). John Calvin will differentiate the role of the two entities of church and state later in our study.

43. Though our focus has been to take note of how Augustine viewed the *nature* of church discipline, we would be remiss if we did not provide a brief critique of the situation and methodology employed by the Catholics. We will address biblical church discipline methods and their application in the church in subsequent chapters.

the emperor for protection, but he never appealed to the state to use force to carry out the discipline *of the church*. Further, the church is never given the authority in the New Testament to "punish" anyone for sins by appealing to the state or by using state-enforced violence or measures, even if its goals are remedial, restorative, or done in "Christian love."[44] So it is important that we see a distinction here between the actions of the state and the mandate of the church to enforce discipline. Later in history, this will become a major issue when the nature of the church is debated during the Protestant Reformation, especially among the Anabaptist movement, to which we will turn to in a moment.[45]

But first, we are forced to conclude that even though Augustine's understanding of the issues at stake, his motives, his pastoral heart, and his theology of church discipline were for the most part notable and praiseworthy, nonetheless, it was not ideal due to numerous problems posed by the union of church and state. The use of physical force (compulsion) is foreign to the descriptive actions and activities of the church in the New Testament. Further, Augustine's use of language is at times troubling. To describe the church's actions as a "persecution," no matter how it is qualified or substantiated, seems unwise due to fact that whenever this term is used in Scripture, it is usually used in the context of describing unwarranted and ungodly hostility toward God's people. It would seem prudent to avoid such connections and to find a new way to talk about the actions of the church/state in a way that would describe the inherently loving nature of these actions and to more closely follow the language of Scripture itself when it comes to the discipline of the church, which we will investigate later in this study.

44. We will investigate this point further later in our study as we deal with the issue of the atonement and its implications for the New Testament Church. It seems ironic that the way in which Augustine brought people into the "spiritual hospital" known as the church was literally inflicting physical abuse that may have placed them in a literal hospital.

45. William Estep notes that Anabaptism saw this union of church and state as part of the "fall of the church." This fallen condition was prevalent since the days of Constantine, when "church and state were joined," and "the church ceased to be the church. Anabaptists, in their attempt at a restitution of the apostolic church, did not deny the right of the state to exist. They did deny it *any jurisdiction in religious affairs*" (emphasis mine). Estep, *The Anabaptist Story*, 194. For a brief but insightful summary of the Anabaptists view of the church and state union, see Littell, *The Anabaptist View of the Church*, 64–7.

THE ANABAPTISTS AND THE BAN

There have been fewer more significant movements throughout church history that have emphasized the importance of church discipline than those radical reformers of the Reformation period known as the Anabaptists. In fact, in a recent essay, John D. Roth has asserted:

> The teaching and practice of church discipline has been a central tenet of the Anabaptist-Mennonite tradition for virtually all groups and for most of our 475-year history. Far from being an eccentric obsession of a few conservative groups, the goal of a disciplined, visible church has been at the heart of our self-understanding . . . to stand within the Anabaptist-Mennonite tradition virtually demands that one engage the question of church discipline.[46]

The Anabaptists espoused church discipline as an *essential element* in the life of the church and individual believer.[47] For the Anabaptist theologian Balthasar Hubmaier, the believer's baptismal pledge included a willingness to submit to church discipline.

> What is the baptismal pledge? . . . It is a commitment made to God publicly and orally before the congregation in which the baptized person renounces Satan and all his imaginations and works. He also vows that he will henceforth set his faith, hope, and trust solely in God and regulate his life according to the divine Word, in the strength of Jesus Christ our Lord, and if he should fail to do so, he therefore *promises the church that he would dutifully accept brotherly discipline from it and its members* . . . (emphasis mine).[48]

Church discipline was woven into the Anabaptists' view of what it means to live a life of discipleship and obedience. It constituted the very nature of the "true church," of which its preservation and holiness was of utmost importance. For these radical reformers, the empty formalism and spiritual slackness of the Roman church and even some select Reformed

---

46. Roth, "The Church 'Without Spot or Wrinkle' in Anabaptist Experience," 15.

47. See Ludwig, "The Relationship Between Sanctification and Church Discipline in Early Anabaptism," 77–85. Ludwig also notes that the Anabaptists distinguished between the "Small Ban," which was exclusion from the Lord's Supper, and the "Great Ban," based on Matthew 18:15–17, which resulted in exclusion from church membership (excommunication) and shunning. Ibid., 78.

48. Hubmaier, "A Christian Catechism," in Pipkin and Yoder, *Balthasar Hubmaier*, 350–51.

churches had watered down the church into a nominal Christianity.[49] But one of the marks of a true church is one that practices "fraternal admonition" or "the ban," as they called it, in keeping with the teachings of Matthew 18 and the epistles. Without it, there was no church.[50]

So for this group, the purity and unity of the church demanded its employment, so that the inner and outer life of the believer was in harmony with faith. Rather than reform by governmental decree, the church would have to be separate from the state in its reform efforts and include people who were freely committed to the pursuit of holiness and Christ-likeness, while being submissive to the discipline of the church.[51] The Anabaptists desired to restore the church to that which most closely resembled the early church and New Testament community.

To this end, the Anabaptists saw church discipline as necessary for the purity, unity, and identity of Christ's church.[52] But more than that, it

49. Littell, *The Anabaptist View of the Church*, 65.

50. Martin Luther considered it a mark of the church's identity as well. He writes, "Now where you see sins forgiven or reproved in some persons, be it publicly or privately, you may know that God's people are there. If God's people are not there, the keys are not there either; and if the keys are not present for Christ, God's people are not present." Luther, "On the Councils and the Church," in Gritsch, *Luther's Works, Church and Ministry*, 153.

51. Estep, *The Anabaptist Story*, 186–7. Thus the Anabaptist movement became a "free church" or "believers' church" tradition. One of the earliest confessions of this tradition was known as the Schleitheim Articles of 1527 written by the Swiss Anabaptist Michael Sattler. In these articles of faith, the church was admonished to be separated from the world and all evil, to be nonviolent, to practice believer baptism, to practice the ban, and to practice a symbol of the Lord's Supper. Oaths were rejected, and pastors were elected and held accountable in the local church. The Anabaptist historian J. Denny Weaver claims, "Schleitheim made the first formal articulation of those elements within the Swiss Brethren which would later constitute the essence of the whole Anabaptist movement." Weaver, *Becoming Anabaptist*, 50. For a further summary of the articles, see Snyder, *The Life and Thought of Michael Sattler*, 114–22; Snyder, *Anabaptist History and Theology*, 60–3; and Ibid., *The Swiss Anabaptists*, 39–42.

52. As to the necessity and identity of the church, Hubmaier stated, "In fact, even water baptism and the breaking of bread are in vain, useless, and fruitless if brotherly discipline and the christian [sic] ban do not accompany them-brotherly discipline with water baptism, and the ban with communion and fellowship." Hubmaier, "On Brotherly Discipline (1527)," in Durnbaugh, *Every Need Supplied*, 29. For the Anabaptists, the "identity" of the church was extremely important in that as a redeemed people they must show the fruit of saving faith and prove themselves to be disciples of Christ, different from the sinful world and the culture surrounding them. They placed great emphasis on the necessity of the visible church.

was to serve as a means of restoration and an expression of the love of Christ.[53]

Perhaps one of the most significant figures in Anabaptism who expressed this understanding was Menno Simons, from whom the present-day Mennonites derive their heritage and name. The Dutch reformer wrote extensively on the subject of discipline, with his *A Kind Admonition on Church Discipline* (1541), *A Clear Account of Excommunication* (1550), and *Instruction on Excommunication* (1558) being his most comprehensive treatments.[54] Simons characterized the spirit of discipline and its purpose in the church in this extended quote.

> Wherefore, brethren, understand correctly, no one is excommunicated or expelled by us from the communion of the brethren but those who have already separated and expelled themselves from Christ's communion either by false doctrine or by improper conduct. For we do not want to expel any, but rather to receive; not to amputate, but rather to heal, not to discard, but rather to win back; not to grieve, but rather to comfort; not to condemn, but rather to save. For this is the true nature of a Christian brother . . . but those whom we cannot raise up and repentingly revive by admonition, tears, rebuke, or by any other Christian services and godly means, these we should put forth from us, not without great sadness and anguish of soul, sincerely lamenting the fall and condemnation of such a straying brother . . . thus we must obey the Word of God which teaches and commands us to do so; and this in order that the excommunicated brother or sister whom we cannot convert by gentle services may by such means be shamed unto repentance and made to acknowledge to what he has come and from what he has

53. It was for this very reason that Anabaptists resisted the use of force in discipline, unlike the Catholic and select Protestant authorities who persecuted them in this way. For, "Anabaptists said that physical violence was not permitted the Christian. Therefore torture, imprisonment, and death were rejected as legitimate means of discipline . . . the physical sword has no place in the church since it belonged to the function of government. The function of government was strictly separated from that of the church . . . moreover, the sword was a punitive instrument. Church discipline, however, should not be punitive in its final purpose, but redemptive." Klaasen, *Anabaptism in Outline*, 211.

54. Other works by Simons that pertain to the topic of discipline include *Instruction on Discipline to the Church at Emden* (1556), *Instruction on Discipline to the Church at Franeker* (1555), *Final Instruction on Marital Avoidance* (1558), and *Reply to Sylis and Lemke* (1560). See Wenger, *The Complete Writings of Menno Simons, 1496–1591*. This info also cited by Roth, "The Church 'Without Spot or Wrinkle' in Anabaptist Experience," in *Without Spot or Wrinkle*, 11, n.8.

fallen. In this way the ban is a great work of love, notwithstanding it is looked upon by the foolish as an act of hatred.[55]

For Simons, then, church discipline was an act of love, not punishment. It was to be an expression of the church's attempts to receive, heal, win back, comfort, and save those who by their actions had gone astray and *removed themselves* from the communion of Christ and his people.[56] In order for the excommunicated brother or sister to see it as such, Simons made it very clear that the church

> . . . in every respect use it and practice it with godly wisdom, discretion, gentleness, and prudence, toward those who have gone astray from evangelical doctrine or life, not with austerity or cruelty, but rather with gentleness; with many tears because of the diseased and infected members whom we cannot cure, and in whose case pains and labor are lost . . . it should be done in such a manner that the erring brother or sister may be ashamed at heart and won back, as was said above.[57]

Though this was said to be the ultimate goal of discipline, there were, however, abuses in Anabaptist circles, and extreme measures taken.[58] Advocates of the strict ban, such as Peter Riedeman and Dirk Philips,

---

55. Simons, "A Kind Admonition on Church Discipline," in *Complete Writings*, 413.

56. I believe the statement that an unrepentant person has "removed themselves" from the fellowship of the church is a proper way to explain excommunication, though this should never be separated from the fact that the church does in fact need to take formal action.

57. Ibid., 413–14. The admonition by Simons for the church to practice discipline this way was a much-needed word, for the history of the Anabaptist movement is full of conflict, abuses, and disagreements. Roth's thesis is that "for virtually all of our 475-year history, the teachings and practices regarding church discipline have been a source of profound disagreements, intense conflicts, and numerous schisms with the Anabaptist-Mennonite church." Roth, "The Church 'Without Spot or Wrinkle' in Anabaptist Experience," in *Without Spot or Wrinkle*, 15. Roth attributes much of the conflict to "personality clashes, high-minded appeals to principle, exegetical differences, political pressures, and economic considerations." Ibid., 16. He additionally remarks that most of the discipline focused on ethical and cultural issues rather than on doctrine. Furthermore, "The manner in which church discipline should be exercised, especially in regards to its severity," and differing understandings "of where the authority to initiate and carry out church discipline" laid played a major role in the conflicts in Anabaptist discipline. Ibid., 16–17.

58. Timothy Fulop points out that Simons "also recognized the imperfect nature of the church's discipline, counseling tolerance and emphasizing that the ultimate judgment lay with God." Fulop, "The Third Mark of the Church? Church Discipline in the Reformed and Anabaptist Reformations," 40.

often skipped the steps of admonition as mandated by Scripture and basically put all who sinned publicly for any reason outside of the church. Philips was an advocate of spousal shunning as well, where a spouse was not even allowed to have marital relations with his or her mate if he or she was placed under the ban.[59] Many were required to do penance (a form of punishment) before being restored to full membership again.[60] Banning or excommunication was quite common then, even to the point that one testimony proclaimed, "There was daily excommunication among them."[61] Philip Marpeck, an Anabaptist leader from Strasbourg, attempted to call for a balance and censured the Swiss Brethren "for their harsh, legalistic way of exercising discipline in their congregations."[62]

Despite the extremes and obvious abuses of discipline at various times and places of the Anabaptist movement, the general tenor of the nature and use of discipline was that it was an act of love. Hubmaier proclaimed, "It is done for the good of the sinner, that he may examine himself, know himself, and desist from sin."[63] This attitude still can be found among modern-day Mennonites and is ingrained into their concept of the church. For example, in discussing the concept of the church as a

59. See Ibid. For a summary of Philips's views and some of his debates with "moderates" like Menno Simons, see Koolman, *Dirk Philips*, 81–98. To be sure, even some of the "moderates" like Simons advocated spousal shunning, though they were more willing to "permit exceptions for all kinds of reasons." Ibid., 93. This tradition was widespread among the Anabaptists, even among the German Baptist Brethren of the eighteenth century where a wife of a banned spouse would not be allowed "to talk to him, sleep with him, or express affection for him in any way." Willoughby, *Counting the Cost*, 75. However, Willoughby notes that "the ban did not proscribe acts of compassion. If a banned member needed food, or shelter, the congregation met that need with kindness." Ibid. Marlin Jeschke rebuffs any idea of marital avoidance today using the principles of 1 Corinthians 7, where a break in a marriage over a spouse married to an unbeliever was not permissible according to Paul. See Jeschke, *Disciplining in the Church*, 97–99.

60. Alexander Mack stated that if any of the vices of Galatians 5:19 were seen in a member of the church, "then it is only just that such a member be expelled from the church according to 1 Corinthians 5:13, until he is cleansed of it by true penitence and repentance." Eberly, *The Complete Works of Alexander Mack*, 68.

61. Grebel, *The Sources of Swiss Anabaptism, The Grebel Letters and Related Documents*, 382.

62. Klaasen, *Anabaptism in Outline*, 212. Klaasen states, "Marpeck's own view was that there was much to do at the first, that is, the admonition stages, but that the final stage of excommunication should only rarely resorted to." Ibid.

63. Hubmaier, "A Christian Catechism," in *Balthasar Hubmaier*, 354.

disciplinary body, the Mennonite historian Harold S. Bender makes this very clear in this extended quote.

> I hesitate very much to use the term "disciplinary body" here, and do so only for want of a better term. In so doing I do not think of a "punitive body," which alas, is what so many among the laity and the ministry seem to mean by discipline, contrary to the New Testament teaching. I think rather of a restorative body, which by the various means of grace at its disposal, builds up the weak, restores the fallen, heals the broken and wounded, strengthen the feeble knees, encourages the fainthearted, equips with weapons those unarmed for the fight, knots the hearts of all together in love. Now such discipline, wisely directed by skilled leaders, is a tremendous source of strength for the individual and in turn for the entire body. It contributes to stability, sturdiness, and defensive strength, building up also resources for the offensive activity for all kinds of ministry. It undergirds the entire body with a cohesive unity which vastly multiplies the strength of the individual. All this is obviously a great contribution to true community building.[64]

Some of the Anabaptists' disdain for the magisterial reformers and other Protestants was due to their disagreement over the use church discipline and the moral life in the church. At the same time, the Reformed Church felt that the Anabaptists were too extreme and that to implement their strictness upon the community would simply result in too much excommunication. For many reformers, "A society governed by 'Christian civil authority did not need discipline.'"[65] But this is not to say that discipline was not important for the Reformers such as John Calvin, whose views we will briefly look at in a moment.

A BRIEF EVALUATION OF THE ANABAPTISTS

To understand the Anabaptists' view of discipline, one needs to have a grasp of how they viewed a life of faith and discipleship. They took great

64. Bender, "The Mennonite Conception of the Church and Its Relation to Community Building," 31. Bender's sensitivity to the use of "punitive" versus "restorative" language in describing the true nature of discipline is noteworthy.

65. *The Swiss Anabaptists: A Brief Summary of Their History and Beliefs*, 61. To be sure, the context would seem to indicate that it did not need the strict *Anabaptist type* of discipline. For an excellent survey and comparison of the Reformed and Anabaptist positions on church discipline during the Reformation and whether it should be regarded as a mark of the church, see Fulop, "The Third Mark of the Church?" 26–42.

pains to emphasize this amidst a culture and time where widespread corruption in the church seemed so prevalent, especially in Roman Catholic circles. Their desire for a visible, set-apart church drove them to great lengths to establish a community that is identified with Christ and is in keeping with one's profession of faith and baptismal pledge. They desired to return the church back to primitive Christianity (i.e., the life of the church in the secular world as characterized in the New Testament). They had a holy and reverential fear of God and a disdain for sin. Though one can admire their zeal, it would seem that it needs to be interwoven with more grace and patience (why *daily* excommunications?), and a well-balanced reflection of just how the community of God will have the greatest influence and witness to the unsaved world while honoring God. The question for the more extreme Anabaptists is this: in light of the visible, separatist model of the church, how can one effectively and strategically engage a world in need of repentance, grace, forgiveness, and God's reconciling love? To be sure, the balance of "living in the world" but not being "of the world" is difficult, but is marital shunning a good way to attract others to the love offered freely in the gospel?[66]

However, in spite of any negative critique one may give toward these extremes, the desire to link discipline with discipleship, correction, and godly, Christ-like love is evident in their theology, and this is much to their credit. The nature of discipline as found in Menno Simons's extended quote noted earlier represents one of the most biblically sound understandings of church discipline we have seen yet.[67] His cry to use discipline with godly wisdom, discretion, gentleness, and prudence seems to be a prophetic one and is one that needs to be heard today. It is unfortunate that sometimes a movement can be characterized, mislabeled, or held

66. Obviously, I am addressing the extremes here, and one should not characterize the whole tradition of the Anabaptists based on the radicals on the fringes of the movement. In private conversation with Kevin J. Vanhoozer, Dr. Vanhoozer raised a very good point, in that it would seem that the extreme Anabaptists may have had such an exaggerated conception of church purity that they may have lost the essence of the church as forgiven, justified sinners being progressively sanctified, or *simul iustus et peccator*.

67. As a reminder, Simons stated, "We do not want to expel any, but rather to receive; not to amputate, but rather to heal, not to discard, but rather to win back; not to grieve, but rather to comfort; not to condemn, but rather to save. For this is the true nature of a Christian brother . . . but those whom we cannot raise up and repentingly revive by admonition, tears, rebuke, or by any other Christian services and godly means, these we should put forth from us . . ." Simons, "A Kind Admonition on Church Discipline," in *Complete Writings*, 413.

hostage by the few who go to extreme measures. For in the case of the majority of Anabaptists, they have rightly placed discipline in its proper context in the life of discipleship!

JOHN CALVIN AND THE NATURE OF CHURCH DISCIPLINE

John Calvin, the great reformer from Geneva, was critical of the Anabaptists for their harshness in applying discipline and for the perception that they wanted to develop a perfect church of elect citizens separated from the rest of society.[68] Calvin advocated discipline but opted for moderation. One could make a case that for the extreme Anabaptists, their insistence that the church be united and spotless often came at the expense of concern for the individual, especially as one considers a strict marital shunning. But Calvin sought to strike a balance here. Fulop explains:

> When it came to the individual, love and unity outweighed Calvin's concern for purity, for church discipline was to reflect the grace and mercy of the gospel. Concern for repentance of the sinner was one reason why Calvin wished to separate church discipline from civil discipline.[69]

68. François Wendel notes, "Calvin was well aware, as Luther and Bucer had been before him, that there could be no question of forming an ideal human community composed of the righteous and saintly, such as the Anabaptists desired, for instance." Wendel, *Calvin*, 297–8. Fulop remarks, "Calvin's theology is weighted towards love and he often chided the Anabaptists for being too rigorous in their discipline." Fulop, "The Third Mark of the Church?," 33.

69. Ibid., 37. It must be remembered that the church and state were once again united in similar fashion to Augustine's time. For Calvin, the Magistracy and the Church should complement one another with regard to discipline. However, because much of the discipline involved spiritual issues, the Magistracy was always to be answerable to the Church. Furthermore, the Church was not to "exercise a repressive and authoritarian power [as opposed to the punishment the state might enforce], but to safeguard good order among its members and perform an educational service in regard to them." Wendel, *Calvin*, 308. The two entities were to remain in different domains, distinct yet functioning together for the good of society and the church. Calvin stated, "The two conceptions are very different. The church does not assume what is proper to the magistrate; nor can the magistrate execute what is carried out by the church." Calvin, *Institutes of the Christian Religion*, 1215. However, as Wendel notes, Calvin "never succeeded in putting the Genevan Magistracy under the tutelage of the Church." Wendel, *Calvin*, 309. For a helpful summary of how Calvin viewed the relationship of the church and state with regard to discipline, see Wendel, *Calvin*, 306–10, and Calvin in his *Institutes*, 1215–9. See also, Baker, "Christian Discipline and the Early Reformed Tradition: Bullinger and

In a similar fashion to the Anabaptists, Calvin linked church discipline to the sacraments or ordinances of the church.[70] He identified two marks of the church: the right preaching of the word and the proper administration of the sacraments. Calvin placed discipline underneath these two marks, whereby the Anabaptists would have made it a mark in and of itself.[71] In Wendel's synopsis of Calvin's thought, the preaching of the gospel, the teaching ministry, and the sacraments all served to awaken and maintain faith, as well as to promote and contribute to the collective sanctification of individual members.[72] Thus if part of the purpose of church discipline was to maintain unity, purity of thought, and personal sanctification (obedience and spiritual growth), then it would fall within these two marks and would not demand a separate category.[73] Interestingly, the most convincing argument as to why Calvin would not have wanted discipline to be a third mark of the church is offered by Kilian McDonnell, who claims that for Calvin, to make discipline a third mark

---

Calvin," in Schnucker, *Calviniana*, 107–19.

70. For the Anabaptists, who viewed baptism as an ordinance, discipline was linked to the life of discipleship and the baptismal vow, as was seen previously in Hubmaier. The Anabaptists felt that discipline was so important that it deserved to be a separate mark of the church. This was not true, however, for Calvin.

71. See Fulop, "The Third Mark of the Church?" 26–7; 32–6. Wendel notes, "To Calvin the discipline was no less important, but not of the very essence of the notion of a Church; it was simply a measure of defence [sic] and a means of sanctification, and, as such, it belonged to the organization and not to the definition of the Church. Though the Church may remain imperfect as long as it exists on earth, it must nevertheless labour [sic] unremittingly at its own sanctification and at that of each of its members at the same time." Wendel, *Calvin*, 301.

72. Wendel, *Calvin*, 292.

73. However, Glenn S. Sunshine in a recent article argues that Calvin's rejection of discipline as a third mark was more of a reaction against the Anabaptists. He states that among Calvin, the Anabaptists, and other reformers in the tradition, such as Martin Bucer, John Knox, and Theodore Beza, "Their differences over what constituted a mark were determined less by internal elements of their theologies than by their historical context and the specific purpose of their writings, factors that have all too often been neglected in analyzing theological developments." Sunshine, "Discipline as the Third Mark of the Church: Three Views," 479. However, later Calvinistic confessions included discipline as a third mark, though Sunshine argues that there seems to be some semantic ambiguities to the use of the term "discipline." The Belgic Confession of 1561, however, included discipline as a third mark of the church, where it would seem that it is specifically referring to correction of sin. See Ibid., 478.

"would have made the existence of the church dependent upon man's fidelity and would be to measure the church with a human rule."[74]

Calvin, however, did in fact place great emphasis on the need for self-examination, renouncing of sin, a reliance on and a hunger for God, self-denial, love, and fellowship among the brethren as prerequisites before coming to the Lord's Table.[75] Thus it was in this context that discipline was to be maintained, and excommunication from the Communion or Lord's Table was "the severest form of discipline."[76]

John Calvin asserted three aims in the use of discipline in his *Institutes*.[77] In the first of these aims, he links the doctrine of God with church discipline. Because of our common spiritual union as those who are the body of Christ, indwelled by the Holy Spirit, and due to our unique fellowship with Christ that we participate in when we receive the sacraments, church discipline was an absolutely necessary practice so that the high honor of God's holy name would not be blasphemed at the able. Thus members were to keep themselves from evil or sinful practices in order to keep the Lord's Table and the church from being unequally yoked or defamed. Calvin writes:

> Outward sacraments are a kind of bonds by which they are united
> to the Lord, and hence also the converse holds true, viz. that those
> who mix themselves up with impure ceremonies, thereby ingraft
> and entwine themselves in fellowship with Idols.[78]

74. McDonnell, *John Calvin, the Church, and the Eucharist*, 174.

75. See his "Short Treatise on the Lord's Supper," in Calvin, *Tracts and Treatises on the Doctrine and Worship of the Church*, 173–77.

76. Fulop, "The Third Mark of the Church?," 33. In Calvin's view of the Eucharist, we participate in a spiritual union with Christ when we partake of the bread and the cup at the Lord's table. It therefore made no sense to him that someone who was participating in sinful acts should be able to unite him or herself to Christ at the Lord's Table and defame it. See Wendel, *Calvin*, 298–9.

77. For further discussion on these three aims of church discipline, see Wendel, *Calvin*, 299–301; and Fulop, "The Third Mark of the Church?," 36. Robert White also discusses these aims and asserts that they "are intimately linked to a theology of pastoral care. Of the three aims assigned to discipline, two have the needs of believers specifically in mind." White, "Oil and Vinegar: Calvin on Church Discipline," 37. These aims are garnered from Calvin's *Institutes*, 1232–4. The specific elements, manner, or methods to which discipline should be carried out is not the focus here but will be alluded to in subsequent chapters.

78. Calvin, "On Shunning the Unlawful Rites of the Ungodly and Preserving the Purity of the Christian Religion," 373. Here Calvin is specifically referring to the "sinful

Therefore, the first aim of discipline was to protect the doctrine and reputation of God within the confines of the church.

Second, Calvin advocated discipline in the church in order to preserve a godly life among God's people, in order to keep the church in proper condition. They were not to be corrupted by the wicked example of the ungodly, for as Paul said in 1 Corinthians 5:6, "A little yeast works through the whole batch of dough." So discipline was advocated to protect the flock from the corruption and "constant company of the wicked" who were "bad examples from right living."[79]

Calvin's third purpose for discipline also sheds light on his view of the *nature* of discipline, which is that it should be implemented for purposes of correction so that "those overcome by shame for their baseness begin to repent."[80] To withhold discipline from one of its erring members would be to lend to the "ultimate dissolution of the church."[81] Further, by the analogy of metaphor he states that discipline

> ... is like a bridle to restrain and tame those who rage against the doctrine of Christ; or like a spur to arouse those of little inclination; and also sometimes like a father's rod to chastise mildly and with gentleness of Christ's Spirit those who have more seriously lapsed ... Now this is the sole remedy that Christ has enjoined and the one that has always been used among the godly.[82]

Godly church discipline was truly Calvin's goal, and he despised the excessiveness that he perceived to be among the Anabaptists, comparing their zeal for perfection to Donatism.[83] To counter the reputation of

---

act" of being united with the Catholic church and participating in their mass, which was regarded by many Reformers as idolatry. Whatever sinful act one would be participating in, whether fornication or idolatry, one was dishonoring the Lord's name by coming to the Lord's Table when one was sharing in such reprehensible conduct. Calvin remarked in the *Institutes*, "For since the church itself is the body of Christ, it cannot be corrupted by such foul and decaying members without some disgrace falling upon its Head." Calvin, *Institutes*, 1232.

79. Ibid., Institutes, 1233.

80. Ibid., 1233.

81. Ibid., 1230. This is a significant point that supports the basic thrust of this book.

82. Ibid. Note Calvin's emphasis on the remedial element to discipline.

83. Calvin writes, "The Anabaptists act in the same way today. While they recognize no assembly of Christ to exist except one conspicuous in every respect for its angelic perfection, under the pretense of their zeal they subvert whatever edification there is." Calvin, *Institutes*, 1239. It is unfortunate that Calvin brands the whole Anabaptist move-

discipline as a harsh practice, Calvin went to great lengths to speak of the nature of discipline in his *Institutes*. He claimed that for lighter sins the verbal rebuke was to be

> . . . mild and fatherly—which should not harden or confuse the sinner, but bring him back to himself that he may rejoice rather than be sad that he has been corrected.[84]

Even for more shameful acts, where the church needed to take a firmer stance resulting in excommunication, he still proclaimed that it was to be a remedial and merciful act, done in gentleness, as the following quotes reveal.

> But we ought not to pass over the fact that such severity as is joined with a "spirit of gentleness" befits the church.[85]

> For in excommunication the intent is to lead the sinner to repentance . . . in this respect we cannot at all excuse the excessive severity of the ancients, which both completely departed from the Lord's injunction and was also terribly dangerous.[86]

> This gentleness is required in the whole body of the church, that it should deal mildly with the lapsed and should not punish with extreme vigor, but rather, according to Paul's injunction, confirm its love toward them [2 Cor 2:8]. Similarly, each layman ought to temper himself to this mildness and gentleness . . . let us not claim for ourselves more license in judgment, unless we wish to limit God's power and confine his mercy by law.[87]

---

ment this way, for certainly some Anabaptists like Philip Marpeck (noted earlier) were not excessively rigid. One could argue that perhaps the arguments often centered on personalities and culture rather than real theological differences. Calvin said of Menno Simons, "Nothing can be more conceited than this donkey, nor more impudent than this dog," as found in a footnote in "True Christian Faith" in *Complete Writings*, 405. For more on the differences between Calvin and Simons, especially in regard to the logistics (i.e., methods and procedure) of discipline, see Girolimon, "John Calvin and Menno Simons on Religious Discipline: A Difference in Degree and Kind," 5–29. It is unfortunate that these two leaders did not get along, for they shared many similar pastoral concerns when it came to church discipline.

84. Calvin, *Institutes*, 1234.

85. Ibid., 1236.

86. Ibid.

87. Ibid., 1237. Calvin here argues that excessive force in discipline goes beyond grace and mercy, leading to the establishment of a Pharisaic-type of rigid law.

Unless this gentleness is maintained in both private and public censures, there is danger lest we soon slide down from discipline to butchery.[88]

Calvin often cited his favorite church father, St. Augustine, when talking about the nature of correction and discipline.[89] In quoting the ancient bishop, Calvin seeks to lay claim to the fact that church discipline in its nature and purpose must seek to keep peace and restore the fallen.

All pious method and measure of ecclesiastical discipline ought ever to look to "the unity of the Spirit in the bond of peace" [Eph 4:3], which the apostle orders us to keep by "forbearing one another" [Eph 4:2], and when it is not kept, the medicine of punishment begins to be not only superfluous but also harmful, and so ceases to be medicine.[90]

A BRIEF EVALUATION OF CALVIN

For Calvin, discipline was to be practiced in moderation and gentleness, was medicinal and remedial in nature and purpose, sought to confirm the love for and restore the sinner, was to protect the flock, and was to uphold the dignity of the name of God and the table of the Lord's Supper.[91] It was "oil and vinegar" to the open wound of the offense.[92] Calvin's pastoral heart is extremely evident in his writings and does indeed reflect the spirit and nature of a biblical view of discipline. For this he is to be commended. Furthermore, Calvin's emphasis on upholding the honor of the name of Christ is a very significant issue that is often forgotten in today's church

88. Ibid., 1238.

89. For more on Calvin's use of the church fathers in his writings and argumentation, see Lane, *John Calvin*.

90. Ibid., 1239. Calvin is quoting from Augustine's "*Against the Letter of Parmenianus.*"

91. These will be common themes that we will discover are a part of the scriptural witness with regard to divine discipline and its purpose within redemption history, as we will see in later chapters. As Richard R. De Ridder has rightly noted, ". . . for Calvin the church's disciplinary functions were divinely given and clearly specified in the Scriptures . . . anyone who denies the necessity of discipline for the church will find no support in Calvin's *Institutes*. Anyone who would use discipline as a stick to punish will likewise find Calvin's pastoral heart reminding the church that true discipline can be effected only in the spirit of patient love." De Ridder, "John Calvin's Views on Discipline: A Comparison of the *Institution* of 1536 and the *Institutes* of 1559," 230.

92. See White, "Oil and Vinegar: Calvin on Church Discipline," 39.

where the hesitancy to perform discipline has more to do with the concern over its effect on human relationships and fear of sitting in judgment upon one another.

Before we move toward a Scriptural survey of divine discipline, there is one other theologian who is worthy of our investigation in order to see how a more liberal church tradition has understood discipline in the church, for certainly there is some merit in seeing how discipline is viewed in a church tradition unlike those previously mentioned. Therefore, let us quickly turn to one of the more preeminent modern liberals, Friedrich Daniel Ernst Schleiermacher.

SCHLEIERMACHER, THE CHURCH, AND THE KEYS

Friedrich Schleiermacher (1768–1834) is known throughout Christendom today as the theologian of religious experience or of "God consciousness."[93] His basic premise was that religion was a

> . . . unique element of human experience, not located in the cognitive or moral faculties, which produce only an indirect knowledge of God by inference, but in intuition which yields immediate experience of God.[94]

This more subjective view of faith, or "feeling of absolute dependence," as Schleiermacher labeled it, marked his understanding of the church and its relationship to the world. Since Christians experience both the church and the world, they need not be so diametrically opposed to each other (like in the separatist Anabaptist thought) but rather make up the whole of the Christian experience of God. According to Schleiermacher, the Christian's first allegiance is to God, but he was also a "citizen of the

---

93. For a helpful summary of the content and context of Schleiermacher's theology, see Welch, "Schleiermacher's Theological Program," in *Protestant Thought in the Nineteenth Century,* 59–85. See also Clements, *Friedrich Schleiermacher,* 7–65; and Niebuhr, *Schleiermacher on Christ and Religion.*

94. Hoffecker, "Friedrich Daniel Ernst Schleiermacher," in Elwell, *Evangelical Dictionary of Theology,* 1064–65. Alister McGrath notes Schleiermacher's greatest critic, Ludwig Feuerbach, who labeled Schleiermacher's experience-based religion as nothing more than a "self-intoxicated, self-contented feeling . . . nothing less than human beings' awareness of themselves. It is experience of oneself, not of God. 'God consciousness' is merely human self-awareness, not a distinct category of human experience." McGrath, *Christian Theology,* 231.

modern world, and he understood that he had a commitment to both."[95]
The implications of this are precarious and a little vague. In his line of
thought, since religion is primarily a personal, more subjective experience, then the "church" is more properly defined as a

> . . . communal relationship...capable of ongoing development in
> both individuals and communities of faith.[96]

There was not to be any final, unchanging, external authority on
matters of faith, which is what an appeal to Scripture or any historical
creedal statement might provide, but rather the individual's experience
of God shared amongst a common group of people who beheld a "common spirit" where authority was to be found.[97] This relegated any idea of
discipline to an executive power

> . . . owing simply to the natural predominance of the common
> spirit over persons—a predominance such as every member of a
> community feels has won his free assent. Should there be someone
> who does not feel this, or who in his own person is consciously an-
> tagonistic to the challenge of the common Spirit, that fact denotes
> an anti-church element in his life, and the predominance of the
> common Spirit must be re-established inwardly before the person

95. Christian, *Friedrich Schleiermacher*, 138.

96. Reed, "Friedrich Daniel Ernst Schleiermacher," in Hart, *The Dictionary of Historical Theology*, 508. Martin Redeker, in his work on the life and thought of Schleiermacher, contends that Schleiermacher held that "the church is in no way a mere loose union of individuals sharing a religious life. No subjective-pietistic emotionalism is to be founded in this doctrine of the church. But neither is it a mere abstract vision of an ideal church remaining in a transcendent other world; rather it is the activity of Christ through his Spirit among the faithful, and the union, founded by Christ, of the total life of the faithful in community with their Redeemer." Redeker, *Schleiermacher*, 188. In spite of Redeker's contention, it is still difficult to see this as the definition that Schleiermacher is work-ing with, especially as we take a look at how this community is defined when it has to take up the matter of discipline, as we shall soon see. For Schleiermacher, the Spirit's authority in the church is based more on communal subjective inclinations rather than what he has spoken through Scripture, a more objective authority. Karl Barth, whose work on Schleiermacher is legendary, states, "Schleiermacher's church is a free-society of like-minded people founded on common love for Christ with the aim of common contemplation, fructification, and extension of the stimulus received from him." Barth, *The Theology of Schleiermacher*, 28.

97. Hoffecker, "Friedrich Daniel Ernst Schleiermacher," 1065. The logical question to this line of thinking is: how can we then set forth Christian truth, doctrine, or practices with any absolute certainty? I am fearful that this line of thinking is starting to pervade the evangelical church more than we might realize.

in whose case it was infringed can again be acknowledged as a true
member of the Church.[98]

This "anti-church element" is a problem for the *common spirit* of the
church, which alone has the power to decide what belongs to the Christian
life.[99] The person cannot be re-established inwardly through the use of
external means, but rather the "sinner's" change of heart is brought about
by a "steady voluntary submission," which "is the very power exerted
by Christ."[100] Furthermore, the power given to the church is the power
to make judgments and pronouncements. Yet this power is limited and
never results in total excommunication. But rather it is the power to

> . . . define the place taken in the community by each individual as
> a consequence of his inward state, and determine whether much
> or little can be entrusted to him.[101]

Additionally, the legislative actions of the church are only to be seen
as temporary, and "all legislative acts within the congregation are always
subject to revision."[102] They can be revised in keeping with the current

98. Schleiermacher, *The Christian Faith*, 661.

99. This is what Schleiermacher calls the "Power of the Keys," referring to Matthew
16:19 and 18:18. His theorem is that "the Power of the Keys is the power in virtue of which
the Church decides what belongs to the Christian life, and disposes of each individual
in the measure of his conformity with these decisions." Ibid., 662. This obviously moves
the church more toward a subjective and relative view of spirituality and Christian living.
But to "dispose" of someone is not to excommunicate him or her, as we shall soon see.

100. Ibid., 661. This power of Christ, according to Schleiermacher, is "manifested
precisely in the fact that impulses coming from Him were recognized as law [i.e. a man's
convictions], and that His judgments regarding men were felt to be final pronouncements
on what is in man—the new community thus becoming His Kingdom." Ibid. So then,
Christ is the one who has to change a person's heart through religious experience. But
Christ is not directly manifesting himself through the actions of the church. According
to Schleiermacher, "It is less easy to describe this power as a prolongation of Christ's
activity, for the difference between legislative and administrative activities essentially
relates to the organized community, while Christ's own activity preceded it. If, then, the
difference has no application to His case, the Power of the Keys as thus defined cannot
in the strictest sense be called a prolongation of His activity, although it does develop the
outline of the common life as Christ drew it, and that without absorbing alien accretions
from without." Ibid., 662.

101. Ibid., 662. Schleiermacher uses the argument that Jesus, when confronting the
scribes and Pharisees, did not expel them from his fellowship but rather simply withdrew
from them. Schleiermacher avoids any discussion of Paul's command to excommunicate
in 1 Corinthians 5.

102. Ibid., 667.

public opinion regarding the Christian life. The locus of authority and the definitive ideal of the Christian life reside solely in the experience of the congregation in union with the Spirit, and in the congregation's public opinions, which may change over time.

It would seem that for Schleiermacher, the unity of the church regarding the experience of the Christian life and the influence of dissidents are the primary concerns of any "legislative action."

> It is clear that the Redeemer's promise entails that the church will judge rightly on the question what, and how much or how little, is to be entrusted to the individual member of the Church, and to what extent his influence on the Church or his collaboration with it ought to be restricted, if the minimum of disturbance is to result from his inward state.[103]

A BRIEF EVALUATION OF SCHLEIERMACHER

As we evaluate the dynamics of Schleiermacher with regard to church discipline, we find little in common between him and the approaches of those we have surveyed before (Augustine, Simons, Hubmaier, and Calvin). For Schleiermacher, there is seemingly no connection between God's holiness and church morality as a redeemed people. Nor does he imply that the purpose of discipline would be for the correction, restoration, or salvation of the sinner, as Christ works through the church. Rather, he focuses on the ideal that the church ought to be in unity with regard to people's religious experience of redemption and that someone whose internal disposition is not in keeping with the majority's "common spirit" ought to be restricted in his or her activities and influence within the community. Holiness is not mandated or emphasized as a priority in living in a sinful world, and Scripture is not followed with regard to procedure or excommunication (Matt 18).[104] Even though he rightly places emphasis on

---

103. Ibid., 665. Schleiermacher specifically is referring to the power of the keys to bind and loose. We will show that this is not the proper understanding of binding and loosing in our later chapters.

104. This lack of excommunication is due to his understanding of the experience of regeneration. "He contended that believers experience regeneration (Jesus's God-consciousness) by participating in the corporate life of the contemporary church, rather than by merely believing in Christ's death and resurrection in history." Hoffecker, "Friedrich Daniel Ernst Schleiermacher," in *EDT*, 1065. Thus Schleiermacher states that "no judgment should seek to terminate the influence of the Church on the individual

church unity, it is not necessarily unity of morality, thinking, or doctrine, but of experience. It is very difficult to see his theology of discipline as useful for our study due to its shaky, unbiblical, weak foundation. It cannot hold high esteem in our understanding of church discipline.

CONCLUSIONS AND SUMMARY

Our goal in this chapter has been to survey a few significant Christian figures or traditions in order to see how church discipline has been understood throughout history, keeping in mind the limitations of such an undertaking. We have sought to understand how these figures or traditions have understood the nature and purpose of discipline while noting the various contexts from which their theology developed. In our overview, a variety of issues have surfaced. First, we have seen distinguishable positions regarding how discipline is to be *carried out*. It ranged from Augustine, whose concept of discipline involved the idea of persecution by the state, to the Anabaptists, who felt the church was to be completely separated from the state and the world, whereby the church was the only one authorized to deal with spiritual matters. In the middle of the spectrum falls Calvin, who wrote within the context of the state-church society and who advocated that the church and the Magistracy were to complement each other, with the Magistracy answerable to the church. Outside of all of this falls Schleiermacher, whose understanding of the Christian life involved a positive affirmation of a union with the world, a collective agreement to a "common spirit," whereby one who behaves or embodies a spirit outside of acceptable public opinion is merely pushed aside but not completely excommunicated, which sounds precariously like many mainstream (and dare I say some moderate *evangelical*) churches today.

Second, the *severity of discipline* ranges from a gentle admonishment that can escalate to complete banishment and marital avoidance (Anabaptists) to rational argumentation that when ignored and scoffed can end up leading to physical force and coercion (Augustine). To be sure, the various understandings of the logistics of discipline seem to be heavily dependent upon the great struggle of applying biblical exegesis and wisdom to the context or culture that the church finds itself in. In many ways the cultural circumstances did much to shape the way the church thought about discipline. This is all the more reason why a biblical theol-

---

who has once been received into its bosom." Schleiermacher, *The Christian Faith*, 668.

ogy of church discipline is necessary.[105] Though such a theology cannot be written in a vacuum, it is nonetheless important that the church realize its cultural, intellectual, and spiritual environment and biases that it brings to the task of implementing church discipline as it seeks to be a faithful witness to Scripture and the embodiment of a new covenant community. The church also must be aware of the past, its triumphs and mistakes, which is why our look at these traditions is valuable.

Yet even though there have been differences with regard to the logistics surrounding church discipline, we have also seen many overarching similarities and overlapping themes throughout our survey regarding the *nature and purpose* of church discipline. Positively, discipline at its heart was seen as an act of love, a mercy of Christ, a correction and remedial action taken by the church in order to help, rescue, win back, receive, and restore those who have fallen into sin or heresy. This was made clear in Augustine, the Anabaptists, and Calvin. It helps foster, protect, and preserve the godly spiritual life of a community in union with Christ, a people redeemed from and forgiven of sin and committed to a life of discipleship.[106]

Negatively, to withhold it was seen as excessive cruelty, a compromise of the commands of Christ and Paul as given to the church, causing the church to be indistinguishable from the world. As ambassadors for Christ, Calvin rightly noted that the church that fails to practice discipline would defame the name of Christ and corrupt the Lord's Table, disrupting the unity and spirit of the church, and would allow sin to reign unchecked. This would do great damage to the individual spiritual lives of the collective believing community as well as to the witness it has to the unsaved world. These similar themes identified above do indeed correspond to the biblical witness concerning the nature and purpose of divine discipline, and it's to this biblical witness that we now turn.

---

105. We will seek to present and defend a biblical theology of discipline in subsequent chapters.

106. It would be well to remind ourselves at this juncture of the excellent point quoted earlier by Harold Bender, the Mennonite historian who said, "Such discipline, wisely directed by skilled leaders, is a tremendous source of strength for the individual and in turn for the entire body. It contributes to stability, sturdiness, and defensive strength, building up also resources for the offensive activity for all kinds of ministry. It undergirds the entire body with a cohesive unity which vastly multiplies the strength of the individual. All this is obviously a great contribution to true community building." Bender, "The Mennonite Conception of the Church and Its Relation to Community Building," 31.

3

Divine Discipline as Manifested in the Old Testament

THE OLD TESTAMENT PROVIDES the initial framework for an understanding of humankind's relationship to God. Here the creation
story—the beginning of life, the fall of humanity into sin, and God's redemptive plan—is set forth, shaping our understanding of God's dealings
with his creation gone astray and priming us for the incredible wonder
of his great salvation. Our survey in the next several chapters intends
to be redemptive historical in nature, as was stated in our introduction.
Specifically, this chapter intends to survey the complexity of the Old
Testament with regard to divine discipline, with special attention given to
Israel as a nation, King David and his line, and other individuals (e.g., the
Psalmists) who experienced the discipline of God *as part of a covenant
relationship.*[1]

In the Old Testament, God's discipline is found primarily in the context of this relationship. Furthermore, the idea of discipline in the Old
Testament often anticipates a resolution—a resolution only to be found in
the One who is the focal center of redemptive history, Jesus Christ, who
bore the punishment for our iniquities. It is due to this resolution that
divine discipline can rightly be said to be temporal and remedial in nature

1. Due to the vast amount of material that will fall into the category of divine discipline
in the Old Testament, it will be necessary to survey only a few representative passages
in the various genres. My goal is to write primarily as a theologian (not as an exegete)
but doing exegesis when necessary and helpful to our overall goals. Divine discipline in
the Old Testament is seen both in a corporate (narratives and prophetic literature) and
individual (Wisdom literature and Psalms) dimension. D. P. Kingdon has noted some
of the great complexity and range of meaning of discipline in Scripture, showing that
it "can connote training (Eph 6:4), education (Deut 8:5), reproof (Prov 9:7), correction
(Zeph 3:2,7), warning (Isa 8:11), chastening (Prov 3:11), and punishment (Hos 10:10)."
Kingdon, "Discipline," in Alexander, Rosner, Carson, and Goldsworthy, *New Dictionary
of Biblical Theology*, 448.

for the believing remnant, and as such is to be differentiated from judgment, where the larger apostate community is cut off, blown away like
chaff, and does not participate in the redemption and resolution found
in the cross.

ISRAEL'S DISCIPLINE IN DEUTERONOMY 8

The nation of Israel in the Old Testament was a people chosen by God,
called out from among the nations to be holy. They were the recipients
of a divine covenant from Yahweh, who had rescued them from the
hand of the Egyptian pharaoh through the leadership of Moses, the great
prophet. As God's people, the sufferings and discipline they experienced
were always to be seen in the context of a covenant relationship, for this
relationship was at the core of their very identity and existence.[2] Walter
Brueggemann has highlighted the Pentateuch's testimony of God's actions
toward Israel in establishing her as his very own. He states that this

> . . . action of Yahweh—this inexplicable, irreversible commitment
> of Yahweh—is rendered in two distinct narratives: the stories of
> the ancestors (Genesis 12–36) and the Exodus-Sinai narrative re-
> volving around Moses (Exodus 1–24).[3]

These narratives capture definitive moments in Israel's calling, identity, and history, and Deuteronomy 8 calls to mind the wilderness experience of the Exodus in order to remind them of God's greater purposes for
them and to assure them of their inheritance of the Promised Land.[4]

> Be careful to follow every command I am giving you today, so that
> you may live and increase and may enter and possess the land that
> the LORD promised on oath to your forefathers. Remember how
> the LORD your God led you all the way in the desert these forty
> years, to humble you and to test you in order to know what was

---

2. Walter Brueggemann remarks, "Israel's existence is rooted in Yahweh's inescapable, originary commitment to Israel. According to its unsolicited testimony, there was a
time when Israel did not exist. Israel came to exist because of the decisive, initiatory . . .
sovereign, free action of Yahweh." Brueggemann, *Theology of the Old Testament*, 414.

3. Ibid.

4. I am indebted to the unpublished doctoral seminar paper of Scott R. Swain (now associate professor of systematic theology at Reformed Theological Seminary, Orlando, Florida)
whose paper entitled "The Fatherly Discipline of God: The Meaning and Significance of a
Biblical Metaphor," has extensively dealt with this chapter in Deuteronomy in explaining
the purposes and theology of God's "fatherly" discipline to Israel.

in your heart, whether or not you would keep his commands. He humbled you, causing you to hunger and then feeding you with manna, which neither you nor your fathers had known, to teach you that man does not live on bread alone but on every word that comes from the mouth of the LORD. Your clothes did not wear out and your feet did not swell during these forty years. Know then in your heart that as a man disciplines his son, so the LORD your God disciplines you. Observe the commands of the LORD your God, walking in his ways and revering him. For the LORD your God is bringing you into a good land . . . (Deut 8:1–7 NIV).

It is in this context (v. 5) that we read of the Lord's discipline (יָסֹר, *ysr*), a discipline couched in the historical language of the covenant (i.e., oath, promise). Its primary purpose here is not temporal punishment but rather instruction. The term *ysr* in its verbal form occurs forty-two times throughout the Old Testament, mainly in Wisdom Literature, and can either carry the connotation of "instruction and admonishment" or "chastisement and punishment."[5] Here at first glance it would seem to

5. E. H. Merrill notes, "In the general semantic field of learning and instructing, the vb. *ysr* specifically relates not to formal education but to the instilling of values and norms of conduct by verbal (hortatory) means, or, after the fact, by rebuke or even physical chastisement." Merrill, "יָסֹר," in VanGemeren, *NIDOTTE*, 479. Similar words in its semantic range include אָלַף (*'lp*), used four times in the OT and mostly in Job meaning "to teach, learn," אָמְנָה (*'omnâ* II) used once in Esther meaning "bringing up," יָרָה (*yrh* III), used four times in Deuteronomy and forty-six times in the OT, meaning "to teach or instruct," לָהַג (*lhg*) used only in Ecclesiastes, meaning "to study," לָמַד (*lmd*) used eighty-six times in the OT and seventeen times here in Deuteronomy meaning "to learn or teach," לֶקַח (*leqah*), a noun used nine times in the OT and once in Deuteronomy, meaning "instruction, teaching, gift of persuasion." The noun form of *ysr* is *mûsār*, found fifty times in the Old Testament, once in Deuteronomy, and it "carries all the nuances of *ysr*, i.e. instruction, correction, chastisement, discipline, punishment. Fundamentally, it has to do with teaching/learning by exhortation and example, with warning as to the consequences of disobedience, and with the application of penalty following failure to adhere." Ibid., 480–1. This noun form is predominately seen in Wisdom Literature as well, occurring no less than thirty times out of the fifty in the book of Proverbs alone, often translated as "instruction" or "discipline." A word often paralleled with ysr and mûsār is יָכַח (*ykh*), a verb appearing fifty-nine times in the OT, mostly in Job (seventeen times) with a semantic range meaning "to dispute, reason together, prove, judge, rule, or reprove." See Hartley, "יָכַח," in *NIDOTTE*, 441–45. For a fuller treatment of Hebrew words related to divine discipline in the Old Testament and their specific relationship to the concept of suffering, see Sanders, *Suffering as Divine Discipline in the Old Testament and Post-Biblical Judaism.* Sanders deals exhaustively with the Hebrew words for discipline (*ysr, mûsār, ykh*) and accompanying conceptual statements. His work is "a special survey of the various literary expressions of divine discipline, with special attention given to the idea that suffering is a form of discipline." Ibid., 3. We will interact with him throughout this chapter.

carry the nuance of *instruction*, as Yahweh led them in the desert for forty years in *order to humble* (`nh* II), *to test* (*nsh*), and *teach* (*yd`I*) his people (vv. 2–3).[6] They enjoyed a steady diet of manna stew, manna muffins, and just plain manna. The point was to teach them that "man does not live on bread alone but on every word that comes from the mouth of the Lord" (v. 6). It was Yahweh who supplied their every need—even the most basic need of physical nourishment, sustaining their life and warranting their dependence. Truly, then, we must conclude that one of God's primary purposes for the wilderness experience was the instruction and teaching of the nation of Israel.[7] In the same way that a human father disciplines his son to instruct and communicate to him essential principles about life (Deut 8:5), so Yahweh disciplined the nation of Israel in order for them to know him as their God (Exod 16:6, 12) and further as their source of strength and blessing (Deut 8:7–10, 18). They were not to forget Yahweh but to remember him (8:2, 11, 14, 18, 19).[8] Nor were they to take pride

---

6. The root (יָדַע, *yd`I*) used in verse three in the hifil infinitive construct, meaning "to inform, announce, or teach" helps nuance *ysr* in verse 5 (Cf. Deut 4:35–36 where we find *yd`I* with *ysr* in the Qal infinitive construct). Yahweh wanted to teach them a lesson about the nature of their relationship, and in testing them he in turn would know what was in their hearts and whether they were inclined to obey him (v. 2b). Further evidence for the instructional nature of the discipline is found in the Septuagint, where the Greek verb παιδεύω is used in translating *ysr* in verse 5, meaning "to train, educate, discipline, or correct." "Know then in your heart that as a man disciplines (παιδεύσαι) his son, so the LORD your God disciplines (παιδεύσει) you." See also verse 16.

7. Kingdon notes, "Since discipline is located in the context of covenant it is to be understood theocentrically, for all discipline comes ultimately from God, and its goals and means are determined by him." Kingdon, "Discipline," in *NDBT*, 448.

8. The commands to "remember" (זָכַר, *zkr*) and not to "forget" (שָׁכַח, *škḥ*) are primary lessons in Deuteronomy as they draw the Hebrew attention toward the covenant God of their forefathers. The root *zkr* is used fifteen times in Deuteronomy (15/222), and *škḥ* is found fourteen times (14/102). Verse 11 forms the central emphasis and point of the chiasm of verses 1–18, repeated again in verses 19–20—that is, that Israel should be careful not to forget Yahweh, lest they become disobedient to his commands and incur judgment. See Wright, *Deuteronomy*, 121. Leslie C. Allen notes, "Memory plays a major role as a positive constraint . . . God's dealings in the desert are meant to stimulate Israel to obedience, while in 8:18 the reflection that Israel's prosperity is God's gift is an incentive to obey and stay loyal to him, rather than worshiping other gods." Allen, "זָכַר," in *NIDOTTE*, 1102. Thus another purpose of discipline, according to Allen, was to *stimulate* Israel to obedience. The link between the themes of obedience and discipline will be common in our redemptive historical survey. For example, see 2 Thessalonians 3:14, where the Apostle Paul calls for church discipline (in this form, disassociation) to be enacted upon one who does not *obey* their instruction.

in their *own strength* (8:17) or think that it was on account of their *own righteousness* (9:4–6). The instructional purpose of divine discipline is made very clear in the text.[9]

Yet we must also remind ourselves that Israel was in the desert for forty years due to her disobedience and refusal to submit to Yahweh's command to take possession of the land. Instead, they rebelled against the command of Yahweh (1:26) and did not believe in him (1:32). They were more fearful of the people they were to conquer than they were committed to obedience to Yahweh. Therefore, Yahweh declared, "Not one of these men of this evil generation shall see the good land I swore to your forefathers" (Deut 1:35 ESV), a judgment against unbelief.[10] According to Deuteronomy 8, then, the wanderings were essentially a remedial lesson from God and additionally a punitive chastisement of the nation of Israel as a consequence of human sin.[11] This lesson is often captured in significant moments of redemption history. Christopher Wright notes:

> Like other events in biblical history (e.g., the story of Joseph, the rise of the monarchy, and ultimately, of course, of the cross itself), the wilderness wanderings is presented to us *both* as arising out of human sin and rebellion *and* as having divine purpose.[12]

9. Scott Swain argues, "The main purpose of the manna experience . . . was to enact a spiritual parable that would carry the Israelites into the Land of Promise." Swain, "The Fatherly Discipline of God," 8. Later in Deuteronomy 11:1–7, the discipline (*mûsār*) of Yahweh in the exodus narrative is cited as being instructional in that it allowed Israel to deeply grasp the character of Yahweh (i.e., "his majesty, his mighty hand, his outstretched arm," his overwhelming power and just judgment, and the "great things the LORD has done" [11:2, 4, 6, 7, NIV]). Cf. Kingdon, "Discipline," in *NBDT*, 449.

10. The exceptions mentioned are Caleb (v. 36) and Joshua (v. 38). They were not like the others who did not believe or trust in Yahweh (v. 32).

11. This punitive chastisement for sin is part of our redemptive historical focus in that it anticipates the culmination of punishment and wrath poured out on Christ on our behalf on the cross. There is where the judgment withheld from the believing remnant was poured out in *fullness* as atonement for sin. Therefore, though indeed there is an element of punitive retribution even in what the Israelite remnant experiences, it is not the full and final retributive punishment for their sin that Christ endured, whereby punitive retribution was satisfied and done away with once and for all in the scheme of redemption history for God's people. One may assert that the punishment that the remnant endured served as a type to the fuller punishment that would be poured out upon and satisfied by Christ, the anti-type.

12. Wright, *Deuteronomy*, 122. There they were to live, multiply, and possess the land (8:1) with the understanding that they were to bless him, (8:10) walk in his ways, and fear him (8:6), while remembering him and his statutes (8:11, 18).

Here, then, is the compatibilistic theology of redemption history echoed by the Apostle Paul in Romans 8:28:

> And we know that in all things God works for the good of those who love him, who have been called according to his purpose (Rom 8:28 NIV).[13]

It is essential to note that this divine discipline is seen in the context of the intimate relationship and love that is to be shared between Yahweh and his people, the nation of Israel. J. W. McKay has successfully shown that in Deuteronomy, there is a close link established between testing/discipline and the command by Yahweh for obedience and love from his people, all of this falling within the context of the covenant relationship.[14] All of these themes are woven together and are inseparable. For example, comparing Deuteronomy 8:1–20 with 13:1–5, we see the testing (*nsh*) of Israel (8:2,16; 13:3[4]) by Yahweh in order to discern the disposition of their hearts, which would be seen in their level of obedience (8:2) and love (13:3[4]).[15] The *past* testing or discipline referred to in 8:1–20 recalls the story of the God who brought them through the wilderness. And the *future* testing of Israel with the false prophets (13:1–5) is brought forth by the *same* covenant God who "brought you out of Egypt and redeemed you from the land of slavery" (13:5). Thus the testing, humbling, and discipline of God are important elements of a personal covenantal relationship

---

13. Israel was called according to God's purpose, and as Swain has rightly pointed out with regard to the reflection in Deuteronomy 8, "The point is that God, as a benevolent and prudent Father, simply transformed their disobedience and its ensuing chastisement into a 'teachable moment' and an opportunity to promote their future blessing (8:16)." Swain, "The Fatherly Discipline of God," 9.

14. McKay, "Man's Love for God in Deuteronomy and the Father/Teacher–Son/Pupil Relationship," 426–35. The father-son motif is often used to characterize the intimacy of this relationship. When it was apparent that the Israelites were in complete violation of the covenant and were not willing to drive out completely the surrounding Canaanite nations during the period of the conquest, Yahweh in turn used those nations to discipline and punish Israel, as a test of Israel's obedience. As Yahweh states in Judges 2:22, "I will use them [the pagan nations] *to test* Israel and see whether they will keep the way of the LORD and walk in it as their forefathers did" (NIV, emphasis mine).

15. Cf. Exodus 15:26, 16:4, 20:20. In 20:20, Yahweh is said to have come to test (*nsh*) Israel "so that the fear of God will be with you to keep you from sinning," and in Deuteronomy 8:16 it is done "so that in the end it might go well with you" (NIV). It would seem then that God's testing of Israel and his calls for her to remember and not forget are means to the positive restraint of sin hinted to earlier by Allen (see footnote 8) and is a profitable component of divine discipline.

between God and his people and are stimuli for the obedience and love of Israel so that "it may go well with them" (8:16). The teaching, instruction, and even the punitive aspects of discipline by Yahweh have a benevolent purpose.[16] It taught them about the character of Yahweh and the nature of the covenant relationship and was a deterrent against sin and apostasy.

DISCIPLINE VS. JUDGMENT

One important distinction that is necessary to see in our study is that the Bible, especially through the narratives and prophetic literature of the Old Testament, distinguishes between that which is temporal and that which is eternal. There is a more *temporal* judgment, chastisement, or discipline that falls on God's people of faith, and then there is a judgment that is *eternal*, or more final in consequence (e.g., Num 33:4, Isa 34:5), falling on those who do not believe. Both may be retributive in nature, but one is more exhaustive and final than the other. Alvin Sanders notes:

> Not all of man's sufferings are interpreted as divine discipline in the Old Testament: God might destroy His people completely or he might punish them for sins committed. It is only when the punishment is interpreted as an opportunity to repent, and is seen as evidence of God's goodness and love that it is to be called divine discipline.[17]

A perfect example of this is found in the passage that we have just investigated, Deuteronomy 8. Israel as a nation came under divine discipline but was not as a whole brought under final condemnation and judgment for her unbelief, where there was no hope for restoration.[18] Not

---

16. This is a dominant theme in Wisdom Literature as well, as we will soon see. Notice in Jeremiah 32:33 that discipline (*mûsār*) is situated in the context of the covenant relationship with Israel and Judah (v. 30). Here discipline's goal was to teach (*lmd*, v. 33) them as they were being punished through Yahweh's anger and wrath (v. 31). Yet the benevolent purpose even of this discipline is that they might experience the blessings of 32:37–41.

17. Sanders, *Suffering as Divine Discipline*, 117. Sanders seems to be assuming, however, that final judgment on the wicked and the nations is never acknowledged as *discipline*, which is not the case, as we will see. Nevertheless, his definition does support our distinction between a temporal versus a final punishment for sin, where suffering with the opportunity for repentance is part of the experience of the former.

18. One Hebrew word that can often embody this latter type of judgment is the root word (הרג, *hrg*). W. R. Domeris has noted that in Isaiah 30:25, the prophet "speaks of the salvation of Israel and the destruction of her enemies on the Day of the Lord—the

all of them perished in the desert. God always seemed to keep a remnant of people who would believe in him, and the affliction would help sort that out. It helped separate the sheep from the goats, if you will. Peter Craigie explains:

> On the one hand, the desolation of the wilderness removed the natural props and supports which man by nature depends on; it cast the people back on God, who alone could provide strength to survive the wilderness. On the other hand, the severity of the wilderness period undermined the shallow bases of confidence of those who were not truly rooted and grounded in God.[19]

The two narratives of the exile and the exodus reveal the perseverance of the remnant in spite of the judgment upon the nation. The prophet Isaiah links both groups as he draws a parallel between the remnant that will return from the exile with those who had experienced the fullness of the wilderness experience in Israel's past.

> There will be a highway for the remnant of his people that is left from Assyria, *as there was for Israel when they came up from Egypt.* In that day you will say: "I will praise you, O LORD. Although you were angry with me, your anger has turned away and you have comforted me. Surely God is my salvation; I will trust and not be afraid. The LORD, the LORD, is my strength and my song; he has become my salvation" (Isa 11:16—12:2 NIV, emphasis mine).[20]

When many in Israel refused to believe in Yahweh in the wilderness (Deut 1:32), God did not cast the nation off altogether and destroy them *completely.* Nor did he do so in the exile (Isa 10:20–22; Amos 9). But rather, as they were his chosen people, God decided to teach Israel a lesson, punish them for and cleanse them from sin, humble them, and

---

day of great slaughter [*hereg*]. Amos 9:1–4 uses the vb. *hrg* to present the theme of God's war against his people . . . the judgment will be final and none shall escape, for even in exile God will command the sword to seek them out (v.4a). Ezek 8–11 and Hos 6:5 use the same theme but include a sense of hope for the remnant." Domeris, "הרג," in *NIDOTTE*, 1056. The similar Hebrew word *ḥērem* also carries this idea of being set apart for a final destruction with no hope of restoration. See Younger, *Judges/Ruth*, 28–30; and also Naudé, "חרם," in *NIDOTTE*, 276–7.

19. Craigie, *The Book of Deuteronomy*, 185.

20. Those who "came up from Egypt" are the remnant who experienced the discipline of God and who subsequently entered the promised land. Other examples of texts where Isaiah names a remnant are 1:9; 8:18; 10:20–22; 11:11–12; 17:6; 24:6; 26:8; 30:18–21; 37:31, 32; 49:5–6; 56:6–8; 65:8–9; 66:19–21.

figuratively speaking, bring them to their knees.[21] Thus, through God's actions they would realize their need and dependence upon Yahweh, who has been faithful to them since the time of their forefathers. This was one of the purposes of the exile, which can rightly be called a meta-narrative concerning divine discipline and judgment.[22] Many perished under God's judgment in the exile due to their unbelief, yet there would be a righteous remnant who would return, be restored, and could properly see the exile as a temporal discipline.[23] This is explicitly portrayed in Jeremiah 30, where the prophet proclaims the word of Yahweh:

21. Yahweh proclaims through the prophet Ezekiel that his judgment in the desert and his judgment in the exile were designed to "take note of you as you pass under my rod" and "bring you into the bond of the covenant," all the while "purging you of those who revolt and rebel against me" (Ezek 20:37–38, NIV.) Previously, Ezekiel feared that God would even destroy the remnant as well in his judgment (11:10–13), but Yahweh assured him the he was their sanctuary and that they would be gathered back to the land where once again they will be restored (Ezek 11:14–20). The unfaithful, however, will face a permanent and decisive judgment, as Yahweh will "bring down on their own heads what they have done" (11:21).

22. However, these are not the only themes. We may also regard the flood narrative of Genesis 6–9 in this same manner where judgment fell upon the earth, yet a remnant of the righteous would be spared, a people who were the recipients of a covenant (6:18). Only Noah is said to be righteous and blameless, however (6:9; 7:1), though some commentators hold that his family fell in this category since they were listed before the corruption of the earth in 6:10. See Wenham, *Genesis 1–15*, 170. Abraham Heschel in his classic work on the prophets remarks, "The divine intention, according to the prophets, is not primarily retributive, to impose penalty in consequence of wrongdoing; but rather deterrent, to discourage transgression by fear of punishment; and reformatory, to repair, to refine, to make pure by affliction: God's purpose is not to destroy but to purify (cf. Isa 27:7–8; 28:29, 'to purge away your dross as with lye and remove all your alloy; . . . afterward you shall be called the city of righteousness, the faithful city' (Isa 1:25–26; cf. 4:3). 'Behold, I will refine them and test them, for what else can I do, because of My dear people?' (Jer 9:7 [H. 9:6]). . . through suffering lies the way to restoration and to the implanting of His will in the hearts of regenerated people (Isa 1:26; Hos 6; 10:12, 14; Jer 24:7; 31:33 f.)." Heschel, *The Prophets*, 187.

23. Note the restoration founded upon repentance in Hosea 14. The remnant was not to fear Yahweh's judgment (Mal 3:5), for he was an unchanging, faithful God whose promise was never to destroy them completely (v. 6). David embraced God's judgment in his psalm of thanks in 1 Chronicles 16 (see specifically v. 33 couched in praise and thanksgiving). For the remnant then, God's judgment was a sign of his faithfulness and righteous rule over the earth (cf. Ps 9:7–10). But on the other hand, he will be quick to judge and testify against those whose deeds are evil (Mal 3:5). They will be like chaff and unable to stand (Ps 1:4, 5). The Psalms often portray the difference between the temporal judgment and one that is more final. For an excellent treatment of the topics of justice and judgment in the Old Testament, see Schultz, "Justice," in *NIDOTTE*, 837–46. Schultz

> I am with you and I will save you, declares the LORD. Though I completely destroy all the nations among which I scatter you, I will not completely destroy you. I will discipline (*ysr*) you but only with justice (*mišpāṭ*); I will not let you go entirely unpunished (Jer 30:11 NIV).[24]

For the nation of Israel, discipline's purpose was to rid them from sin, call them to obedience to the law, and shape their hearts for loving him (Deut 6:4–6) and in doing so pave the way for the future blessing that was ahead.[25] And this discipline was based on justice and righteousness and was an act of grace, as David W. Baker rightly notes.

> God's grace is not only manifest in his election of Israel, his establishing a covenant with them, and his forgiveness of them when they broke the covenant, but also in the *whole area of discipline*, the punishment that follows wrongdoing. This is an area not often considered in discussions of grace (emphasis mine).[26]

In light of preceding discussion, then, one could ask why it is important that God would choose a remnant to endure temporal discipline

---

notes the various nuances of divine and human justice (מִשְׁפָּט), noting the theological dimensions where he states that the "Psalms both exalt God's universal displays of justice, especially towards Israel (99:4), and his acts of delivering individuals who trust and obey him [i.e. the remnant], even if this demands the destruction of the wicked (9:4, 7, 16 [5,8,17]); such people plead not simply for justice (for no one is truly righteous) but for mercy (143:1–2)" (844). See again the quote by Sanders in note 17.

24. Cf. 40:28.

25. By contrast, the Old Testament records situations where discipline will be enacted upon the surrounding nations. This idea is seen in the form of a rhetorical question found in Psalm 94:10, where the Psalmist asks, "Does he who disciplines nations not punish?" (NIV). Here the Psalmist reminds Israel that the nations (גּוֹיִם) will undergo discipline (*ykḥ*) by Yahweh. However, the purpose of this discipline is not primarily to bless or express covenant love to those nations, but simply to chastise or rebuke them for their wickedness (v. 3), evil (v. 16), and arrogance (vv. 2, 4), the result being destruction (v. 23). Yet to those in Israel, the upright in heart (v. 15), they are considered blessed for Yahweh's discipline, and are granted relief from trouble (v. 13), and he will never reject or forsake them (v. 14). The blessing of Yahweh in discipline on Israel and in judgment on the nations stood as a testimony to his lordship, so that even the Egyptians "will know that I am the LORD when I stretch out my hand against Egypt and bring the Israelites out of it" (Exod 7:5 NIV). Alvin Sanders notes that this is a prevalent theme in the writings of Ezekiel as well as the nations (e.g., Ammon, Moab, Edom) are punished (see 25:7, 11, 17; 26:6; 28:22–24, 26; 29:6, 9, 16; 30:8, 19, 25–26; 32:15; 39:6, 28). Sanders, *Suffering as Divine Discipline*, 95. Incredibly, some in the nation of Egypt will respond to Yahweh in faith (see Isa 19:20–22).

26. Baker, "Aspects of Grace in the Pentateuch," 12.

rather than send the whole nation into a final, decisive judgment like those unbelieving Israelites (and other nations).[27] A variety of reasons may be offered for this, but we will only offer a few of the most significant. First, God had covenanted with Israel through her forefathers that he would make her name great and that all peoples of the earth would be blessed through them. There would always be a *people of faith* who God would work his purposes through. Therefore, to wipe out even the remnant would be to go back on a promise made to Abraham, Isaac, Jacob, and the nation that Moses had brought up from Egypt. The destruction and final judgment for any sin that they would commit would be stayed, so that God's redemptive historical plans for humankind would continue to be in effect, and so that his promises would hold true.

Second, and perhaps most significantly, God would in fact inflict a thorough and just punishment upon human sin to pay for the punishment that even Israel (the believing remnant) deserved. A final judgment

27. For more on the topic of collective retribution, see Krašovec's, "Is There a Doctrine of 'Collective Retribution' in the Hebrew Bible?," 25–89. He argues that with regard to collective retribution and Israel, "God makes use of it only in special circumstances. On the one hand, human institutions are not allowed to practice it. Consequently, general statements of collective divine punishment should not be regarded as a doctrine or principle, but as an anthropomorphous expression of the fact that operation of natural law implies collective or inherited punishment. The point is that children are victims of 'natural' consequences of their father's guilt" (35). I believe that Krašovec rightly argues that children suffer the "natural" consequences of their father's guilt. But one must ask if there is indeed more to this. Do they also *directly* suffer from imputed guilt? Though he does not deal with the issue, Romans 5 would seem to implicate that as our head, Adam's corruption and guilt were passed on to his progeny (unless one takes the Semi-Pelagian or Pelagian views) and that God holds us *directly* responsible for Adam's sin. For we know that the direct imputation of Adam's guilt is the basis for arguing positively for the direct imputation of Christ's righteousness (Rom 5:18–19). But isn't this a special circumstance? It would seem that federal headship is not an exact parallel to the sins of the fathers being visited upon the children. For if indeed we receive imputed guilt from our parents due to their sin, then conversely one might have to conclude that we receive imputed righteousness from them as well. This is not a conclusion that many, including this writer, would want to keep. Therefore, in the same way that 1 Corinthians 7:14 is a promise of blessing (but not salvation) upon the children of a believing parent, so it would seem that the sins of the fathers would have natural consequences upon the children. But it does not follow that this would include direct imputed guilt. Whatever the case, these sinful consequences are not fatalistic, like Israel was arguing in Ezekiel 18:2. The prophet suggests (vv. 3–32) that the consequences of the father's sins can be removed or the cycle is broken through repentance and faith manifested in righteous actions. Further, Israel seems to have lost sight of the fact that they were also paying for their own sins, and Ezekiel was not going to let them off the hook by passing blame.

would come, but it would not be realized until later when there would be One (Christ) who would serve vicariously as the propitiation for her sins—past, present, and future.[28] Isaiah foretold this when he said:

> Surely he took up our infirmities and carried our sorrows, yet we considered him stricken by God, smitten by him, and afflicted. But he was pierced for our transgressions, he was crushed for our iniquities; *the punishment (mûsār) that brought us peace was upon him*, and by his wounds we are healed. We all, like sheep, have gone astray, each of us has turned to his own way; and the LORD has laid on him the iniquity of us all (Isa 53:4–6 NIV, emphasis mine).[29]

Further, the New Testament affirms that Jesus Christ was in fact the substitute sacrifice for all the sins of God's people (or in this case, the

---

28. We will discuss the doctrine of retribution and penal substitutionary atonement in chapter 5 of this work as we reflect theologically and note the redemptive historical impact of Christ's work on the doctrines of divine discipline and punishment for sin.

29. The nominative form of *ysr (mûsār)* is used here. From the context, where the suffering servant is seen as afflicted, stricken, crushed, and pierced, carrying infirmities, sorrows, and iniquities, it is hard to dismiss the argument that this use of *mûsār* is a vicarious *punishment* for sin. John N. Oswalt states that the context "demands this understanding." Oswalt, *The Book of Isaiah, Chapters 40–66*, 388. However, see letter (c) by Merrill, "יסר," in *NIDOTTE*, 481. This vicarious punishment is hotly debated in the study of Isaiah and the atonement. The amount of scholarly material is immense. For a brief summary of some of the argumentation, see Childs, *Isaiah*, 415–23. Though Childs defends the vicarious punishment of the servant for sin (418), he rejects the idea that this primarily was a *specific* prophecy pointing directly to fulfillment by Christ. Rather, it is linked by its substance, and by analogy, where Christ is not said to *actually be* the suffering servant of Isaiah 53 but fits that role for Israel and the world (423). I disagree with Childs on this point, however, because the context of Acts 8 suggests that Philip is directly answering the Ethiopian's specific question with regard to the identity of the servant. It is a stretch, in my opinion, to read into this account that Philip is only presenting Christ as an analogy that fits Isaiah. Notice that Philip never recognized that the servant might be Isaiah himself (the very question the eunuch was asking), or Israel as a nation, but rather he taught the Ethiopian with regard to Jesus. It is implied in preaching about Jesus that he is indeed the servant of Isaiah 53, in the same way that he is the fulfillment of other prophecies that have come to fruition and are now explained by the apostles in the book of Acts. One must keep in mind what the book of Acts is seeking to do by presenting Jesus (and the Spirit) as the fulfillment of the OT prophetic witness while the new covenant is being enacted and preached. And it will only be Christ in the epistles who will bear the sin of (2 Cor 5:21) and have the ability to justify the many (Rom 3:26), echoes of the prophet. Mikeal C. Parsons rightly identifies the citation of Isaiah 53 in Acts 8 as a Lukan "intertextual echo" to Luke 24:25–27 and 24:44–46 where Luke is attributing both factuality and significance to Christ's suffering. See his "Isaiah 53 in Acts 8: A Reply to Professor Morna Hooker," in Bellinger and Farmer, *Jesus and the Suffering Servant*, 104–19.

remnant) for all times, bearing the eternal judgment that was due their sin.[30] Paul would state:

> God presented him as a sacrifice of atonement, through faith in his blood. He did this to demonstrate his justice, because in his forbearance he had left the sins committed beforehand unpunished—he did it to demonstrate his justice at the present time, so as to be just and the one who justifies those who have faith in Jesus (Rom 3:25–26 NIV).[31]

He stood in their place as the object of God's just wrath against sin. Thus, the remnant was spared judgment and anticipated the resolution of that judgment that had been stayed, and this was fulfilled when the Christ "died as a ransom to set them free from the sins committed under the first covenant" (Heb 9:15 NIV). Therefore, we see the Christological anticipation and focus of redemption history.[32] To be sure, Israel did in part face *temporal* punishment and chastisement for her sins (i.e., discipline), but it was not a *decisive judgment*, or punishment in the fullest sense, like that rendered to the apostate community. This was reserved and poured out on Christ. Thanks be to God.

KING DAVID AND DIVINE DISCIPLINE IN 2 SAMUEL 7

The complexity of divine discipline in the Old Testament continues as we now turn our attention to the dynastic oracle given to King David in 2 Samuel 7.[33] Within this chapter we see an unconditional covenant, a promise of Yahweh to build a dynasty and an everlasting kingdom through the progeny of one man who was to be a recipient of Yahweh's steadfast

---

30. The double jeopardy argument against unlimited atonement (which is that it is not right that Christ paid the penalty for the sins of unbelievers who are now paying for it *again* eternally) holds weight here in my opinion. These generations of unbelieving Israelites perished as a penalty for sin and unbelief, whereas a remnant survived and is restored in keeping with the fact that Christ would in the future receive their punishment the same way he did ours, including us in the promise of eternal life. Cf. Hebrews 11:40.

31. Cf. Hebrews 2:17; 1 John 2:2; 4:10. He is the "sacrifice of atonement *through faith* [διά, denoting agency] in his blood." His atonement, however, is capable of being sufficient for the entire world.

32. Michael S. Horton proclaims, *"The cross and resurrection form the horizon of expectation for the people of God*, holding in check overrealized and underrealized eschatologies, respectively" (emphasis mine). Horton, *Covenant and Eschatology*, 7.

33. See Calderone, *Dynastic Oracle and Suzerainty Treaty*.

love.[34] It is another one of the defining moments for the people of Israel. The narrative focuses around the theme of the building of a house (בַּיִת, *bayit*). This wordplay on the term "house" (used fifteen times in this chapter alone) ironically had both a literal and figurative (*eschatological*) sense to it.[35] For as the story goes, it is David's desire to build Yahweh a house or temple, an idea that even Nathan the prophet initially thinks is a good idea (vv. 2–3).[36] Yahweh reminded David through Nathan the next day that this was not needed or important, for it had not been a part of his past history with Israel (vv. 5–7). Nevertheless, Yahweh states that indeed a house would be built, but it would not come from him but from his son (v. 13).[37] Further, God would be the one who would build *David* a house

34. Baldwin notes, "even though that word 'covenant' does not occur in Nathan's pronouncement, it is used in later references to David's dynasty (2 Sam 23:5; Pss 89:3[4], 28[29], 34[35]; 132:12), and confirms that it was regarded as an enduring, unconditional promise, sworn on divine oath." Baldwin, *1 and 2 Samuel*, 213. Arnold calls this "one of the most important chapters of the Bible." Arnold, *1 and 2 Samuel*, 472.

35. With regard to its eschatological sense, Gerald H. Wilson notes that due to the failure of the Davidic kings to usher in this "eternal kingdom," there became a shift in emphasis to look for a future king who would rule justly forever. "As a result of this promise and the growing eschatological interpretation of its fulfillment, Davidic lineage became an important element in messianic thinking and theology." Wilson, "בַּיִת," in *NIDOTTE*, 656. Cf. Hebrews 1:8. Of course, in hindsight, this was Yahweh's intention.

36. Though there were apparent political implications to this in the Ancient Near East, it may also be seen as an expression of the relationship that David had toward God, who had given him rest on all sides (v. 1). "Now that God has given David rest from his enemies, what could be more natural than acknowledging the favor?" Craig, "The Character(ization) of God in 2 Samuel 7:1–17," 163. For more on the common practice of temple building in the Ancient Near East, see Hurowitz, *I Have Built You an Exalted House*, 473, n. 9.

37. Peter R. Ackroyd suggests that it more preferable to read verse 12 in light of verses 14–16. Thus the comment from Yahweh is not necessarily a promise for Solomon his son, but rather on the royal line. "The word is 'seed' in the sense of 'descendants'; it is *his kingdom*, i.e. that of David's line of descendants, which is to be established perpetually." Ackroyd, *2 Samuel*, 78. However, this does not preclude the idea that the prophecy may have a fulfillment in multiple senses. Further, the line of David would "build a house for my Name," a reflection of the Immanuel concept hinted to earlier in Deuteronomy 12:11–12 where "access to the great God" was permitted for God's people. Baldwin, *1 and 2 Samuel*, 215–6. However, Arnold suggests, "God's choice of a place for his name to dwell refers simply to God's reputation, not to some mystical hypostasis of God's presence, as is often assumed in Old Testament scholarship since the nineteenth century." Arnold, *1 and 2 Samuel*, 473, n. 8. It is hard, however, to not have Exodus 29:42–46 in the back of our minds, where the tabernacle of meeting fully communicated to Israel the immanence of even a transcendent God. Cf. 1 Kings 8:27–30. The foreshadowing of the Son of David, the Christ who dwelt (lit. "pitched a tent," John 1:14) among us, seems

(v. 12), and this house would not be a literal one but a figurative one, a dynasty that would endure forever (v. 16).[38]

It is in this context of the covenantal promise that Yahweh professes his unconditional, steadfast love (*ḥesed*) for David and his lineage (v. 16). And this intimate relational love will be expressed in many ways, including a *punitive discipline* (*ykḥ*) of the sin of David and his line, a sort of fatherly correction or chastisement.[39] Whereas before, the word *ysr* in Deuteronomy 8 carried a strong nuance of instruction and training, here *ykḥ* in this context carries a slightly different shade of meaning. It connotes the punitive aspect of divine discipline, here couched in love.[40] It is a discipline not to be seen out of the context of a loving relationship. Yahweh has benevolent intentions in his punishment, as he desires obedience to the law and a change of heart toward sin so that "it might go well" with them.[41] Thus to chastise the believing sinner was an overall sign of God's general favor and approval upon one's life. As a righteous, just, and holy God, he appropriately chastises in keeping with the truth *because he*

---

prevalent. Further, William Schniedewind notes, "The concept of the name in both Near Eastern and biblical literature indicates that to put one's name somewhere meant to claim exclusive ownership," which surely fits the idea that Yahweh is their God and they are his people (cf. Exod 6:7; Lev 26:12). Schniedewind, *Society and the Promise to David*, 85.

38. Baldwin writes, "He [David] received far, far more than he could have ever hoped to give, and any disappointment at having to allow someone else the privilege of building the Temple was far outweighed by the assurance of blessing that extended into eternity." Baldwin, *2 Samuel*, 217.

39. Interestingly, the Chronicles account does not include the promise of punishment for sin. See 2 Chronicles 17:11–14. This may have been a desire to put a more positive spin or outlook on the house of David on behalf of the Chronicler.

40. We briefly touched on the word earlier in footnote 6. The verb (יכח, *ykḥ*), as seen here in its hifil perfect form, is a strong form of rebuke, correction, or punishment in response to sin (Cf. the nominative form *tôkaḥat* accompanied by *ysr* in Ps 39:11[12] where the rebuke is a correction for iniquity). The punitive aspect is further accentuated with the use of the phrase "the rod of men, with floggings inflicted by men." The root is also seen in another nominative form *tôkēḥâ* in 2 Kings 19:3 (cf. Isa 37:3), where King Hezekiah (one of David's line) laments in the "day of rebuke or punishment *tôkēḥâ*" brought on by God through the Assyrians due to Israel's disobedience (2 Kgs 18:12). And in support of the idea that this is a thorough judgment for some but a temporal punishment for others, Hezekiah asks that Isaiah "pray for the remnant that still survives" (Isa 37:4). The punishment for them is not full and final, even though the pain is real.

41. These are the words again of Deuteronomy 8:16 and 5:29, where Yahweh's desire to bless is made very clear. In 5:29, Yahweh exclaims, "Oh that their hearts would be inclined to fear me and keep all my commands always, so that it might go well with them and their children forever" (NIV).

loves his children.[42] It is what is best for them, as the wisdom of Proverbs echoes.

> My son, do not despise the LORD's discipline *(mûsār)* and do not resent his rebuke *tôkēḥât*, because the LORD disciplines *(ykḥ)* those he loves, as a father the son he delights in (Prov 3:11–12 NIV).

Thus the punishing of the Davidic line for their sin was to be seen as a sign of his favor.[43] The narrative further characterizes this special status or relationship that David has with Yahweh. The very fact that God calls David his *servant* (vv. 5, 8) and that he has given him rest from all his enemies (v. 1) further accentuates the uniqueness of the relationship. Yahweh was with him (v. 3; Cf. 2 Sam 5:10), and as such David received blessing (v. 29), even the blessing of correction *(ykḥ)*. This type of nuance where punishment is a sign of God's favor was true for David's line and is *also* reverberated in Job 5:17–18, where it says:

> Blessed is the man whom God corrects *(ykḥ)*; so do not despise the discipline *(ysr)* of the Almighty. For he wounds, but he also binds up; he injures, but his hands also heal (Job 5:71–18 NIV).[44]

Though the promise of punishment was for David's line, David's own life and experience in many ways embodied this promise, as he found great blessing but also great tragedy in that Yahweh punished him for his

42. It is extremely necessary to stress the idea that God *appropriately* chastises in *keeping with the truth* so that there is a clear understanding that this is a just and proper punishment. As such, it would be appropriate in measure, similar to the equity of punishment of sin in violation of God's law (Lex Talionis). It is not unreasonably harsh, arbitrary, unfair, or grossly insensitive to the needs and sensibilities of the people of Israel, or an abuse of God's proper authority as Creator. (Descriptions here of this type of discipline are taken from Lincoln's, *Ephesians*, 406. Likewise, Bill Arnold notes, "Yahweh will graciously restrict his punishment to that appropriate to humans." Arnold, *1 and 2 Samuel*, 476. The feminists and others who see God's discipline or punishment as "divine child abuse" have not understood its appropriateness and balance in keeping with the truth, and we cover this in more detail later in our theological reflection on the atonement.

43. Scott Swain provides a valuable insight as he remarks that "even as a subset of the major illocutionary force of [the Davidic] promise, the metaphor [fatherly discipline, v. 14] serves as an encouraging role as it stands in contrast to the fate of Saul's house." Swain, "The Fatherly Discipline of God," 18. God's favor was taken away from King Saul, "whom I removed from before you" (v. 15). Arnold also compares and contrasts David and Saul and their reactions to God and his prophets. See his *1 and 2 Samuel*, 476–7.

44. The man who receives *ykḥ* and *ysr* is qualified as a "blessed man." Cf. Deuteronomy 32:39, where in the song of Moses similar ideas are found. Though Eliphaz was right in principle, he was wrong in application in asserting that Job needed correction for sin (1:8).

sin. His sin with Bathsheba and murder of Uriah wrought divine discipline that brought death in the form of a sword that would never depart from his house (2 Sam 12:10), even costing the life of his child (12:14).[45] Further, there was a public humiliation by the fornication done to his wives , betrayal by his own family, famine, and plague. Yet in all of this Yahweh still delivered David and loved him, establishing his throne forever.[46]

AN EXAMPLE OF DISCIPLINE IN THE MONARCHY

It is worthwhile for us to pause and take a very brief look at how the truth of this promise made to David was manifested in the history of the monarchy, as we take a look at how one of the Davidic kings named Uzziah exemplified the truth of this promise.

Our context is this. The nation of Israel was soon divided after King Solomon's death into two kingdoms (Israel and Judah). This was due to the sin of Solomon (David's son), who intermarried and followed foreign gods (Ashtoreth and Molech), built a high place for Chemosh the god of the Moabites, and in general "turned his heart after other gods," lost his devotion to Yahweh, and did evil in the eyes of the Lord (1 Kgs 11:1–13). He was just the first of the Davidite kings who was punished by Yahweh in keeping with the promise to David. Though he was punished, Yahweh was still faithful to keep a remnant together, and one tribe (Judah) that remained in the kingdom was given to David's line due to the blessing and favor of Yahweh upon the house of David.

Biblical history portrays all of the kings of Israel as doing "evil in the sight of the LORD," prostituting themselves to foreign gods, sacrificing their children, practicing divination, and following the ways of the pagan nations. Eventually this led to the total demise of the kingdom of Israel, and its ten tribes were "rejected" by Yahweh and received his judgment of exile into Assyria.[47] They became altogether worthless (2 Kgs 17:15). The

45. An interesting study of David's *sin and punishment* as embodied in 2 Samuel 10–20 is done by Gillian Keys, where he argues this is the primary theme of this section. See Keys, *The Wages of Sin*, 127–55.

46. In fact, Yahweh often relented from destroying his people in light of the covenant He promised with David (Cf. 1 Kgs 11:12, 13, 32, 32; 2 Kgs 8:19; 19:34; 20:6; Isa 37:35).

47. An even more ominous conclusion is sounded about these ten tribes as Scripture describes them as being "torn away from the house of David" and "thrust" or "removed from the presence" of Yahweh (2 Kgs 17:20, 21, 23). Yet even among these tribes, God still preserved a remnant. Some of them even left their tribes and joined themselves to

kings of the nation of Judah were often no better, yet among them there was a remnant of godly men who led the nation during their respective reigns (e.g., Asa, Jehoshaphat, Jotham, Hezekiah, and Josiah, to name a few). Some of Judah's kings (e.g., Joash, Amaziah) started out well, pursuing the ways of the Lord, but fizzled out and grieved Yahweh toward the end of their reigns. One of those worthy of our attention is Uzziah (or Azariah), a king with a lengthy reign of fifty-two years (approx. 791–739 BC). We find his account in 1 Kings 14–15 and 2 Chronicles 26.

Uzziah is portrayed as a powerful man who loved the Lord and the land and "did what was right in the eyes of the LORD" (2 Kgs 15:3). But he was still lacking in that he was not fully bringing in the necessary spiritual reform (v. 4). When his eyes were on Yahweh, he reigned and fought in battle with much blessing (2 Chr 26:5ff.). One might even possibly surmise that this was one reason why his reign was so long, for it was blessed. But like many a man's downfall, Uzziah struggled with the issue of pride. His power seemingly went to his head, and he felt that there was almost nothing he couldn't do, including the sin of entering the temple and burning incense on the altar of the Lord (2 Chr 26:16). This was part of a ritual of atonement "most holy to the LORD" (Exod 30:10), reserved for the priests alone (v. 18).[48] When confronted, Uzziah became agitated and contentious, and the subsequent punishment of Yahweh for his sin is quite apparent in the narrative.[49]

Benjamin and Judah (2 Chr 15:9) when they saw that Yahweh was with King Asa of Judah. Scripture tells us that "only the tribe of Judah remained loyal to the house of David" (1 Kgs 12:20), though even their sin would eventually result in being thrust from Yahweh's presence (2 Kgs 24:20). It was from this tribe (Judah) that the "Lion of the tribe of Judah, the Root of David," or Christ the Messiah would emerge (Rev 5:5–6).

48. Cf. Exodus 30:1–10. To be sure, we are not told Uzziah's motives for entering the temple. Traditionally, "One offers incense in reverence to a being whom all one's allegiance is pledged because one depends on that being for sustenance and survival and because one wants to garner the favor of that being." Taken from "Incense" in Ryken, Wilhoit, and Tremper, *Dictionary of Biblical Imagery*, 419. This burning of incense was abused in Israel's history, as its people often burned incense in allegiance to other gods (cf. Jer 7:9; 44:3). But Uzziah enters none other than the temple of Yahweh. Though on the surface his actions seem to be an honorable declaration of allegiance and a desire to seek Yahweh's favor, it was clear that Uzziah already had the Lord's favor by the blessings of his reign. Thus this violation of the temple law by usurping the role of the priest should be seen as an act of pride and disobedience. It is only by God's grace that Uzziah was not immediately put to death by Yahweh (cf. Num 18:7).

49. It is interesting to note that Uzziah was confronted ('*md*) by at least eighty "courageous" priests, led by Azariah (vv. 17–18). These "men of valor" were in keeping with the law, whereas Uzziah is described as acting unfaithfully. Their number and their actions serve to highlight the seriousness of the violation and are tantamount to a heavy rebuke.

Uzziah, who had a censer in his hand ready to burn incense, became angry. While he was raging at the priests in their presence before the incense altar in the LORD's temple, leprosy broke out on his forehead. When Azariah the chief priest and all the other priests looked at him, they saw that he had leprosy on his forehead, so they hurried him out. Indeed, he himself was eager to leave, because the LORD had afflicted him. King Uzziah had leprosy until the day he died. He lived in a separate house—leprous, and excluded from the temple of the LORD (2 Chr 26:19–21a NIV).

The priests, almost prophetically, announced to Uzziah, "You will not be honored by the LORD God" (v. 18). Uzziah's punishment was a physical affliction, the type of skin affliction that would quickly temper a man's pride. It is often translated as leprosy, though it could easily be a variety of skin eruptions.[50] Regardless, it seems ironic that it was on his head, the very source, figuratively speaking, of Uzziah's problem.[51] The priests, as well as Uzziah, recognized this as a visible mark of divine discipline, reaffirmed in the text by the fact that they left in a hurry due to the "affliction" of Yahweh (v. 20). Ceremonially, Uzziah was unclean (a point quickly observed by the priests) and as such was excluded the rest of his days from the house of the Lord and from the discharging of his duties as king, especially those related to the temple.[52] His son Jotham was then enlisted to help rule, overseeing the palace and governing the people of the land and eventually becoming king himself.

Sara Japhet holds that only Azariah made the rebuke. See Japhet, *1 and 2 Chronicles*, 886. However, I believe it is better understood as a communal rebuke in light of Uzziah's position of authority and his powerful reputation.

50. See "Leper, Leprosy" in Ryken, *DBI*, 507. Also, see Hulse, "The Nature of Biblical Leprosy," 87–105, as noted by Thompson, *1, 2 Chronicles*, 332, n. 96. Flavius Josephus, the Jewish historian, claims that in addition to the leprosy that fell upon Uzziah, an earthquake also took place that split a mountain in half and destroyed roads as well as the gardens of the king, which, if true, could be another form of divine punishment manifested on the land that Uzziah so loved (2 Chr 26:10). See Whiston, *The New Complete Works of Josephus*, 327. In the original it would be found in Josephus, *J. W.* 9.10.4, 225. Could this be the earthquake referred to in Zechariah 14:5?

51. Further, it brings out a powerful contrast as it was the place where Aaron the high priest was to wear a plate of pure gold where it was engraved, "HOLY TO THE LORD" (Exod 28:36). Obviously, Uzziah had trespassed and violated that which was holy to Yahweh. For more on this point, see Beentjes, "They Saw That His Forehead Was Leprous (2 Chr 26:20): The Chronicles Narrative of Uzziah's Leprosy," in Poorthuis and Schwartz, *Purity and Holiness*, 67.

52. Thompson, *1, 2 Chronicles*, 332.

Uzziah's story of chastisement essentially embodies the promise of Yahweh to David and his line (2 Sam 7:14), that as a sign of God's favor, retributive punishment or discipline would follow sin, but full rejection would not.[53] Though there were consequences to his sin, this did not mean the end of the Davidic line in the kingdom of Judah. For as was earlier stated in Chronicles, Yahweh was going to honor his promise despite the sins of the kings.

> Nevertheless, because of the covenant the LORD had made with David, the LORD was not willing to destroy the house of David. He had promised to maintain a lamp for him and his descendants forever (2 Chr 21:7 NIV).[54]

Biblical history reveals that Yahweh did indeed severely punish David's line, and at one point there was only one heir to the throne left (Joash), but in keeping with the promise, he survived the evil plots of Athaliah, the only queen of Judah, and assumed the throne (2 Chr 22–24). Divine discipline for sin upon David's house would culminate in the vicarious punishment placed upon Jesus Christ, the Son of David. He is the central fulfillment of the Davidic Covenant (Luke 1:32–33) in its climactic sense and the one who will be seated upon David's throne here on earth upon his return (Jer 23:5–8). The crucifixion account in Matthew 27 exemplifies the language of the promise of 2 Samuel 7:14, where the Christ is said to have been beaten by the soldiers who "took the staff and struck him on the head again and again" (Matt 27:30 NIV).[55] In the person and work of Christ, the Father-Son relationship and promise is seen in a dynamic new fashion. So among the descendents of David, where we see discipline nuanced as a retributive punishment for sin, we also find redemptive, restorative, and benevolent overtones to it. Ultimately, then, it is a sign of God's favor and blessing for those united to him through faith, and it anticipates the cross.

53. Uzziah seems to have only been excluded from the temple and from performing kingly duties. One difference between what we see here and the promise given to David was the punishment for wrongdoing was to be inflicted by "the rod of men, with floggings inflicted by men." This was often embodied by the surrounding nations and their conquests of God's people, culminating in the exile. One could argue, however, that Uzziah's sin was a part of the larger whole of the sins of Judah and their kings that eventually cast them into exile, and so the "rods of men" was inflicted indirectly. The affliction here seemed to have come directly from God.

54. Cf. 1 Kings 11:35.

55. Compare this with "I will punish him with the rod of men, with floggings inflicted by men." Jesus as our substitute bore the sin on his shoulders (2 Cor 5:21) and received the punishment that we ourselves deserved.

THE INDIVIDUAL AND COVENANTAL DISCIPLINE

We have looked at how divine discipline has been manifested to the nation of Israel and to the David and his line, all within the context of a covenant relationship. We have also differentiated between a temporal punishment (discipline) upon God's people of faith that anticipates resolution in Christ and a more final judgment that is poured out on those who do not believe. Further, we have seen discipline nuanced in a remedial, more educative sense, and also its punitive side. We now turn to look at how discipline was seen by the individual Israelite as we move from the more communal sense of the narratives and prophetic voice to the more individualistic tone of the Psalms and Wisdom Literature. Due to the vast amount of material, our space will be limited to a few representative passages.

THE DISCIPLINE OF PROVERBS

The idea of discipline takes many forms (e.g., instruction, rebuke, and punishment) in the text of Proverbs, but its primary sense is that of discipline in the remedial or educative sense to the one who will heed.[56] The topics of "educational learning" and the "acquisition of practical daily wisdom and discernment" are the dominant themes in the book of Proverbs, and the admonishment is to pursue this under the rubric of the "fear of the LORD."[57] Relationship is key in acquiring wisdom and receiving the blessings that come from discipline. In Proverbs we find the discipline of God as well as the human/parental discipline of children.[58] With regard to its primary function, D. P. Kingdon notes:

> Discipline in Proverbs is aimed at the shaping of godly character, character that reflects something of the wisdom and righteousness of God.[59]

56. By contrast, it also paints a picture of the one who refuses it. Those who reject it are said to be stupid or foolish (1:7; 12:1; 15:5), despises himself (15:32), invites punishment (16:22), are mere mockers (13:1; 15:12), come to poverty and shame (13:18), leads others astray (10:17), and are a willing contributor to their own death (15:10).

57. True wisdom must begin and be acquired, then, in relationship and reverence for Yahweh, where Yahweh is also recognized as the Creator, as well as a Sovereign and knowable God, as Daniel J. Estes points out. See his, *Hear, My Son*, 19–39.

58. The context of Proverbs uses the father-son relationship primarily, which is how the last chapter in the book should be read, as instructions from a father to the son on the kind of girl he should marry. (This chapter is not often seen from this perspective.) However, the teaching received from the mother is indeed mentioned (1:8; 6:20; 31:1).

59. Kingdon, "Discipline," in *EBT*, 449. Both human and divine subjects have this as a

Our focus will be mainly on divine discipline, and a more specific look at a few passages will also reveal that this discipline, which, on occasion, may be applied with severity, follows directly out of Yahweh's love. The idea of divine retribution in Proverbs is in many ways like the act-consequence format outlined earlier in the book of Deuteronomy, where in the covenant relationship, blessing and curses follow the actions of God's people.[60] Much of this thought is contained in the proverbial genre, but there is undoubtedly an upward focus to divine discipline where the teacher helps the pupil process the motives of Yahweh's direct actions upon his life. There is no more explicit place than Proverbs 3 where this is taught, in a passage we noted earlier.

> My son, do not despise the LORD's discipline (*mûsār*) and do not resent his rebuke (*tôkahat*), because the LORD disciplines (*ykh*) those he loves, as a father the son he delights in (Prov 3:11–12 NIV).[61]

---

goal. It is significant to note then that Jesus Christ is the perfect fulfillment of discipline's instructional purpose, as he exemplifies perfect obedience to God the Father and embodies the wisdom, justice, and righteousness of God, so one could say that God as the "Father" of Israel uses discipline to achieve in her what will be seen perfectly in Christ. We will discuss the Christological fulfillment and focus of discipline (both in terms of instruction and punishment) further in our later chapters.

60. Duane A. Garrett notes, however, "Deuteronomy does tend to stress more the concept of punishment or reward being direct acts of God whereas Proverbs tends to speak more of each action containing within itself a link to reward or punishment." Garrett, *Proverbs, Ecclesiastes, Song of Songs*, 54. Thus it is a more natural law approach, though not exclusively. For more on the doctrine of retribution in the Hebrew Bible, with specific emphasis on the book of Deuteronomy, see Gammie, "The Theology of Retribution in the Book of Deuteronomy," 1–12. Gammie, after tracing some recent and invaluable history with regard to the doctrine, sets forth the idea that retribution is not merely anthropocentric, but is rather theocentric as well, existing side by side (10). He avoids the direct cause-effect dogmatism that seemed to creep into the Hebrew mind, where everything bad was due to sin and everything good was due to man's virtue. After some excellent exegetical insights, he concludes with a good balance, noting that "the message of the Book of Dt [sic] then is that the say of man significantly affects his destiny but that man's is not the last say" (12).

61. Here we see our nominative (*mûsār*), meaning "instruction or discipline," where as we identified earlier in note 5, is found no less than thirty times in Proverbs out of fifty occurrences in the Old Testament. Merrill notes that with regard to the nuance of instruction, "the nom. *mûsār* appears at the beginning of Proverbs (1:2, 7) as a virtual synonym of *hokmâ*, wisdom; *bînâ*, insight; and *da'at*, knowledge (cf. 23:23)." He further notes that with regard to the nuance of punishment, for those who heed it, its purpose is restorative. "It issues from true love (13:34) even though the disobedient hate it (5:12). Those who truly love will not withhold it (23:13)." Merrill, "יסר," in *NIDOTTE*, 481.

The teacher asks the pupil to receive Yahweh's correction and reproof with the understanding that it is an expression of his love. It is primarily instructional in nature, even though, as Garrett points out, the idea of punishment and retribution may also be in the background.

> It is analogous to military training, in which, although the threat of punishment is present, even stern discipline is not necessarily retribution for offenses. Hardship and correction are involved, however, which are always hard to accept.[62]

The recipient is admonished not to despise or reject (מאס) this discipline. As Daniel J. Estes rightly notes:

> The motivation for the learner's response to the teacher's commands is the recognition that this way is advantageous to him . . . it is in the learner's best interests to submit to the directions of the teacher.[63]

A willing and receptive child will identify with fatherly love, and here Yahweh's love is compared to such so that it will be received with the idea that submission to it prolongs life and brings prosperity, bringing *assurance* of Yahweh's love for him (vv. 2, 12).[64] A prudent and wise son will accept that which flows from the heart of God. It is part of the way that Yahweh expresses his *acceptance* and is part of the development of a pious heart toward God.[65] Knowing the truth about this discipline will make one wise

---

62. Garrett, *Proverbs, Ecclesiastes, Song of Songs,* 81. Both nuances (instruction and punishment) seem to be present here then, though *mûsār* seems to carry the primary nuance of instruction because the corrective/rebuke aspect of the discipline seems to be carried more by the use of *tôkaḥat*.

63. Estes, *Hear, My Son,* 112.

64. We will speak more about the father-son metaphor as a vehicle for communicating divine discipline in our next chapter. Verses 11–12 stand in connection to verses 1–2 in the structure of the section. Paul Overland has noted that there are no less than four internal features that shape the frame of this passage: "(1) the occurrence of 'for' or 'because' (*kî*), (2) the occurrence of 'son' (*bēn*), (3) the concept of training, and (4) the ratio of verbs expressing imperative in contrast to those expressing incentive." Overland, "Did the Sage Draw from the Shema? A Study of Proverbs 3:1–12," 426. F. Delitzsch also notes that prosperity must be thought of in the opposite direction as well, so that in the same way that "God should not be forgotten in days of prosperity, so one should not suffer himself to be estranged from Him by days of adversity." Delitzsch, *Proverbs, Ecclesiastes, Song of Solomon,* 64.

65. Garrett remarks, "This section emphasizes piety toward the Lord rather than devotion to the abstractions of wisdom and righteousness," and that the name יהוה is used at least once in every quatrain in verses 5–12. Garrett, *Proverbs, Ecclesiastes, Song of Songs,* 80, and n. 49. Overland provides an intriguing study on Proverbs 3:1–12 and its

concerning the relationship between God and man and will educate one with regard to the nature and character of Yahweh, and this is insight (wisdom) that will bring further blessing, wisdom, and understanding (v. 13).

It will be this passage that is quoted by the writer of Hebrews (12:5–6) in the New Testament as he seeks to encourage them in the midst of hardship, asking them to regard their painful trials as divine discipline. Reminding them that this is one of the ways that God expresses his covenant love and their adoption as God's people (vv. 6–9), the writer also places great emphasis on how discipline is part of the training ground that God uses to instill godly character (here holiness, righteousness, and peace, vv. 10–11).[66]

The one who heeds and accepts discipline in Proverbs is said to be wise and receives the blessing of a rich and full life, as the following selective Proverbs show:[67]

> For these commands are a lamp, this teaching is a light, and the corrections of discipline (*tôkaḥ*) are the way to life (6:23).

> Whoever loves discipline (*mûsār*) loves knowledge, but he who hates correction (*tôkaḥ*) is stupid (12:1).

> A wise son heeds his father's instruction (*mûsār*), but a mocker does not listen to rebuke (*geʿārâ*) (13:1).[68]

> He who listens to a life-giving rebuke (*tôkaḥ*) will be at home among the wise (15:31).

---

likely connections and interpretive expansions on the Shema (Deut 6:4–9), whereby "the product was a sapiential rendition of classic covenantal piety" (440).

66. By contrast, the one who would withhold *mûsār* does not love but rather "hates" (שֹׂנֵא) his son (13:24).

67. All citations come from the NIV.

68. The nominative גְּעָרָה (*geʿārâ*) is a word that bears the meaning of "shout, outcry, rebuke, reprimand, or threat." Hartley, "גער," in *NIDOTTE*, 884–7. It is used fifteen times in the Old Testament, primarily in Wisdom Literature (three times in Proverbs) where it usually is translated as a "rebuke" or "threat." It is very similar to *ykḥ*, which we have covered earlier, and *khh* II (כהה), a hapax (1 Sam 3:13) meaning "to rebuke." Hartley remarks that "a rebuke was a powerful tool of discipline for the teacher. A responsive student accepts a teacher's rebuke, mindful that it is designed either to deter from harm or to sharpen skills. A discerning person is thus more affected by a single rebuke than is a fool by a hundred blows, for the rebuke goes deep into the conscience and motivates that one to improve his conduct (17:10)" (886).

A rebuke (*gᵉʿārâ*) impresses a man of discernment more than a hundred lashes a fool (17:10).

Discipline (*ysr*) your son, and he will give you peace; he will bring delight to your soul (29:17).

In summary, both divine and human discipline in Proverbs is part of an intimate relationship characterized by love. Its benefits and purposes are not to harm us, but to give us life, knowledge, wisdom, discernment, and peace and to save us from the folly of the fool and even death (15:10; 19:18; 23:14).[69] We are encouraged to joyfully receive and respond to this discipline (whether verbal rebuke, instruction, or chastisement) with the understanding that we are loved and accepted. Though at times it may be painful, blessings will abound.

DISCIPLINE IN THE PSALMS AND JOB

Our attention now turns from the book of Proverbs to the Psalms and Job, where discipline is often not understood by the one receiving it. This could not be truer for the righteous Job, who from the human perspective suffers a horrific and tragic ordeal under the watchful eye of Yahweh for no apparent reason. Yahweh early in the narrative recognizes Job as a righteous man. "There is no one on earth like him: he is blameless and upright, a man who fears God and shuns evil" (Job 1:8 NIV).[70] Not only did Yahweh recognize his righteousness, but Satan did as well as he

69. Kirk J. Muller notes the benefits not only for the one receiving it, but for the one giving it as well. "Love truly calls for discipline when it is observed that the discipline will produce the benefits of a long and honorable, secure, full, and pious life for the disciple, as well as comfort and delight for the disciplinarian." Muller, "The Concept of Discipline in the Book of Proverbs," 42.

70. This is an astounding pronouncement by Yahweh himself, to be sure. Job (and later his friends) has no idea of the spiritual test that is going on in the spiritual realm as Satan seeks to test Yahweh and his "servant Job." This does not mean that Job was a perfect man, but is rather a statement about the current state of fellowship shared between Job and Yahweh. There apparently was no unconfessed sin in Job's life, though Eliphaz in Job 5:17 is seemingly implying that Job needs correction for sin. He makes it even more explicit in 22:23 where he advises Job to "return to the Almighty" so that "you will be restored." But this will only be done "if you remove wickedness far from your tent." With regard to Job's friends, John E. Hartley has recognized that "their understanding of retribution leads them to conclude that Job has sinned and has escaped worse punishment only through the mercy of God. Therefore, they earnestly exhort him to repent in order to enjoy God's favor again." Hartley, *The Book of Job*, 44. They tempted Job to repent in order to seek reward, rather than God himself, as Hartley rightly notes (44).

quickly acknowledged Job's reverence (1:9) and questioned its integrity by essentially asking, "How hard can it be when you're blessed?"[71] While Satan was allowed to run roughshod with Job's life, Job saw no reason for his suffering, for he even saw himself as "righteous in his own eyes" (Job 32:1).[72] He even begins to question whether God is just.[73] So the context of the story gives us the impression that this "discipline" that Job is experiencing is not due to sin that needs correction or reproof but is rather a test. As Steven W. Isom has rightly noted, "Discipline is more than punishment. In the case of Job, it is instruction in loyalty through the temptations and trials."[74]

The instructional purposes for Job are that he completely surrender, submit, and trust in God in light of any circumstance, even if he does not understand, for God is sovereign over all things. Further, there are lessons for the reader as well. First, suffering or even divine discipline is not necessarily directly related to sin on *every* occasion.[75] Second, we should be cautious when we open our mouths and claim to speak authoritatively for God or pretend to know what is going on in the spiritual realm where we cannot have full access and understanding. Third, seeing things from a

71. This writer's paraphrase of 1:9.

72. This comes after a long discourse of Job (chapters 26–31) where he pleads his case. This is a confession of introspection (Hartley calls it "an avowal of innocence," *Job*, 45) and is not to be confused with the unrighteous lives of the Israelites who "did what was right in their own eyes" during the period of the judges. Francis Anderson notes that in the Qumran Targum of Job (IIQtgJob) this line is left blank, and this may be due to the astounding nature of the statement. See Anderson, *Job*, 245, n. 1.

73. "And Job continued his discourse: 'As surely as God lives, who has denied me justice, the Almighty who has made me taste bitterness of soul . . .' (27:2)" (NIV). This brought a rhetorical rebuke from Yahweh later, as he says to Job, "Will the one who contends (*yissôr*) with the Almighty correct him? Let him who accuses (*ykḥ*) God answer him" (40:2, Cf. Kingdon, "Discipline," in *EBT*, 449). The nominative *yissôr* is found in the Old Testament only here in Job and can be translated as "faultfinder." See Merrill, "יסר," in *NIDOTTE*, 480. See his comments on emendation as well.

74. Isom, "The Concept of *Mûsār* in the Old Testament," 17. Similarly, Sanders states that the basic meaning of *ysr* in Job is "that of learning or teaching a lesson," and that in Job, discipline must be instructional since there is "blameworthiness on the part of the recipient of the lesson." Sanders, *Suffering as Divine Discipline*, 31–2.

75. Was not this one of the lines of thinking Jesus was seeking to contradict with regard to the man born blind in John 9? Yet, as the Apostle Paul makes very clear in 1 Corinthians 11:30, sometimes it may be a result of sin, as some who were receiving communion in an unworthy manner found themselves directly under the judgment of God, becoming weak and for some succumbing to death.

higher (or detached) perspective, in this case Job's misfortune, challenges us to trust God's plan with regard to our own experiences in life. Here for Job it was a test, and the discipline he encountered was severe and painful, but as we have often seen with God's people of faith, their discipline can rightly be recognized as temporal. In the end, it brings abundant blessing and a full life, which is what was indeed said of Job when this discipline had subsided (42:10, 12, 17).

The book of Psalms presents discipline in a variety of ways, and we will be limited in our coverage of content. As we noted earlier, this discipline includes the people of God who are blessed by it (94:12; 141:5), as well as the surrounding pagan nations and apostate who are cursed and receive it as punishment or rebuke for wickedness (80:16[17]; 94:10; 119:21). When the Lord judges the earth, he is a "refuge for the oppressed, a stronghold in times of trouble" for his people who will place their trust in him (9:9[10], 10[11]). These faithful people will "see the punishment (שִׁלֻּמָה) of the wicked," (91:8) a fate that will last forever (81:15 [16]), in answer to their prayers (59:5[6]; 119:84).[76] In fact, in an ironic fashion, the people of God may at times actually be the instrument that God uses to inflict his punishment on the wicked, as Psalm 149 illustrates:

> For the LORD takes delight in his people; he crowns the humble with salvation. Let the saints rejoice in this honor and sing for joy on their beds. May the praise of God be in their mouths and a double-edged sword in their hands, to inflict vengeance on the nations and punishment (*tôkēḥâ*) on the peoples . . . to carry out the sentence (*mišpāṭ*) upon them. This is the glory of all his saints. Praise the LORD (Ps 149:5–7, 9 NIV).[77]

---

76. The word (שִׁלֻּמָה, *šillumâ*) is the feminine form (seen only here) of the nominative *šillûm* (seen four times in the OT), where in the negative sense, as we see here, means a "repayment or retribution." Philip J. Nel notes that "negatively it refers to retribution for the sins of Israel (Hos 9:7) . . . positively, it designates Yahweh's rewarding of Zion when her enemies are punished (Isa 34:8)." Nel, "שׁלם," in *NIDOTTE*, 133.

77. The reality of and call for the punitive sense of final judgment on the wicked is very prevalent in the Psalms (cf. 1:5; 7:9[10], 11[12]; 9:5[6], 17[18]; 11:6, 7; 17:13; 28:3-5; 31:17[18]; 34:21[22]; 36:11[12], 12[13]; Psalm 37; 43:1; 50:16, 21; 55:23[24]; 58:9[10], 10[11]; 59:5[6]; 68:2[3]; 75:7[8], 8[9]; 82:4, 8; 91:8; 92:7[8]; 94:13; 101:8; 104:35; 106:18; 112:10; 119:119; 125:3; 139:19; 141:10; 145:20; 147:6). Willem A. VanGemeren remarks that the reference to the sword may favor and lead one to believe that indeed the ones carrying out God's punishment are his people. "However, the psalms ascribing kingship to the Lord make it clear that the victory is the Lord's (cf. 96:13; 98:1-3)." VanGemeren, "Psalms," in Gaebelein, *The Expositor's Bible Commentary*, 877.

The psalmists often cry out for Yahweh's judgment upon the nations who oppress them so that their suffering may cease. In addition, they also pray that Yahweh will not put them under *his hand* of discipline, due to the nature of the unpleasant experience. "O LORD, do not rebuke (*ykḥ*) me in your anger or discipline (*ysr*) me in your wrath" (6:1[2]; 38:1[2]).[78] They often express that discipline is a painful mystery to them, for they do not understand, and ask how long it will last.[79] However, as King David at times recognized, submission to the blessing of rebuke is the proper attitude that one should have. For it helps to restrain sin in one's life and furthers the development of a pious, godly character.

> Let a righteous man [or the Righteous One] strike me—it is a kindness; let him rebuke (*ykḥ*) me—it is oil on my head. My head will not refuse it (Ps 141:5 NIV).

Both senses of discipline as *instruction* and discipline as *punishment* for sin are seen in the Psalms. A section of Psalm 94 undoubtedly carries the former while Psalm 39 carries the latter in the following two citations.

> Blessed is the man you discipline (*ysr*), O LORD, the man you teach (*lmd*) from your law (Ps 94:12 NIV).[80]

> You rebuke (*tôkaḥat*) and discipline (*ysr*) men for their sin; you consume their sin; you consume their wealth like a moth—each man is but a breath (Ps 39:11[12] NIV).[81]

There are two Psalms that are especially noteworthy due to their strong affiliation with the idea of divine discipline. Psalm 78 is nothing less than Asaph's didactic narrative of Israel's history that is nothing less than the embodiment of divine discipline on the remnant and judgment upon a

---

78. Kingdon has noted these following psalms as well. Kingdon, "Discipline," in *EBT*, 449.

79. Cf. 6:3[4]; 13:1[2], 2[3]; 79:5; 89:46[47]; 90:13.

80. The instructional aspect of the discipline is nuanced by the instruction in the Torah.

81. The vivid imagery used by David would register powerfully with the Hebrew mind, where moths would easily destroy crops and wool harvested in abundance and squelch their source of income. David identifies this discipline as the "scourge or affliction" (*nega'*) of Yahweh that overcomes him. VanGemeren rightly remarks that "for the child of God, disappointments, adversity, and fatherly discipline are reminders of his father's concern." VanGemeren, "Psalms," in *EBC*, 316.

stiff-necked and apostate people![82] In addition, Psalm 89 is a vivid reminder of the promise of love and discipline that we spoke of earlier with respect to the Davidic Covenant (2 Samuel 7). This powerful Psalm reminds us:

> If his sons forsake my law and do not follow my statutes, if they violate my decrees and fail to keep my commands, I will punish (פָּקַד) their sin with the rod, their iniquity with flogging; but I will not take my love from him, nor will I ever betray my faithfulness. I will not violate my covenant or alter what my lips have uttered (Ps 89:30–34[31–35] NIV).[83]

As noted earlier, the punishment for sin was conditional based on fidelity to the law, and the Davidic covenant guaranteed a response from God when the king would not walk in the prescribed ways of Yahweh. Though the kings would break the covenant, we are reminded in this Psalm that Yahweh will not compromise the unconditional aspects of the promise, for *he will not violate* that which he has declared. So then, we see that Yahweh's discipline and punishment are distinguishing marks of not only retribution for sin but also of his very faithfulness to the covenant relationship, where his love (*ḥeseḏ*) is made manifest.

---

82. The primary message, however, is about God and his faithfulness to Israel in spite of her rebellion, with a pro-David polemic at the end, so as to encourage Israel that indeed God will establish her forever. Thanks be to God that he works through us and with us in spite of us! Marvin Tate notes, "Yahweh's wrath flared up because the Israelites did not trust him enough to depend upon his saving work," and so punishment for sin rested alongside instruction about dependency. Tate, *Psalms 51–100*, 291. It's very interesting to see how Asaph distinguishes between the final condemnation of those who did not believe (vv. 21, 22, 31–33, 59, 62–64) versus the restraint that he had due to the remnant (vv. 38, 39, 68) and his love of David (vv. 70–72). The condemnation of Egypt is recalled as well, and once again we are given insight into the spirit world (like in Job) where we are told that God's wrath against the Egyptians was helped carried out in part by a band of destroying angels (v. 49).

83. The qal perfect (פָּקַד, *pqd*) is a very broad term meaning "to attend to, take note of, care for, punish, muster, assemble, record, enroll, commit, appoint, call to account, or avenge." Williams, "פָּקַד," in *NIDOTTE*, 657. Of the nine times it is used in the Psalms (302 in the OT), only twice does it carry the strong negative connotation of punishment (but it is abundant in prophetic literature, like Jeremiah, Isaiah, and the Minor Prophets, where the covenant violators are announced their fate). Here the negative meaning is "to call to account and punish" due to the sin of forsaking Yahweh's law and commands.

SOME PRELIMINARY CONCLUSIONS
FROM THIS CHAPTER

Our brief survey of divine discipline in this chapter is but a cursory look at the idea as seen in the various genres and contexts of the Old Testament.[84] Specifically, we have looked at the nature and purpose of divine discipline as encountered by Israel as a nation, the Davidites, as well as individuals—all who experience the discipline of God within the context of the covenant relationship. We have not sought to be exhaustive, for this would be an immense task. Why so? This is because the idea of divine discipline is woven so deeply and intricately into the very identity, redemptive stories, and personal experiences of the people of God in covenant with Yahweh. It is a prominent part of the story of redemption. It is part of God's design to handle the problem of sin for his people to know and love him and follow him and his commands while recognizing his holy and sovereign rule over them and the world.

Discipline in the Old Testament is depicted both as a medium for instruction and training as well as a punitive chastisement and judgment upon sinfulness.

As *instruction*, discipline teaches Israel about the character and sufficiency of Yahweh and the nature of their covenant relationship (which includes his steadfast love and favor) and stimulates them to love and obey Yahweh and his law and walk in his ways (Deut 8). His correction and rebuke (with punitive undertones) is his loving concern for their well being and the way in which he imparts wisdom, so that they might experience and know God and the fullness of his promises for blessing, protection, an inheritance, and mighty salvation.

As *punishment*, discipline is part of God's redemptive plan as he executes judgment and retribution on sin (2 Sam 7). On one hand, for the believing remnant, this can rightly be seen as a temporal chastisement and an experience of suffering that separates the faithful from the unfaithful (e.g., the wilderness and exile). Further, it can have a cleansing and restorative effect and serves as a deterrent from sin. Their stay of execution anticipates a future atonement in redemptive history that will pay their debt in full as judgment for sin is poured out on their Substitute sacrifice

---

84. The challenge and task of the theologian is to be able to do theology on a wide redemptive historical scale while at the same time being sufficiently cognizant of the immediate historical contexts and literary devices used from which one's biblical and systematic theology must emerge.

on the cross, who experiences the penalty they rightly deserve (Isa 53). This aspect of discipline stems from Yahweh's promise to the patriarchs, Israel's forefathers, and King David to redeem and restore a people for himself and establish his rule upon the earth, a rule characterized by justice, righteousness, and peace. This type of discipline is part of the way Yahweh expresses his everlasting love, assurance, and acceptance of his chosen people in spite of their sin. It is a way in which he instructs and calls them to persevere in purity and holiness, so as to rid sin from their midst. It is a restorative act of grace. To joyfully receive it like a growing child is to understand it rightly, as it is a sign of God's fatherly care and adoption as his children. To be sure, it is not often understood this way, even by the believing Israelites themselves, as the Psalms testify.

Yet on the other hand, punitive discipline can connote judgment that will fall on the unbelieving nations and apostate Israelites and will be the source of their demise as they are cut off and destroyed from the presence and promises of Yahweh. It is his just wrath on those who have turned away and have refused to repent of their evil and wicked ways. It is a decisive judgment and holds no hope for restoration. This is an altogether different aspect of discipline than that issued to the believing remnant, and it legitimately comes directly out of Yahweh's just and righteous rule of the earth.

So then, there are two slightly different categories that fall under the heading of "discipline as punishment." For the remnant, it is a temporal chastisement that anticipates complete retribution for sin to be fulfilled upon the cross, and for the apostate and unbelieving it is more of a final and decisive judgment with no hope of restoration. The difference between the two has everything to do with whether one is standing or living in covenant relationship with Yahweh.

We have also noted that for *believers,* the idea of discipline is a valuable part of the covenant relationship between a holy God and sinful humanity. As we have surveyed various texts, we have seen different ways in which the intimacy of this relationship is expressed (e.g., the ownership idea of the covenant formula that exclaims, "They will be my people and I will be their God"). There is another extremely powerful metaphor that is often used to qualify the intimacy of the relationship that is worthy of further review and discussion. It is proper that we should ask: to what extent can divine discipline be rightly understood as "fatherly" discipline? We have seen this idea employed in various texts that God regards the discipline he performs as analogous to the father-son relationship. What does this metaphorical terminology add to the idea of discipline, and what ramifications does it have for the way we respond to it? Is there perhaps a redemptive historical link that can be understood and established under the umbrella of "fatherly" discipline as we relate it to Israel, Christ, and the life and practices of the church? Are their potential objections to this? It is to this important theological inquiry and reflection that we now turn.

4

When Divine Discipline Is Classified as a "Fatherly" Discipline

A S WE HAVE SURVEYED some representative texts in the Old Testament concerning the nature and purpose of divine discipline, it has become apparent that the Scriptures occasionally employ the metaphor of God as a "father" to Israel within the context of discipline. The metaphor can either be explicit or implicit in the text.[1] This was especially true for Deuteronomy 8, 2 Samuel 7, and Proverbs 3 and will also be true of Hebrews 12 in the New Testament. Let us look again at these references where the metaphor is indicated.

> Know then in your heart that as a man disciplines his son, so the LORD your God disciplines you (Deut 8:5 NIV).[2]

> He is the one who will build a house for my Name, and I will establish the throne of his kingdom forever. I will be his father, and he will be my son. When he does wrong, I will punish him with the rod of men, with floggings inflicted by men (2 Sam 7:13, 14 NIV).[3]

> My son, do not despise the Lord's discipline and do not resent his rebuke, because the Lord disciplines those he loves, as a father the son he delights in (Prov 3:11, 12 NIV)[4]

1. To be more precise, we can "distinguish between paternal analogies [where the metaphor is implicit] and the naming of God as Father [where it is more explicit]." Witherington and Rice, *The Shadow of the Almighty*, 1.

2. Here the metaphor is implied in a paternal analogy and the parallel conveys the idea that Yahweh considers Israel as his "son." The language of the adoption of Israel in spiritual sonship is pictured.

3. The metaphor of God as father is explicit, as discipline becomes a mark of the assurance of the father-son relationship and promise of God. This language helps shape the uniqueness of the relationship that undergirds the actions of Yahweh, who will deal with the sin of David's line.

4. The assumption is that the Lord disciplines because he loves, like a father (paternal

79

And you have forgotten that word of encouragement that addresses you as sons: 'My son, do not make light of the Lord's discipline, and do not lose heart when he rebukes you, because the Lord disciplines those he loves, and he punishes everyone he accepts as a son.'

Endure hardship as discipline; God is treating you as sons. For what son is not disciplined by his father? If you are not disciplined (and everyone undergoes discipline), then you are illegitimate children and not true sons. Moreover, we have all had human fathers who disciplined us and we respected them for it. How much more should we submit to the Father of our spirits and live! Our fathers disciplined us for a little while as they thought best; but God disciplines us for our good, that we may share in his holiness. No discipline seems pleasant at the time, but painful. Later on, however, it produces a harvest of righteousness and peace for those who have been trained by it (Heb 12:5–11 NIV).[5]

Some questions naturally surface. What does the use of this metaphor for God teach us *about discipline,* and how we are to receive or embrace it as the people of God? Is it important to see God's discipline as fatherly, and what is meant by that qualifier in our texts? This will be our specific focus, and a few of the more recent biblical theologies concerning God's fatherhood will assist us in this matter.[6] For clarification purposes, it is beyond the scope of this work to enter fully into the inclusive language debate regarding the designations of and names for God, though we cannot avoid the "elephant in the room" either. Modern controversies loom over the legitimacy of seeing God as our heavenly Father, and therefore we will briefly discuss the role of the metaphor, the nature of

---

analogy), and the recipient is to receive it in this light, for the father's best interests for the child are in mind. The parallel communicates to us that as the Lord is disciplining us, he is delighting in us as well. So for the recipient, submission to Yahweh's discipline is wisdom in practice.

5. The Hebrews writer loosely quotes from Proverbs 3:11, 12, and then adds or expands upon the significance and meaning of the discipline in light of their adoption as children of God. The author describes how their current circumstances might possibly be seen as fatherly discipline, so as to develop a willingness to embrace it while describing its long-term effects and ultimate purpose in their lives. The Lord is explicitly named as the Father of our spirits. We will deal with this significant passage in detail later in this chapter.

6. See, for example, Thompson, *The Promise of the Father*; Witherington and Rice, *The Shadow of the Almighty*; and Wright, *Knowing Jesus through the Old Testament*. It must be emphasized that it is not our intent to fully develop a complete biblical theology concerning God's fatherhood, but rather to see what this metaphor contributes to our understanding of divine discipline.

biblical language concerning the theology of God's fatherhood, and the frequency of the idea. Further, this chapter will build off Marianne Maye Thompson's recent work *The Promise of the Father,* where she highlights the redemptive historical (or eschatological) link within the relationships of God as the Father to Israel, the Father of Jesus, and Father of the new community or church in the New Testament. I will suggest that discipline can be framed within the context of these relationships, setting the stage and preparing us for further theological reflection in the following chapters on the nature of church discipline itself.

THE FATHERHOOD OF GOD
WITHIN OUR DISCIPLINARY TEXTS

The Scriptures we just reviewed are unique in the way they present divine discipline. Discipline is not simply communicated in a vacuum apart from a context or delivered from a transcendent God whose character and nature are completely unknown to his chosen people. Though there are some exceptions (e.g., Job), the purposes of divine discipline are for the most part apparent in the surrounding context of each passage.[7] Further, unless it is described as a decisive judgment against unbelievers, discipline in the Old Testament is always to be found in the framework of the covenant relationship between God and his people. Its purposes, *depending on context,* can either be to teach, test, and stimulate one to obedience or remembrance; to provide assurance, acceptance, or hope; or to employ temporal chastisement so as to cleanse and restore.[8] In the midst of these different senses is the thought that Yahweh is exercising discipline as a father to Israel or David and his line, whether by direct designation or by analogy. It is an affirmation of his covenant love (*ḥeseḏ*) and his fatherly care. Couched in familial language, this discipline communicates powerfully to the recipient its nature and purpose and the nature of the relationship they have with their Creator-Redeemer.

---

7. But even the reader has a "bird's-eye view" of what was happening in the heavenly realm in Job's situation, as chapter 1 of the narrative would suggest, and so we can gain a measure of understanding of its purposes as a test.

8. It is important that the reader remember not to import all the associated nuances of discipline in any one passage and commit the fallacy of "illegitimate totality transfer." The context of the passage sets limits on what the specific purposes of discipline might be in that case. See chapter 3 for the specific purposes of discipline in our selected passages. It is true that discipline may have a multiplicity of purposes in any one passage.

In Deuteronomy 8, Yahweh disciplines Israel to test them, and like a father who is teaching, instructs them to rely upon the sufficiency of God and his word. Further, he was also punishing them for their sinful lack of trust or faith in his command to seize the Promised Land. So in many ways, the actions of Yahweh are likened to the proper role that a human father should play in his child's life as he grows and learns.[9] Wright notes:

> Here the emphasis is on God's parental discipline of the growing child who needs to learn life's lessons. This was the purpose of the Sinai theophany (Deut 4:36). The wilderness, then, was the time of Israel's adolescence, in which God taught them and disciplined them through hardship and suffering.[10]

He is their *Redeemer* from the Egyptian enslavement. He is their *Sustainer* in that he kept their clothes from wearing out and provided the manna that fostered life. And he is their *Father* in that he is *teaching, training, and correcting Israel*.[11] He guides them into a different direction from where they were currently headed, which was down the path of *disobedience*, the consequence of which led them to nowhere but a wandering in the desert itself, a barren land.[12] He gives them a deeper understanding

9. We will discuss how biblical metaphor works in this fashion in our next section.

10. Wright, *Deuteronomy*, 124.

11. This too seems to be the major emphasis in the similar paternal analogy we saw earlier in Proverbs 3:11, 12. J. W. McKay remarks, "Discipline constantly receives the highest commendation from the wisdom teachers as the best foundation for a good relationship between father/teacher and son/pupil." McKay, "Man's Love for God in Deuteronomy and the Father/Teacher–Son/Pupil Relationship," 432. Willem A. VanGemeren has noted a few of the different ways Yahweh functions as a father in the Old Testament where the metaphor of fatherhood is coupled with something else or a further action. "Yahweh is Father in his acts of electing, providing (Deut 32:6; cf. vv. 9–14; Mal 1:6) redeeming (Isa 63:16), compassion (Ps 103:13–14), protecting his people (68:5, where 'Father' is synonymous with 'Judge'), restoring broken relationships with Israel (Jer 3:4, 19) and special covenantal relationship with David and his descendants (2 Sam 7:14; cf. 1 Chr 17:13; 22:10; 28:6; Ps 2:7; 89:26)." VanGemeren, "*Abba* in the Old Testament?," 392–3.

12. Christopher Wright suggests that the fatherhood metaphor was not primarily an emotional metaphor. "Rather it was a matter of authority on the one hand and obedience on the other, within the framework of a trusting, providing and protective relationship." Wright, *Knowing Jesus through the Old Testament*, 121. He notes that there are two complementary meanings to God's fatherhood of Israel. First, there is the attitude of God as a Father *toward* Israel, where he embodies "concern, love, pity, and patience with the son [Israel] . . . it is a desire for his best interests, which therefore includes discipline (cf. Deut 1:31; 8:5)." Second, there is the expectation of God as a Father *from* Israel, where

of who he is and his purpose for them. He was their strength (Deut 8:17) and their righteousness (Deut 9:4–6). All of this is couched in "fatherly" language and accentuates the way he is *functionally relating* to them, highlighting the paternal relationship.[13] Witherington and Rice remark that with regard to the father language of the Old Testament,

> . . . it suggests God's compassion and care, God's creating and sustaining roles in relationship to Israel, or God's official adopting of the king as his son.[14]

Yet the father language of the Old Testament includes more than just how Yahweh is acting or functioning like a father to Israel (i.e., he adopts, creates, or sustains), but does indeed include the idea that Yahweh is father by *designation*, and thus it says something about God and the status of the relationship.[15] This is made very clear in our text of 2 Samuel 7. Here the text explicitly declares that Yahweh *will be a father* to the Davidic king, and he will be Yahweh's son (more than just by function, but by designation).[16] Of course we are speaking metaphorically here, since it is

---

"he is to be viewed as a trustworthy, protective authority to be respected and obeyed." God expected Israel to see him this way as in Malachi 1:6; Deuteronomy 14:1; Isaiah 1:2f.; Jeremiah 3:19; and Hosea 1:11f. "These show how God felt towards his son and what was expected in return." Ibid., 120–1.

13. God can also be said to be *functioning* like a mother in Scripture as well, cf. Isaiah 42:14, 66:13, and see the discussion in VanGemeren, "*Abba* in the Old Testament?," 394–5. Yet there is a clear difference between God *functioning* like a mother and actually *designating* God as Mother, which the Bible never does. John W. Cooper rightly notes, "All of Scripture's feminine references to God are imagery. They figuratively attribute feminine characteristics to a linguistically masculine person–cross-gender imagery. No feminine term is used as general appellative ('God is a mother'), title ('God the Mother'), or proper name ('Mother') for God. To speak of God as Scripture does in general means, therefore, that *we should occasionally use feminine and maternal imagery for God, but not as frequent references or standard titles and names for God.*" Cooper, "The Motherly Touch of Our Heavenly Father: The Language of Biblical Christianity," in *Our Father in Heaven*, 275.

14. Witherington and Rice, *The Shadow of the Almighty*, 3.

15. Francis Martin remarks, "If I say God is Father, I am saying something, rightly or wrongly, about *God* . . . in keeping with the theory of metaphor, I am speaking of God *relationally* and not merely of the relation." Martin, *The Feminist Question*, 259. Similarly, Marianne Maye Thompson has suggested, "In speaking of God's mercy, compassion, and love, and the way in which God as Father is turned toward Israel for Israel's salvation and wholeness, we are speaking of the 'very nature of God.'" Thompson, *The Promise of the Father*, 38.

16. A similar designation is made in the extrabiblical book of Jubilees, where we read, "And their souls will cleave to me and to all my commandments, and they will fulfill my

not biological fatherhood that is spoken of.[17] To be sure, it is the language of adoption and the election of one who is the head and representative of all God's people.[18] Punishment for the sins of the Davidic line of kings is to

commandments, and I will be their Father and they shall be my children. And they all shall be called children of the living God, and every angel and every spirit shall know, yea, they shall know that these are my children, and that I am their Father in uprightness and righteousness, and that I love them" (Jub 1:23, 24).

17. Thompson has suggested, "No passage in the Old Testament pictures God as the physical father of any people or individual," however "there is a sense in which the predication that God is 'father' of Israel is a literal statement. God is Father of Israel as its founder, the ancestor of the 'clan' of the Israelite nation insofar as he brought it into being (Jer 31:9; Deut 32:4-6; cf. Deut 32:18)." Thompson, *The Promise of the Father*, 40–1. The point, then, is that he is not their biological father in the sense that they came from his physical human body (which he did not have) in the way we understand biological fatherhood today. Witherington and Rice conclude, "It is of course true, and important, that the Father language sometimes shows up in texts where the actual subject is not physical creation but rather the re-creation or redemption of Israel as a people. In such texts it of course does not refer to actual begetting but rather to the process of rescuing and forming a people." Witherington and Rice, *The Shadow of the Almighty*, 13, n. 16. Paul Ricouer has further noted that two familial descriptions and relations are mentioned in Jeremiah 3:19–20 of God and Israel. One is of a father-son relationship and the second is of a husband-wife relationship. Thus he writes, "By means of this strange mutual contamination of two kinship figures, the shell of literality of the image is broken and the symbol is liberated." Ricouer, "Fatherhood: From Phantasm to Symbol," in Ihde, *The Conflict of Interpretations*, 489.

18. Christopher R. Seitz notes, "It is finally the case that *election* is the pivot on which the question of God's fatherhood turns." Seitz, "The Divine Name in Christian Scripture," in *Word without End: The Old Testament as Abiding Theological Witness*, 251. In his in-depth study, W. Marchel notes, "Il en est le Père, non pas en tant que Créateur des Israélites, comme il l'est de tous les hommes, mais en tant que, dans un amour tout particulier, il est créateur de l'existence nationale d'Israël, *par son élection*, et par l'Alliance conclue d'abord avec les Patriarches, puis tout spécialement au Sinaï" (emphasis mine). Marchel, *Abba, Père!*, 51. Francis Martin also states, "The source of Israel's belief in God as the Father of his people was their theological reflection on the mystery *of God's choice of Israel*, expressed in his action by which they were rescued from slavery in a given land" (emphasis mine). Martin, *The Feminist Question*, 271, quoted as well by Thompson, *The Promise of the Father*, 36. It is, however, more than just Israel's reflection that matters, but is rather how God has directly termed himself in Scripture as the "father" of his elect people that substantiates the conclusion. Seitz further classifies God's fatherhood as a "fit metaphor from the Old Testament, used there for the primary purpose of stressing *close familiarity* between God and Israel, God's son; or God and king [as seen here], called 'son' in Psalm 2" (emphasis mine). Seitz, "Reader Competence and the Offense of Biblical Language," in *Word without End*, 294. A similar conclusion is held by Thompson, who claims that though the metaphor of "father" can be used in connection with the creation of all humanity (cf. Isa 45:9–13), it "refers specifically to God's purposes and blessings for Israel." Thompson, *The Promise of the Father*, 41.

be seen in this light, where the metaphor of fatherhood characterizes the forgiving, correctional, instructive nature and intimacy of the covenant relationship that Yahweh longed for with the king.[19] Gerald Blidstein writes:

> It is also most significant that the forgiveness of God is consistently described—from Biblical times on—as the forgiveness of a father towards his children. "As a father has mercy on his children—so have mercy on us, O Lord" is a frequent liturgical refrain modeled on Ps 103:13. This pervasive recognition is surely representative of the Jewish ethos of parenthood, and helped mold it.[20]

Thus it is clear that father language amidst chastisement reminds the king and Israel of their special relationship and calls them to an even deeper, more intimate understanding of it.

Further, Yahweh's fatherhood to the Davidic king in 2 Samuel 7 also plays a significant role in affirming that there indeed was to be an *inheritance* that came from God as "Father" (a common birthright in the father-son relationships in Israel).[21] Here in this context it is not your typical

19. It was not only the Davidic king, but Yahweh longed for this type of relationship with all of Israel as well. The prophet Hosea richly notes, however, how strained the relationship was. "When Israel was a child, I loved him, and out of Egypt I called my son. But the more I called Israel, the further they went from me . . . my people are determined to turn from me" (Hos 11:1, 2a, 7, NIV). Note the designation of the "sonship" (election) of Israel and in the following verses the intimate language that characterized Yahweh's love. "It was I who taught Ephraim to walk, taking them by the arms; but they did not realize it was I who healed them. I led them with cords of human kindness, with ties of love; I lifted the yoke from their neck and bent down to feed them" (Hos 11:3, 4, NIV). Witherington and Rice suggest that one of the reasons why God is not called Father more in the Old Testament is because they had not reached the intimate stage in their relationship with him like that of Moses. "Therefore God did not fully reveal the divine character to Israel in those terms. Yahweh was prepared to relate to Israel in this way, but they were not prepared to respond in such terms. In fact, we notice in later prophetic evidence that Father language is used to chastise Israel from moving away from the possibility of such an intimate relationship." Witherington and Rice, *The Shadow of the Almighty*, 6–7.

20. Blidstein, *Honor Thy Father and Mother*, 130. As cited in Mawhinney, "God as Father: Two Popular Theories Considered," 186.

21. Cf. Psalm 89:26–28. We are not saying the parallel is exact here, for God is not male, a point we shall discuss later. The inheritance is simply analogous to the inheritance given the firstborn in the Hebrew father-son relationship. In a wider sense, the Old Testament speaks of Israel as being Yahweh's firstborn son as well. See, for example, Exodus 4:22; Jeremiah 3:19; 31:9. Christopher Wright also notes that there is an eschatological dimension that is contained in the idea of Israel being Yahweh's firstborn son. He writes, "The idea of Israel being Yahweh's firstborn son certainly envisages the possibility, indeed the definite expectation, that other nations will become sons. But that expecta-

human father-son inheritance but the type of inheritance that can only be granted by Yahweh himself, that of an eternal kingdom and throne granted to One (The Messiah) who would come from the Davidic line (Messiah). Thus the fatherhood metaphor assured the king of the future hope for his descendants and the remnant of Israel, the inheritance that was theirs, and that proper atonement would be made for sin, both in an immediate sense to the king and in a wider redemptive historical sense through the Messianic, Davidic king, from which all Israel would profit. Christopher Wright notes:

> The father-son relationship between God and Israel contained within itself an element of permanence, which injected hope into an otherwise hopeless situation . . . the father could not ultimately disown his son.[22]

THE CHALLENGE IN UNDERSTANDING GOD AS FATHER

The metaphor of God as Father is in some circles a very controversial way to address God nowadays, and this we cannot avoid. One thing is for certain, however. Though it is difficult to describe God in human terms, nevertheless he condescends and allows human terms or language and descriptions (anthropomorphisms) to designate his person and work, though never with complete adequacy with regard to God in his fullness. Jože Krašovec remarks:

> The Hebrew Bible emphasizes unceasingly that God is absolute, all-embracing, unfathomable, incomprehensible, utterly different from human beings. Consequently, the portrayal of the divine is in theory prohibited, although in practice God is presented through analogy, allegories, symbols, and expressions that are used to depict human nature, with all its extremes of feeling.[23]

---

tion in turn depended on Israel fulfilling the demands of *its own* sonship—i.e. that they should live in loyalty and obedience to Yahweh. From this point of view, the sonship of Israel can be understood as a 'missionary' concept." Wright, *Knowing Jesus Through the Old Testament*, 130. Due to Israel's failure to live in such loyalty and obedience, the necessity of Jesus as God's Son to live a perfect life is all the more necessary to God's redemptive purposes for Israel and the nations. On another note, the idea of adoption as a son and inheritance is further expanded in terms of a spiritual inheritance in Christ later in the New Testament. See Galatians 4:7.

22. Wright, "אב" in *NIDOTTE*, 222.

23. Krašovec, "Is There a Doctrine of 'Collective Retribution' in the Hebrew Bible?," 84.

Janet M. Soskice rightly notes that theological realism "accommodates figurative speech which is reality depicting without claiming to be directly descriptive."[24] God as a Father, then, is essentially a biblical metaphor, a way of speaking about God that registers with the human mind. And with regard to metaphor, Soskice defines it as "a speaking of one thing in terms which are seen as suggestive of another."[25] Thus God's fatherhood *in discipline is suggestive* of the type of discipline seen in a proper, godly father-son relationship. Here discipline is exercised appropriately in order to encourage the child to learn, mature, and grow, and to correct and chastise when fallen into self-destructive disobedience, learning the essential lessons of life under Yahweh's loving hand. The underlying subject of the metaphor, or the *tenor*, as it is often named, is the intimate relationship between Yahweh and his people or the king, and the *vehicle* or description of this relationship is found in the terminology of the fatherhood of God. Thus the idea of God in "fatherly" discipline is essentially a metaphor that draws upon the interanimation of two different networks or set of associations to communicate the idea that is being set forth. This, however, does not mean that the associations are exactly a perfect parallel or is the same in *every way*. For even though fatherhood is often *a model* associated with God's actions and his loving concern, painting a picture of the intimacy and status of the unique relationship, this does not warrant that we conclude that God is male by simple use of this metaphor.[26]

24. Soskice, *Metaphor and Religious Language*, 148.

25. Ibid., 49. Soskice defends and outlines her theory of metaphor in pages 24–53. Similarly, Kevin J. Vanhoozer defines metaphor as "indispensable cognitive instruments that enable thought to perceive resemblances between things that would not otherwise be observable. Metaphor is the imagination making creative connections, thinking laterally, talking out loud." Vanhoozer, *Is There a Meaning in This Text?*,129. Building off of Paul Ricoeur's theory of metaphor, Vanhoozer notes that metaphors are "now seen to be a matter not only of words, but of sentences . . . thanks to metaphor, we can set the unfamiliar [in this case, God] in the context of the familiar in order to understand it in new ways . . . it is a 'reworking' of the language, that 'enables us to see things differently." Ibid., 129. With regard to God, then, metaphors allow us to grasp in some measure that which is difficult to understand with our finite minds. And the key to understanding God as a father is by understanding how it is being used at the linguistic level of the sentence, and essentially, what is being communicated as a part of the wider narrative's purpose and context.

26. Ibid., 55. She further writes, "To say that a statement is metaphorical is a comment on its manner of expression and not necessarily on the truth of that which is expressed." Ibid., 70. It was the feminist Mary Daly who misunderstood the biblical language and its use of metaphor and subsequently made the unfortunate illogical leap when she coined

Christopher Seitz calls this latter conclusion the "paradox" of bibli-cal language.

> The very book that uses masculine address for God is the same book that insists that God is neither male nor female but the wholly other Creator God, Lord of all creation—who is not to be constrained by any image, "in heaven or on earth," as the second commandment puts it . . . the Bible asserts that God is above hu-man sexuality; yet then it speaks of God with masculine address and masculine metaphors.[27]

This, for Seitz, is merely the "language of address" that is fitting for the close relationship believers have with the Israelite God, but it does not necessarily connote maleness. He argues that this is one of the ways Jesus used it to connote his unique relationship with the "wholly other God of Israel," who as the Heavenly Father was not a man like the incarnate Christ.

> What could be closer than the personal language he uses? The lan-guage also serves to indicate that God's intention with Israel, first-born son, is now embodied in Jesus, son [sic] of God. "Mother" is further unfit in this instance as a term of address because Jesus' mother is Mary, a woman. But Jesus' father is not a man, on crude analogue with Mary the woman, but the wholly other God of Israel, who, nevertheless, is spoken to on the most intimate terms possible [the paradox]. By speaking of God as Father, Jesus points the way to a particularly intimate and personal relationship with God, one that he himself knows and then offers to the world at large. This is not an act of sexual oppression but an act of sheer grace and mercy.[28]

---

the phrase, "If God is male, then male is God." Daly, *Beyond God the Father*, 19.

27. Seitz, "Reader Competence and the Offense of Biblical Language," in *Word with-out End*, 293. Francis Martin argues that with respect to the engendered language, "In the Hebrew Bible the use of masculine forms for God reflects the unique teaching of God as creator. This linguistic procedure is necessary in order to mediate consistently the otherness of God, not because of language itself, but because the image mediated in and through language. It is a transcultural fact that as natural images, *male* mediates transcendence and otherness and *female* mediates immanence and closeness." Martin, *The Feminist Question*, 251. Martin critiques the feminist rejection of male language for God and discusses "the manner in which biblical language for God creates background images" in pages 248–52.

28. Seitz, *Word without End*, 294.

Seitz questions why calling God Father has become so controversial today, which is a relatively modern issue.[29] He reminds us that doing away with the idea of God as father is paramount to casting off the biblical language about God (or to borrow a phrase from Hans Frei, to "eclipse the biblical narrative").[30] This is an indictment of the biblical illiteracy prevalent both in and outside of the church and the academy today. Yet we cannot dispense of the father or male language in Scripture, for this is how God and his actions are described in the texts.[31] He notes that most

29. Gary Badcock has captured the current tendency well when he states that "maleness, religion, and the language of God the Father are indeed now inter-related in popular imagination and in much contemporary polemical theology." He notes, "What is especially troubling about this is that a leap (an occasionally rather vicious one, I should say) is frequently made from maleness to oppression (patriarchy), as if the two were one and the same, to a supposed ideological sanction for this in religious belief about the maleness of God." Badcock, "Whatever Happened to God the Father?," 11. One classic feminist work that draws such conclusions and reacts strongly against any male or hierarchal terms for God is Ruether's, *Sexism and God-Talk.* See especially pages, 47–71. Badcock notes, "An adequate theological response can only come from the basis of a more satisfactory doctrine of God the Father than we currently posses, and a more satisfactory understanding of maleness than many men possess." Ibid. John Frame, in his recent work on the doctrine of God, lists several reasons why the overwhelming preponderance of masculine imagery has theological importance. See his *The Doctrine of God*, 383–6.

30. He calls this "the thoroughgoing loss of the biblical world as a key agent in informing our world in the modern age and the loss of confidence in how to read and live into these biblical stories, from Old and New Testament." Seitz, *Word without End*, 296. Thompson draws a similar conclusion and suggests, "Part of the point, then, of giving closer attention to the witness of the scriptures is to equip ourselves for the catechesis of a generation for whom the language of scripture and confession is too often alien and empty." Thompson, *The Promise of the Father*, 158. Frame reminds us that in Scripture "God names himself. His names, attributes, and images are not the result of human speculation or imagination, but of revelation. He has not authorized any change in the balance of male and female imagery, and we should not presume to make such changes on our own authority." Frame, *The Doctrine of God*, 384. Casting off the biblical language about God then is essentially casting off revelation.

31. So it is more than just a translation issue, it becomes a textual issue as well. Seitz cautions us, "One should always be suspicious of enlightened efforts to cleanse and modify the Bible's own language—are we to swap the collective wisdom of the ages for the wisdom of some new power group? Where will the swapping end? . . . the trinitarian language 'Father, Son, and Holy Spirit' is to be retained because it belongs to a set story about Jesus that the church did not invent but inherited. To sever our link with that story, including details we may not like, is to begin to sever our link with the person and events themselves. Revelation will become only a personal individual thing, having to do with our experiences, our inward longings, and even our strongly held convictions, and not with a fuller story, with a corporate claim, a social history, and an ultimate link with real people in real times and places, among them the prophets and apostles and a Jesus who

opposition to this is due more from human experiences and modern agendas being projected back on to the language used to describe God.

> That is, because of the sheer passion and concern about male and female equality in the modern age, the paradox of biblical language is forgotten and misunderstood, whereby masculine language of address did not describe God's maleness so that men could feel included, but was simply the fittest language for insisting on God's nonsexual character.[32]

We live in an age where many have forgotten how biblical language can work and at times even be paradoxical, especially when the effort is to describe the indescribable in linguistic terms. We have often failed to enter the biblical world in all of its linguistic complexity in speech about God. As a result, there is a tendency to fall prey to oversimplification and subsequent sweeping conclusions when we transfer our fallible human experiences and modern-day assumptions about language back on to the naming of God that we find in Scripture.[33] Seitz challenges the modern-day agenda by "flipping the coin," if you will.

---

spoke of God as Father in heaven." Seitz, *Word without End*, 298.

32. Ibid., 296. Thomas F. Torrance remarks, "In the sphere of divine revelation an *epistemological inversion* takes place in our knowing of God, for what is primary is his knowing of us, not our knowing of him. This is precisely how we are to understand God's Fatherhood, for all other fatherhood is properly to be understood from its relation to his Fatherhood and not the other way around." Torrance, *The Christian Doctrine of God, One Being, Three Persons*, 105. Describing the indescribable is to project human experience back on to human language about God, especially since we often deal with anthropomorphisms and metaphors that help us conceptualize to a small degree God and his actions. However, the potential for abuse is there, and I would suggest that this has been done when any unhealthy human experiences may cause us to balk at the "now uncomfortable" biblical voice whereby we desire to eclipse the biblical narrative or re-conceptualize God in ways that are foreign to the text and its own language. Seitz reminds us, "Individual details cannot be swapped or exchanged like so many negotiable bits and pieces without final damage being done to the larger organic story itself, its saving purpose, and its faithful representation of the divine life." Seitz, *Word without End*, 298. With regard to the direction of the metaphor, I believe we have to say that it originates with the model of human fatherhood, whereby that model is used to depict the actions of God. However, in depicting the actions of God, God's fatherhood can then in turn serve as that which is primary and a definitive statement and correction of the actions of human fathers. One should be cautious, however, about drawing perfect parallels between the two.

33. Consider, for example, the comments by J. C. L. Gibson, who states with regard to the motherhood language in the Old Testament, "By having God travail with, give birth to, carry his folk from the womb, dandle them at the breast, it subverts from within, perhaps without realizing it, the anti-female prejudice so evident in its pages elsewhere."

The chief task before the church is not to sanitize and correct the Bible from the outside, but rather to learn again from the inside the connected universe of the Bible's presentation; to learn to become competent readers again of a scripture whose intention is not only to include, but to address and judge and cleanse and save.[34]

In an effort to protect fatherhood theology from modern-day criticism, some theologians have backed off considerably from what fatherhood seems to be portraying about God in the text and have simply said that to see God as Father is simply to *name* him only. This erroneous notion is perhaps notably seen in the previously cited article written by Gary Badcock, where he concludes:

Of much greater importance is the fact that the word "Father," when used in the Christian sense of God, is not an image or a

---

Gibson, *Language and Imagery in the Old Testament*, 134. Gibson's assumption is that speaking of God in male terms along with the patriarchal culture of Israel promotes an anti-female prejudice, and thus he is appealing to the motherhood imagery to refute the "prejudice." To be sure there are abuses in every culture, even in biblical culture (cf. Judg 11:29–40; Judg 19), but his statement that there is an anti-female prejudice to the Bible is a bit of an overstatement. Elsewhere he claims, "We cannot go back to these days and model women's position in our society on the Scriptures." Ibid., 12. With these types of sweeping generalizations and overstatements in print today, it is little wonder that paradoxical language about God is misunderstood and critiqued. However, it is interesting to note that there is little criticism in theological circles about motherhood imagery for God on the same level of that of fatherhood imagery. It does not seem to be that modern human ideals of motherhood are above reproach either, and it causes this writer to question why this does not cause problems when motherhood actions are projected back on to God. This could be due, however, to the fact that God is never named "Mother" in the Scriptures, but certainly he has motherly actions, as noted earlier.

34. Seitz, *Word without End*, 299. William P. Alston remarks with regard to the fatherhood metaphor for God, "At least in its earliest employments an ideal picture of fathers as loving, providing, caring, protecting and so on was used as a source of suggestions for thinking of God . . ." This is certainly true, but today, "instead of having more or less clearly delimited set of properties that are fixed as the theological meaning of *father*, people generally work with some idealized picture of human fathers (that may well differ for different people) from which they draw various features in thinking of God." Alston, "Literal Talk of God: Its Possibility and Function," in Kimel, *This Is My Name Forever*, 154. Thus part of the agenda to "sanitize" the Scriptures of the father image for God (which is the biblical language) is undoubtedly due to the shattered condition of the metaphor, where imperfect experiences with human fathering differ so much from the biblical ideal that for some people it nearly becomes impossible to call God a "father," even if we are speaking metaphorically. Thus Seitz's call to connect with the universe of the Bible becomes all the more critical, so that we can learn once again what an ideal, loving father looks like since this is a metaphor that the Scriptures use to speak of God.

metaphor (as is generally supposed) but a name; that is to say, as a name, the use of the word Father in reference to God is not supposed to connote maleness or fatherliness but rather, to denote the one to whom or of whom one speaks.[35]

Yet as we have shown and stated earlier, God as father is more than just a naming of God or designation. But rather as a "father," his fatherhood is a metaphorical model associated with his actions and loving concern for his people, which paints a picture of the intimacy and status of the unique *covenant relationship*, especially in the context of *discipline*.[36] Marianne Maye Thompson has rightfully critiqued the view expressed by Badcock when she states that this view basically extracts "the designation of God as Father from the biblical narrative," and then defends

> . . . the abstracted concept as though its meaning were to be explicated quite apart from the historical or literary contexts in which it appears. This is tantamount to a neglect of the biblical narrative in practice.[37]

Therefore we cannot merely say it is only a name, but it is a powerful metaphorical tool used by the inspired writers of Scripture that not only attempts to explain who God is and what he does, but further defines the very identity of God's people as those who have been chosen and adopted by God. And this plays a key role in how they are to receive and relate to the discipline they receive from him.

35. Badcock, "Whatever Happened to God the Father?," 12. There is certainly some truth to the idea that this is the language of address, as we noted in Seitz's argument, and this then excludes the conclusion that God is male, but it does not exclude the metaphor of being father-like, or practicing fatherliness in order to nuance the type of relationship Israel or the church has with God. Even the divine names for God communicate something about God and are more than just a mere naming. James Daane remarks, "He who is a father communicates something of himself to that which he fathers in such a way that the other has not merely his source in the father, but also the nature of the father's reality." Daane, "Father," in Bromiley, *The International Standard Bible Encyclopedia*, 285. A helpful chart of the divine names along with their significance or meaning and accompanying Scripture references can be found in House, *Charts of Christian Theology and Doctrine*, 51–2. See also Lang, *The Hebrew God*, 202–8.

36. Dennis J. McCarthy notes in Jeremiah 31:9 that the restoration of the father-son relationship is the restoration of the covenant relationship. "Thus in the mind of Jeremiah the covenant relationship and the father-son relationship were not incompatible, they were essentially the same thing." McCarthy, "Notes on the Love of God in Deuteronomy and the Father-Son Relationship between Yahweh and Israel," 147.

37. Thompson, *The Promise of the Father*, 167.

THE (IN)FREQUENCY OF THE METAPHOR

The metaphor of God as a Father in the Old Testament is not as overly prevalent as one might think. Though the Scriptures do at times characterize the intimate relationship Yahweh had with Israel and the king this way, especially in the context of discipline, it is still relatively a rare occurrence.[38] Scholars have noted that the surrounding Canaanite cultures, along with the fertility cults of other pagan nations, were a constant problem for monotheistic Israel. The Scriptures stand as a witness to this as well.[39] With the pagan male and female gods and their willingness to call their gods "father" or "mother," there may indeed have been hesitance within Israel's "official theology" or among the true Yahwists to use this type of language to describe the Israelite deity.[40]

In the Ancient Sumerian Hymns, the temple poets often call their god Enlil the "father."

> When Father Enlil seats himself broadly on the holy dais, on the lofty dais . . . the earth-gods bow down willingly before him . . . the great and mighty lord, supreme in heaven and earth, the all-knowing one who understands the judgment, has set up his seat in Duranki . . .[41]

This is not just on occasional reference to Enlil as "father," for in another short hymn (an irshemma-song) of twenty-five lines to this

38. Helmer Ringgren surmises, "It follows from all of this that the idea of God as father of the people of his own possession does not occupy a central place in the faith of Israel. This is only one of many figures which the OT uses to describe the relationship between Yahweh and Israel." Ringgren, "אָב," in Botterweck and Ringgren, *The Theological Dictionary of the Old Testament*, 18. Wright agrees that it did not figure prominently in Israel's "official" theology, but it was a "significant strand in OT theology that informed Jesus' and the NT's concept of sonship." Wright, in "אָב," in *NIDOTTE*, 222.

39. See, for example, Israel's tendency to forsake the covenant and seek after other gods as documented in Judges 2. Daniel I. Block notes, "The onomastic, epigraphic, and iconographic evidence suggests that even while the Israelites and later Judeans were professing primary faith in Yahweh, many were also enamored of the gods of the nations, integrating pagan beliefs and cultic practices into their own religious structures . . . however, in sharp contrast to the religious situation outside Israel, and in stern reaction to the historical reality within, the Old Testament portrays Yahwists as consistently and vehemently opposed to the worship of any gods alongside or in competition with Yahweh." Block, *The Gods of the Nations*, 69.

40. See Wright in "אָב," in *NIDOTTE*, 222. He notes that kingship and covenant metaphors are more common.

41. Pritchard *Ancient Near Eastern Texts Relating to the Old Testament*, 573.

Sumerian god and his wife he is called Father Enlil (here portrayed as the god of fertility) no less than ten times while being named lord eight times. Note the following excerpt from this hymn,

> . . . Father Enlil, lord of all lands, Father Enlil, lord of the rightful command, Father Enlil, shepherd of the blackheads, Father Enlil, insightful in his calling . . .[42]

In an Akkadian vassal treaty of Esarhaddon (cf. Ezra 4:2), king of Assyria, the heading of the treaty reads,

> Seal of the god Ashur, king of the gods, lord of all lands, which is not to be altered; seal of the great ruler, the father of the gods, which is not to be contested.[43]

Willem A. VanGemeren further notes examples from Hittite, Canaanite, Egyptian, and other cultures that surrounded Israel that readily employed the terminology of fatherhood to their gods, thus revealing that the nations

> . . . held to a mythological understanding of a relationship between the worlds of the gods and men. In this context the writers of the OT cautiously referred to Yahweh as "Father." Yahweh is not El, the father of "the gods." He is not Baal, the god of fertility. Yahweh is the Creator of everything and is sovereign (Lord, King, Ruler) over the nations.[44]

---

42. Ibid., 576.

43. Ibid., 534. In the Ugaritic writings the Near Eastern god, 'Ēl portrays the "figure of the divine father" who is the "primordial father of gods and men, sometimes stern, often compassionate, always wise in judgment . . . In Akkadian and Amorite religion as also in Canaanite, 'Ēl frequently plays the role of 'god of the father,' the social deity who governs the tribe or league, often bound to league or king with kinship or covenant ties." Cross, *Canaanite Myth and Hebrew Epic* 42–3.

44. VanGemeren, "*Abba* in the Old Testament?," 392. Witherington and Rice quote VanGemeren here as well but suggest that he is only partially correct, for father language was still being applied to foreign gods (and even the emperor) during the time of the writing of the New Testament, which explicitly uses "Father" for God. They hypothesize, "Since Christianity was a missionary religion, it actually looked for points of contact in its God language with that of the larger culture, whereas Hebrew God talk was primarily concerned with stressing what distinguished Yahweh from other deities." Witherington and Rice, *The Shadow of the Almighty*, 5. Though their former hypothesis sounds like a good idea, it is largely unsubstantiated, and it is more likely that Father language was used more in the New Testament for decidedly different reasons, as we will see. To their credit, they preface their hypothesis with "perhaps." For more on the religious use of the father image in the ancient world, see Schrenk, "πατήρ," in Friedrich, *The Theological*

Though the Ancient Near Eastern pagan religions often employed the use of fatherhood language for their gods, nevertheless the characterization of these gods were altogether different from the characterization of Yahweh, a point that John W. Miller raises.

> The assumption that biblical father religion is simply continuous with wider ancient Near Eastern patriarchalism is unsupported by a comparison of the portrait of God as father in the Bible with divine father figures in several contemporary ancient Near Eastern mythologies. Only in biblical tradition is it believed that a father-god truly worthy of being hallowed is fully in charge of the cosmic home.[45]

This may further substantiate why in the Old Testament the fatherhood of Yahweh is declared more by what he does rather than by the designation of "Father." For the model of fatherhood in the religious life of the ANE religions and as exemplified in their myths and literature was an altogether different concept than the model used for the metaphor of calling the Israelite deity a Father to his people. By contrast:

> The certainty that God is Father and Israel his son is grounded not in mythology but in a unique act of salvation by God, which Israel had experienced in history.[46]

Dictionary of the New Testament, 951–9.

45. Miller, *Calling God "Father,"* 35. So also Block, who states, "Deuteronomy is emphatic about the qualitative difference between the God of Israel and the gods of the other nations," and even further, "We observe several strong denials of the objective realities of other national deities." Block, *The Gods of the Nations*, 70–1. Miller, in his text, surveys some of the mythological portrayals of the divine father figures in the Babylonian creation story, the *Enuma Elis*, the Mesopotamian narrative known as the *Gilgamesh Epic*, as well as mythological tales in Canaanite and Egyptian cultures. He argues that unlike Yahweh, the pagan divine fathers are at times portrayed problematically in that they may embody "marginality, cruelty, incompetence, and powerlessness," and "more often than not, pose dilemmas to which mother, son, or daughter deities must respond either by defending themselves or by taking action to uphold the universe in their stead." Ibid. By contrast, Yahweh is portrayed as "one God and one God only to be worshiped and served. He is a divine father, yet not cowardly or withdrawn like so many of his paternal contemporaries, but alert rather, vigorously involved and uniformly just, kind, and compassionate. 'After all, you are our Father . . . you, Yahweh, are our Father, 'Our Redeemer' is your name from of old (Isa 63:16).'" Ibid., 43.

46. Jeremias, *The Prayers of Jesus*, 13, quoted in Geffré, "Father as the Proper Name of God," in Metz and Schillebeeckx, *God as Father?*, 44.

Perhaps one of the most recent insightful reasons given as to why explicitly calling God Father in the Old Testament was a relatively rare occurrence has been provided by Christopher Seitz. It is true that it is more common for the Old Testament to portray God as a Father by implication rather than by explicit designation. The title is there, it just isn't used that much. Yet even when it *is* implied, we notice something else in connection with it that is much more explicit. It is quite common to see Israel or the Davidic king as having received the status of "sonship." This more prevalent use of sonship language (e.g., Hos 11:1) might simply be a matter of perspective and who is speaking in the narrative. Seitz argues:

> In the Old Testament the filial relationship is described *from God's perspective*, hence the overwhelming preponderance of "son" over "Father" as descriptive of the divine-human relationship. This preponderance changes in the New Testament . . . the change is perspectival. The filial relationship is the same as in the Old Testament, but in the New it is described *from the standpoint of the Son,* Jesus. Where "son" appeared in the Old Testament, in the New we have "Father."[47]

This may very well be part of the reason why Father is not used more in more formal narrative or speech in the Old Testament. It has everything to do with the angle being taken.

Finally, as we noted earlier (note 19), Witherington and Rice suggest that a reason why Israel did not relate to God explicitly as their Father more often in their literature might have something to do with the fact that they had not reached an intimate stage in the relationship like that of Moses.

> It is as if God increasingly attempts to reveal the divine nature in intimate terms, not just to individuals but to the chosen people as a whole, but the response in prayer and praise using the Father language is generally lacking.[48]

They suggest that the phrase given to Moses to identify the God who is sending him to Egypt to release the Hebrews from Pharaoh's hand,

47. Seitz, "The Divine Name in Christian Scripture," in *Word without End*, 258. Witherington and Rice also sight Seitz here and emphatically agree, "This is essentially the correct answer [to why Father is not used more in the OT]. It is Jesus himself who places the emphasis on God as Father, and this explains why the usage in the NT is so much more prevalent than in the OT." Witherington and Rice, *The Shadow of the Almighty*, 5.

48. Witherington and Rice, *The Shadow of the Almighty*, 7.

namely, "I AM WHO I AM," in Exodus 3:14, is not *merely* about who Yahweh is in his divine essence (though this is true), but rather "who Yahweh is or will be in relationship to his people—in his self-revelation."[49] They make a convincing case for the idea that this God is later said to be known by what he has done, so that "in all the subsequent accounts of Israelite history God is said to be known as the one who brought Israel out of Egypt" (Exod 20:2).[50] What this tells us, then, is that God, his name, and his nature are to be continually revealed in more intimate and even fuller ways as God initiates and salvation history progresses.

> God will choose when and where the divine name will be revealed through actions and speech. This narrative then suggests not only intimacy between God and his people, but also an ongoing story with more yet to be revealed. It suggests a set of circumstances in which God's people would look forward to and expect God to continue to progressively reveal the divine character and plan and purposes. *One of the ways that was to happen was by the drawing of analogies between God's activities and that of a human father, and even the naming of God as Father, the creator and sustainer of a people who relates to those people in an intimate, even if sometimes intimidatingly open and frank fashion* (emphasis mine).[51]

They further argue that there was a growing tendency in later prophetic and intertestamental literature (e.g., Wisdom Literature, Qumran writings, later Targums and Talmud) to use father language for God.[52] This obviously takes on an even greater significance and *frequency* when Jesus breaks on the scene and the New Testament era brings to us an even fuller revelation of the God of Israel seen in incarnate flesh. I would suggest, however, that the revelation of God as Father had less to do with how intimate the covenant relationship *was becoming* based on human faithfulness, but is rather due more to how *salvation history was progressing* whereby God began to initiate and reveal his divine plan in a fuller

---

49. Ibid., 11.

50. Ibid., 12.

51. Ibid., 13.

52. See their discussion and presentation in ibid., 13–6, as they have built off of Thompson, *The Promise of the Father*, 48–55. Thompson lists a number of texts in Second Temple Judaism that characterize and invoke God as Father. Ibid., 48, and especially footnote 22. Proof that this is true can be found in John 8:41, where it would seem to suggest that indeed calling God Father was indeed an idea the Jews were willing to embrace at that time.

sense.[53] God was further to be dwelling among them, literally in Jesus and then later with the giving of the Spirit. It was a result of this initiation of his salvific plan that the intimacy subsequently followed, whereby we can now cry out "Abba Father" to the triune God of Israel. Therefore, when we consider the significance of using fatherly language in the context of discipline, we may postulate that it not only describes how God desired intimacy and how he longed to characterize the covenant relationship, but also how in disciplining them he was revealing his ongoing plan of redemption and priming them for an even fuller future hope, whereby in the end, the dwelling place of God will be with his people. "He will dwell with them, and they will be his people, and God himself will be with them as their God" (Rev 21:3 ESV).

Though we have listed a multiplicity of reasons for why God is not addressed as a Father more often in the Old Testament, we cannot make the broad statement that says that the idea was not a significant strand of theology that permeated the daily life and thoughts of the common Israelite. This is ever more brought to the fore when we consider the fact that the individual Israelite was not afraid to proclaim his or her spiritual allegiance through the use of theophoric names, and this includes the idea of seeing Yahweh as a father, as has become evident in the study of onomastics. Daniel Block explains just what exactly we are referring to.

> In contrast to our own culture, in which names are often selected arbitrarily or simply on euphonic grounds, in the ancient Near Eastern world names borne by individuals were much more than mere means of identification. Names generally expressed some aspect of the personality or character of the person who bore or of the person who gave the name. Many Semitic names expressed theological ideas, particularly when they incorporated divine names. These theophoric names were in effect expressions of faith, reflecting the spiritual allegiance of the bearer . . . the onomastic evidence for popular devotion to Yahweh in Israel is both abundant and clear.[54]

---

53. This can be argued by the fact that the "spiritual leaders" of Israel as portrayed in the gospels are seemingly clueless and worthy of Jesus' rebuke when it comes to knowing and understanding the things of God. See, for example, Jesus' dialogue with Nicodemus in John 3.

54. Block, *The Gods of the Nations*, 40. Block also notes (footnote 21, same page) a detailed study done by J. H. Tigay where more can be found on theophoric names in Israel. See Tigay, "Israelite Religion: The Onomastic and Epigraphic Evidence," in Miller,

Though divine elements in names such as '*ēl* (God) and *yāh* (the Lord)[55] were abundant, Israel also readily recognized the role of the father and the fatherhood of God in these personal names. Willem A. VanGemeren has pointed out a few of these names that are worthy of mention. Names like Abinadab, "(My) Father is Generous" (1 Sam 7:1; 16:8); Abiezer, "(My) Father is a Help" (2 Sam 23:27); Abiel, "(My) Father is God" (1 Sam 9:1); Joab, "Yahweh is Father" (2 Sam 8:2); and Abijah, "(My) Father is Yahweh" (2 Kgs 1:3, 4, 8, 12) are just a few of the names that express the Israelite belief and deep thanksgiving for Yahweh's fatherhood.[56] So from the perspective of the individual Israelite, God's fatherhood and their sonship or adoption as a people is clearly seen in these theophoric names, which are expressions of their personal identification with the God of Israel, their Father. This would seem to support Seitz's thesis that the perspectival approach to God's fatherhood does explain its apparent lack of use in the Old Testament *narrative*. For when we actually take a look at life *from the eyes of the individual Israelite*, Yahweh's fatherhood is indeed a common conviction, as is seen from the prevalence of the idea from these theophoric names.

FATHERHOOD AS A CONCEPTUAL BRIDGE IN REDEMPTION HISTORY

The metaphor of God's fatherhood is a foundational understanding of God and his nature within Israel's redemptive history and experience. It further helps define their election and covenantal theology as well as their whole approach to the pietistic family life of the common Israelite. The metaphorical idea of Yahweh's fatherhood, or Israel's sonship, however one wants to say it, seems to surface and become a central idea and basis

---

Ancient Israelite Religion, 157–94. Allen P. Ross notes that in general, "Names were given and explained to express the faith of the parents (Judah, 'may he be praised,' explained by 'I will praise'), record significant circumstances at birth (Jacob's grabbing the heal, Esau/Edom, born hairy [Seir] and red), or preserve the memory of supernatural events (Bethel, the house of God). At times, names were changed to reflect a new status or vision (Abram changed to the dialectical variant Abraham to recall the sounds of 'father of a multitude . . ."" Ross, "שֵׁם," in *NIDOTTE*, 149.

55. A shortened form of Yahweh. See Lang, *The Hebrew God*, 206.

56. VanGemeren, "*Abba* in the Old Testament?," 393. For more on theophorous names that exemplify fatherhood, see Gottfried Quell's section in "πατήρ," in *TDNT*, 969.

of appeal both *by God*, and from Israel's perspective, *to God*, when we look at some of the most pivotal moments in Israel's salvation history.

For example, it is part and parcel to their identity as a people of God's possession rescued from Egypt and disciplined in the wilderness (Deut 8:5; 32:6, 9, 18).[57] Following the conquest, the dark period of the judges in the land of Canaan, and the establishment of the monarchy, it becomes an overarching idea within the promise of 2 Samuel 7. Here a truly redemptive-historical hope is given to the Davidic line of kings, who were to stand as the representative head of God's people. Further, God's fatherhood is also the basis of God's appeal to Israel and his indictment of their disobedience prior to the exile. For in Jeremiah we read Yahweh as saying:

> I myself said, "How gladly would I treat you like sons and give you a desirable land, the most beautiful inheritance of any nation. I thought you would call me 'Father' and not turn away from following me. But like a woman unfaithful to her husband, so you have been unfaithful to me, O house of Israel," declares the LORD.[58]

Wright notes that remarkably, after Israel's punishment and discipline in the exile, it is God's fatherhood that *Israel* appeals to in Isaiah 63 and 64 as "the basis for a fresh act of redemption and a restored relationship."[59]

> But you are our Father, though Abraham does not know us or Israel acknowledge us; you O LORD, are our Father, our Redeemer from of old is your name . . . yet, O LORD, you are our Father. We are the clay, you are the potter; we are all the work of your hand. Do not be angry beyond measure, O LORD; do not remember our sins forever. O, look upon us, we pray, for we are all your people (Isa 63:16; 64:8, 9 NIV).[60]

57. Wright reminds us, "In the narrative texts, the declaration that Israel was Yahweh's firstborn son came *before* the exodus and the making of the Sinai covenant (Ex 4:22)." Wright, *Knowing Jesus Through the Old Testament*, 126.

58. Jeremiah 3:19, NIV.

59. Wright, *Knowing Jesus Through the Old Testament*, 126. So also Robert Hamerton-Kelly, who writes, "The father symbol is not only a foil for the indictment, but also a basis for the plea of pardon . . . they [Israel] appeal to God as Father in the light of him as creator who determines their lives in every aspect, and as their redeemer, whose care for them in history surpasses that of their own fathers Abraham and Israel." Hamerton-Kelly, *God the Father*, 48. In this way, Hamerton-Kelly calls the declaration of God as Father a "prophetic device." Ibid., 45. Israel's appeal to God as their Father here connotes the idea that Israel saw the exile as a none other than a fatherly discipline.

60. Wright, *Knowing Jesus through the Old Testament*, 127.

As salvation history progresses, the New Testament will testify to the new covenant of God in Christ and how the idea of the fatherhood of God will find a deeper and fuller expression in the life of God's chosen people—both Jews and gentiles who are brought into the kingdom.[61] Hear the testimony of Galatians 4.

> But when the time had fully come, God sent his Son, born of a woman, born under law, to redeem those under law, that we might receive the full rights of sons. Because you are sons, God sent the Spirit of his Son into our hearts, the Spirit who calls out, "*Abba*, Father." So you are no longer a slave, but a son; and since you are a son, God has made you also an heir (Gal 4:4–7 NIV).

God's fatherhood takes on new emphasis, development, and even levels of intimacy in the language and teachings of our Savior, Jesus Christ, the Son of God. Jesus' primary language of address to the God of Israel is "Father," and though to be sure he has a unique Father-Son relationship with God within the context of the Trinity, he further invites his disciples to address God as "our Father" in teaching them to pray (Matt 6:9).[62] John Frame notes the difference here.

> God is not our Father in the same sense that he is the Father of Jesus; we are not God. Jesus delicately distinguishes the two fatherhoods

61. Wayne Grudem brings this progression of fatherhood and renewed sense of adoption to the fore when he remarks, "Even though there was a consciousness of God as Father to the people of Israel, the full benefits and privileges of membership in God's family, and the full realization of that membership, did not come until Christ came and the Spirit of the Son of God was poured into our hearts, bearing witness with our spirit that we were God's children." Grudem, *Systematic Theology*, 737.

62. Thompson remarks, "In speaking of God as 'my Father' and 'your Father,' Jesus appropriates the relationship of Father and Son to himself, and of Father and children to his own community. Jesus did not proclaim that a relationship with God formerly unavailable was now possible. Rather, he revivified the reality of God's Fatherhood for Israel by speaking of God's mercy and faithfulness, calling for repentance, and insisting that there could be no devotion to that God without corollary commitment to one's brothers and sisters." Thompson, *The Promise of the Father*, 85. Though he does recognize the salvation historical implications of Jesus' use of Father for God, Hamerton-Kelly puts more of a sociological spin on it when he states that when Jesus uses the term Father for God, "The effect . . . was to deprive the patriarchy, along with everything else which is compared with the sovereignty of God, of its absolute power. The fact that Jesus chose the 'father' symbol for this purpose suggests that he intended to direct his message especially at the patriarchy and to reorganize it by freeing people from its clutches." Hamerton-Kelly, *God the Father*, 102–3. This seems to read more into Jesus use of "father" than is warranted and may be more of nuanced argument in support of a modern agenda.

of God when he speaks with Mary Magdalene after his resurrection: "I am returning to my Father and your Father, to my God and your God" (John 20:17). Elsewhere in the New Testament, the term *adoption* is used to describe our relationship to the Father (Rom 8:15, 23; 9:4; Gal 4:5; Eph 1:5). Jesus is the son by nature; we are sons by adoption. Jesus is the eternal Son, but God confers sonship upon us in time (cf. John 1:12–13). But the distinction is not a total separation. We are "coheirs with Christ," for "we share in his sufferings in order that we may also share in his glory" (Rom 8:17).[63]

Further, as we just noticed in our Galatians passage, and as will be true in Romans 8:15–17, the Spirit of God in the hearts of God's people cries out in the intimate language of "*Abba*, Father."[64] This is the Aramaic language that our Savior used in the gospel of Mark during his moments of intense emotional suffering, as he anticipated vicariously receiving God's just punishment for human sin upon his shoulders.

> Going a little farther, he fell to the ground and prayed that if possible the hour might pass from him. "*Abba*, Father," he said, "everything is possible for you. Take this cup from me. Yet not what I will, but what you will" (Mark 14:35, 36 NIV).

The *Abba* language in context seems to correlate nicely with the fatherhood-sonship relational themes of trust and obedience seen through redemptive history as cited earlier by Wright (see note 12).[65] For Christ

63. Frame, *The Doctrine of God*, 372–3. Thomas F. Torrance draws a sharp distinction to the two fatherhoods, "An entirely different kind of relation obtains in each case, for one is ontological and belongs to the intrinsic life and eternal Being of God, and the other is contingent and relates to the temporal existence of the creature." Torrance, *The Christian Doctrine of God*, 207.

64. The Romans passage reads, "For you did not receive a spirit that makes you a slave again to fear, but you received the Spirit of sonship. And by him we cry, 'Abba, Father.' The Spirit himself testifies with our spirit that we are God's children. Now if we are children, then we are heirs—heirs of God and co-heirs with Christ, if indeed we share in his sufferings in order that we may also share in his glory" (Rom 8:15–17, NIV). By contrast, those Jews or anyone else who rejected Christ had no grounds from which to claim that God was their Father, as Jesus taught in John 8:41–44.

65. I am in agreement, as this chapter would surely suggest, with Willem A. VanGemeren that Jesus' use of the term *Abba* was not a new or novel teaching that was Jesus' distinctive contribution to the metaphor of fatherhood in Israel (reacting to Joachim Jeremias in his *New Testament Theology*, 61–8). "Rather, Jesus restored the OT teaching of Yahweh's love, forgiveness, readiness to listen to prayer, and fatherly concern. Jesus intensified this relationship in that he, as the Son, lived among us and taught more about the uniqueness and the glory of our relationship with our Heavenly Father."

was trusting in the Father for whom all things are possible, and he was willing to surrender his human will to the will of the Father in obedience.[66] And this is what we are called to do as well (John 14:1, 15) as the children of God who, in the words of the old hymn, are to "Trust and Obey."[67]

Though the New Testament deepens and intensifies our understanding of God as Father to his people who live by faith (Gal 3:26), especially as the indwelling Holy Spirit testifies to our status as adoptive sons,[68] we still have not fully realized our adoption in its fullest and final sense. This is the teaching of Paul in Romans 8, whereby all of creation and we ourselves as "firstfruits of the Spirit" (v. 23) long for God to bring to consummation his plan of salvation. Here our adoption and sonship will be made complete, whereby we experience entire sanctification and will live with Christ in a glorified state with a resurrection body at his second advent. This is our hope and is the climactic fulfillment of Jeremiah 31:1 for Israel (see also Rom 11:26).[69]

Therefore, we may say that God's fatherhood and the elective sonship of his people holds a prominent place throughout salvation history, from the Old Testament all the way through the New Testament.[70]

VanGemeren, "*Abba* in the Old Testament?," 397. Thompson critiques VanGemeren as misrepresenting Jeremias (32, n. 37), though she would agree with VanGemeren's conclusions about Jesus' intensification of the fatherhood relation in an eschatological perspective by use of this word. See Thompson, *The Promise of the Father*, 21–34.

66. See Thompson, *The Promise of the Father*, 161. Note also the words in Hebrews 5:8, 9 in the NIV. "Although he was a son, he learned obedience from what he suffered and, once made perfect, he became the source of eternal salvation for all who obey him." As Christ was obedient, so we are to be obedient, even if this involves suffering. Trust in and obedience to Christ are the foundations of eternal salvation for those in the new covenant community and is evidence of our sonship as well.

67. Indeed, the fatherhood of God implied the ethical and spiritual obligations of sonship. Allen Mawhinney writes, "The writers of the NT repeatedly develop the ethical responsibilities of the Christian in the context of his sonship. For example, in Eph 1:4–5 Paul expresses the Christian's holiness and blamelessness as the goal or purpose of his election and predestination to sonship . . . similarly, when laying the groundwork for his plea for Christian service in love Paul reminds the Ephesians that there is (among other things) 'one God and Father of us all' (4:6)." Mawhinney, "God as Father: Two Popular Theories Considered," 188.

68. I am using this in a generic sense, including the idea that we are daughters as well.

69. Paul reminds us that the full number of gentiles included in Christ will experience this consummation as well (Rom 11:25).

70. We must not say that it is the *only* conceptual bridge, but is rather a prominent one.

Thompson calls this the "eschatological trajectory of God's Fatherhood."[71] Furthermore, we have discovered that discipline in the Scriptures is often characterized as a fatherly discipline. *It is therefore evident, then, that divine discipline and the accompanying fatherhood language or idea is purposefully woven together in order to powerfully communicate to God's people his overall redemptive historical purposes. It characterizes the intimacy, promises, and hope within the covenant relationship, and God's deep desire to restore them fully from sin and show them his steadfast love while bringing about their full adoption as sons.*

Divine discipline has a decidedly salvation historical thread to it, as God uses it to bring his people back to himself. As his treasured possession, we are to embrace discipline as God's fatherly love, and to recognize that it is the assurance of his adoption, election, and the promise of an eternal inheritance, whereby he works to restore us fully into Christlikeness so that we ourselves may be like the One who is holy. Since his design from the beginning was that we be a kingdom of priests and a holy nation (Exod 19:6; 1 Pet 2:9), he uses "fatherly" discipline to achieve that end. There is perhaps no more explicit passage in all of Scripture where these truths are taught and expanded for us than in Hebrews 12, a passage we cited at the beginning of this chapter. Here we see the "fatherly" motif in the context of discipline reiterated with great continuity in the New Testament, solidifying our conclusions about its nature and purposes from the Old Testament and throughout salvation history. And in support of the thesis of this book, we will see that it is a valuable tool used by God as part of his redemptive plan.

GOD'S FATHERLY DISCIPLINE IN HEBREWS 12

The context of our passage in Hebrews 12 follows what is known as the great "faith chapter," where the writer of Hebrews has briefly taken a redemptive historical look at some of the great men and women of faith

---

71. Thompson, *The Promise of the Father*, 156. For more on her survey of God's fatherhood under what she calls the eschatological trajectory, see pages 158–64. See also Wright, who notes the same in his *Knowing Jesus through the Old Testament*, 129–35. Paul Ricouer suggests, "Eschatological royalty and fatherhood remain inseparable right into the Lord's Prayer; this begins with the invocation of the Father and is continued by 'petitions' concerning name, kingdom, and will which are only understandable only in the perspective of an eschatological fulfillment." Ricouer, "Fatherhood: From Phantasm to Symbol," 490.

in the Old Testament. Many of them faced horrible circumstances, great trials, and died with only the hope of salvation through faith in their God. They now, along with us, can be made perfect due to the perfect sacrifice of Jesus Christ. All saints, both old and new, now can rejoice in the hope found in the person and work of Jesus Christ, who is the author and perfector of our faith.

Though trials and persecutions remain, as noted here in this context, we are to turn away from and struggle *against* sin,[72] cultivate endurance, and take special comfort in knowing that even our incarnate Lord suffered hardships and trials that were far worse than any sufferings we ourselves have had to endure.[73] And it was he who endured such trials, opposition, and abuse who is now reigning "at the right hand of the throne of God." Therefore, we should not grow weary or lose heart, for our victory and glory lies ahead as well.

The writer of Hebrews then seeks to give a little perspective on what God might be doing with them even now, amidst their trials. His is an invitation to look at it from a different angle as they "run the race marked

---

72. Though this is indeed true in a theological sense, here in Hebrews 12:4 the idea of sin is personified in those that are persecuting them. As David A. DeSilva rightly notes, "The author's labeling of the opposition as 'sin' casts the believer's detractors and abusers in a strategic light; they are to be seen as agents of sin (the same as the hostile 'sinners' in 12:3). The very way of life toward which the neighbors try to reassimilate the addressees then comes to be viewed as that which alienates from God. The possibility of resisting 'to the point of blood' shows that, while the addressees must battle the internal temptations to yield to social pressures, the contest is not strictly internal." David A. DeSilva, *Perseverance in Gratitude*, 446–47.

73. Earlier in the book of Hebrews, the author asserts, "Although he [Jesus] was a son, he learned obedience through what he suffered" (Heb 5:8 ESV), which suggests that the discipline he incurred had a remedial nature to it in keeping with Jesus' active obedience (a perfect righteousness that will be imputed to believers through faith). We should note the father-son metaphor in the context of such training is found here as well, as the writer emphasizes Jesus' sonship (though this was in a unique fashion as more than just an Israelite, but the very Son of God). This reminder of sonship in the context of the remedial discipline will lay a foundation (or one might say, is the basis for appeal) for how the church is to understand their sufferings addressed in Hebrews 12, which is to be seen as a remedial fatherly discipline from God for the purpose of training one in holiness and righteousness (cf. Heb 12:10, 11), which we will soon look at in more detail. If the church considers him who endured such opposition (suffering), then they may find encouragement from the fact that they have gained a significant new way *to identify with* Jesus (the suffering servant), as they themselves endure suffering. The Apostle Paul longed to identify with and know Jesus better, and he knew that participation in his sufferings was a way in which such knowledge might be attained (cf. Phil 3:11).

out" for them. They had not yet been called to pay the ultimate cost for their faith—that of "shedding blood" or death. But rather, as F. F. Bruce rightly notes:

> They ought rather to realize their present hardships were a token of their heavenly Father's love for them, and the means by which he was training them to be more truly his sons.[74]

Their adoption as the children of God makes all the difference, and they are now called to view their trials as fatherly discipline from God.[75] Though we did cite this passage at the beginning of this chapter, it will be worth our while to see as a whole again for purposes of review.

> . . . And you have forgotten that word of encouragement that addresses you as sons: "My son, do not make light of the Lord's discipline, and do not lose heart when he rebukes you, because the Lord disciplines those he loves, and he punishes everyone he accepts as a son."
>
> Endure hardship as discipline; God is treating you as sons. For what son is not disciplined by his father? If you are not disciplined (and everyone undergoes discipline), then you are illegitimate children and not true sons. Moreover, we have all had human fathers who disciplined us and we respected them for it. How much more should we submit to the Father of our spirits and live! Our fathers disciplined us for a little while as they thought best; but God disciplines us for our good, that we may share in his holiness. No discipline seems pleasant at the time, but painful. Later on, however, it produces a harvest of righteousness and peace for those who have been trained by it (Heb 12:5–11 NIV).

The author quotes Proverbs 3:11, 12, and recalling this passage, he designates it as an "encouragement."[76] Therefore discipline is right away characterized as an encouraging affirmation of God's fatherly love, since

---

74. Bruce, *The Epistle to the Hebrews*, 342.

75. The invitation to view it as fatherly discipline should have a comforting effect, for "as a father has compassion on his children, so the Lord has compassion on those who fear him" (Ps 103:13, NIV). He knows their limit.

76. The Greek παράκλησις (cf. 6:18) is a feminine noun here seen in its singular genitive form and is an "act of emboldening another in belief or course of action," as "encouragement or exhortation." This seems to be its purpose here, but elsewhere it can also be a "strong request, or a lifting of another's spirits, a comfort or consolation." Taken from Danker, *A Greek-English Lexicon of the New Testament and other Early Christian Literature (BGAD)*, 766.

they are "addressed as sons" (v. 5). The citation reminds them that when indeed they are disciplined (παιδεία),[77] rebuked (ἐλέγχω),[78] or punished (μαστιγοῖ),[79] they are not to make light of it or lose heart, for it is a sign of God's love, in keeping with their adoption.[80] This discipline is a natural part of their covenant relationship with God, who, as their Father, is treating them as sons through the use of secondary causes (v. 7).

In order to expand upon this idea of discipline as a sign of true sonship, the author inserts an illustration from human family life and the relationship that a father has with his son, for whom discipline is assurance of legitimacy. Negatively speaking, those who are not disciplined are not legitimate, true sons (v. 8). When our human fathers disciplined us

77. Here carrying the strong sense of "instruction or training."

78. Seen here in its present passive participial form, meaning "to rebuke, reprove, or chastise." Thus church discipline, insofar as it is seen as a rebuke, should be seen as "fatherly" discipline.

79. A present active verb that means "to beat, scourge, or chastise." The underlying idea of the verb is to a flogging with a whip or scourging. This idea expressed in μασ– τιγοῖ in the last section of the verse is not found in the MT (where it simply reads "as a father the son he delights in," NIV), but is rather taken from the LXX. DeSilva comments, "The LXX . . . obscures the quality of analogy inherent in the MT, and the verse becomes testimony to actual adoption by God ('every child God receives') rather than a useful analogy for describing God's chastening ('like a father . . .'). This modification makes the LXX version more useful for the author's purposes." DeSilva, *Perseverance in Gratitude*, 448. Paul Ellingworth thinks that the LXX translation used may be based on a more "primitive Hebrew text." Ellingworth, *The Epistle to the Hebrews*, 648. See also Bruce, *Hebrews*, 342, n. 66. Ellingworth further comments that "flogging is an aspect of discipline which the writer of Hebrews ignores as inappropriate to his argument" (649). This use of punishment does pose an interesting theological question. In what sense could this be regarded as punishment in light of the punishment and atonement for sin poured out for us on Christ, which now allows Paul to say that "there is therefore now no condemnation for those who are in Christ Jesus" (Rom 8:1)? This critical question will be a major part of our discussion in the following chapter. But here, DeSilva convincingly argues that the context warrants that the author is not speaking of a punitive discipline in this recontextualization of Proverbs 3, but rather the vocabulary, imagery, and general conversation of the author suggests it is an educative training, where the "emphasis is on the positive fruits that the courageous endurance of such trials will produce in the trainee." DeSilva, *Perseverance in Gratitude*, 449–50. See also the argument against a punitive understanding of παιδεία as well in Croy, *Endurance in Suffering*, 197–9. Croy remarks, "While it is true that the author of Hebrews appeals to a text in which παιδεία implies 'punishment,' his recontextualization exploits the nuances of 'discipline' or 'education.' The more punitive nuances of παιδεία are not relevant to his rhetorical situation. God is not punishing the readers by their afflictions, but is educating them." Ibid., 199.

80. Though their *trials are at the hands of persecutors*, the author desires for them to endure the suffering as a discipline *from the Lord*.

as children, they did it in keeping with the idea that this indeed was for our profit as the recipient, and as the recipients, we as children paid them their due respect. If indeed we were willing to submit to the discipline of our human fathers, then "how much more," the author asks in verse 9, "should we submit to the Father of our spirits and live!"[81] Here again God is called our "Father," who is worthy of our complete trust, and the discipline he shows us is "for our own good." It is wholesome and beneficial. Bruce remarks:

> If our Heavenly Father also imposes discipline on us, shall we not accept it willingly from Him? Our earthly fathers may sometimes have been mistaken in their estimate of the discipline we needed; our Heavenly Father, in the perfection of his wisdom and love, can be relied upon never to impose any discipline on us which is not for our own good.[82]

For what good is God's fatherly discipline exercised then? We have already seen in one respect that submission to our heavenly Father's discipline brings *life* (ζάω, v. 9), and since this verb is found in the future tense, it must surely include our current spiritual life now and also life in the future.[83] The fruit of submission to divine discipline is that it brings life today and eternal life tomorrow. Thus there is an *eschatological theme* in mind.[84] To show that this indeed is true, we only need to look at what divine discipline's ultimate end is according to this passage. The author tells us that God's fatherly discipline is designed for our good, "so that *we may share in his holiness*" (v. 10). As we stated earlier in this chapter,

---

81. This is the only place that God is called "Father" in Hebrews other than in the quotations about Jesus' divinity and relationship to God within the Trinity in 1:5. Here it is used with respect to our relationship to God, especially as our Creator-Redeemer. It is an interesting parallel the author is making. Since we submit to our earthly fallible fathers, we ought all the more to be willing to submit to our perfect heavenly (spiritual) Father, the result not being death but life (ζάω).

82. Bruce, *Hebrews*, 344. William Lane remarks that within the analogy between paternal correction and divine discipline, the "contrast expressed in the formulation οἱ μὲν γὰρ . . . ὁ δέ, 'for they . . . but he,' is sharp." Lane, *Hebrews 9–13*, 424.

83. Lane notes that life here "recalls the summons to life issued in the framework of covenant obedience in Deut 30:11–20. Submission to divine discipline is integrally related to the enjoyment of eschatological salvation." Lane, *Hebrews 9–13*, 424.

84. Perhaps a recollection of the words of Jesus in John 10:10b might bring about further clarification as to the kind of life God intends "for our good." The Savior said, "I have come that they may have life, and have it to the full" (NIV).

we are to embrace divine discipline because it is how God as our Father works to restore us fully into Christlikeness so that we ourselves may be like the One who is holy.[85] In this way, discipline is a means God uses in our progressive sanctification. One might say that it is part of his methods of transforming us by which we learn to "participate in the divine nature and escape the corruption of the world caused by evil desires" (2 Peter 1:4). The hardship and trials may indeed be at times an unpleasant and painful discipline, like gold being refined in fire, if you will. Nevertheless, it has a purifying effect in our lives. The author reminds us that this discipline, or perhaps in the words of Jesus this "pruning" (John 15:2), is not so much a punishment for sins (for that is not encouraging) but is rather to be regarded as instructional in nature, producing a *"harvest of righteousness and peace for those who have been trained by it"* (v. 11).[86] The ideas of righteousness and peace are truly eschatological concepts (Isa 32:17; 60:17; Rom 14:17), and here it conveys the idea that God's people will experience a taste of what lies ahead in a fuller sense as a result of submitting to divine discipline. So then, God's fatherly discipline is a way in which he instills hope, brings life, purifies us, and leads us on the path toward holiness. While being properly trained, it leads to bearing fruit for God (John 15:2) as it produces in us a harvest of righteousness and peace.[87] In fact, for God's people, "their own honor as sons and daugh-

85. It is interesting to note that Peter's admonition given to the church to be holy is found alongside his acknowledgment that the church can call on God as our "Father" in 1 Peter 1:17. The two ideas can go hand in hand because of what Christ has done for us (vv. 18–21).

86. "It is only after the fact, when the results of the discipline emerge, that its relative value can be determined." Lane, *Hebrews 9–13*, 425. The Greek literally can be translated, "the peaceful fruit of righteousness." Its instructional sense is notably seen in that God's people are "trained (γυμνάζω) by it." γυμνάζω is here seen as a perfect passive participle and means "to train or undergo discipline." Danker, *BGAD*, 208. It is from here where we get our word *gymnasium*. See DeSilva, *Perseverance in Gratitude*, 453. Further, N. Clayton Croy has noted that the athletic and educative language seen here in Hebrews is not unique to Greek literature, and he lists several examples. Here in Hebrews, both "γυμνάζω and παιδεία are overlapping. Both denote a process of 'training,' the former obviously veering toward physical training, the latter toward social and intellectual training." Croy, *Endurance in Suffering*, 158.

87. We will notice that church discipline has precisely the same goals in chapter 6, and thus can rightly be called a "fatherly" discipline.

ters of God depends on, and is manifested by, their experience of this discipline."[88]

So in summarizing all this, the fatherhood language, the idea of discipline, and God's redemptive historical (eschatological) and restorative purposes for his people are woven together nicely. The fatherhood language and the reality of our sonship are powerful metaphors drawn from Old Testament covenantal language that calls us to a willing, obedient, and beneficial submission to God.[89] It calls for our trust in his sovereign, redemptive ways as he is at work in our lives, disciplining us "for our own good." William Lane helpfully summarizes.

> The positive role that disciplinary sufferings play in molding of Christian character furnishes the writer with the basis of his argument. Far from being an occasion for discouragement, the imposition of the discipline of suffering must stimulate confidence and a renewed sense of dignity, since it attests to the filial relationship with God that Christians enjoy.[90]

Also in this chapter we learned that the idea of God as Father is not overly prevalent in the Old Testament, but this may be due to a variety

---

88. DeSilva, *Perseverance in Gratitude*, 454.

89. It is worth noting that in the recently released translation known as the *TNIV*, published by Zondervan, the metaphor of sonship is stripped from the text. It reads, "And you have completely forgotten this word of encouragement that addresses you as children . . . endure hardship as discipline; God is treating you as his children. For what children are not disciplined by their parents" (Heb 12:5, 7, *TNIV*). A similar translation is in the NRSV. Besides translating the masculine singular father (πατήρ) into "parents," which usurps the fatherhood analogy trying to be made in verses 9 and 10 between human fathers and our spiritual Father, there is the consistent translating of son(s) (υἱός) into "child" or "children." Though in a dynamic equivalence translation theory this may be an acceptable way to interpret the Greek, it nevertheless lacks adequate theological reflection. There is seemingly little justification for stripping the passage of the powerful Old Testament father-son metaphorical language that has provided assurance of the nature and purpose of the discipline that God's people have experienced throughout the history of their redemption. Furthermore, it breaks up the language that is so part and parcel to the eschatological trajectory of God's fatherhood that we have noted in salvation history that is so connected to his redemptive purposes (in this case, to lead one to holiness, v. 10). I fear that in the translation committee's motives for making the language as inclusive as possible, they have circumvented the covenantal language of the Jewish people, which may lend to a deeper feeling of exclusion for them all the more in the age of a gentile prevalent church. This language is their source of hope and assurance, and the original Greek would have had a powerful comforting effect upon its first-century readers.

90. Lane, *Hebrews 9–13*, 420.

of reasons. It may be due to the surrounding pagan cultures that used it often to denote their qualitatively different gods. It may be infrequent due to Israel's lack of intimacy as a result of their disobedience. Further, as Seitz has pointed out, it may be infrequently mentioned simply from the fact that the narratives are written more from the perspective of God through the prophet or writer. Yet, God's fatherhood has indeed been a significant theological theme throughout salvation history and even in the mind of the individual Israelite family where theophoric names reflected the piety of a people who recognized Yahweh as their loving, compassionate, and protective Father. And this was more than just a name, but as Father, Yahweh was communicating his purpose and plans for Israel, and the very essence of his nature as Creator and Redeemer of a particular people. God as a Father becomes an especially meaningful designation as God initiates his plan in a wider sense throughout history, whereby we now identify with Christ, and through the indwelling Holy Spirit may cry out to him as our *Abba, Father*. We await our adoption in fullness and can recognize the fatherhood language within discipline as a source of hope and assurance of our covenant relationship and inheritance with God, and his perfect plan to set apart a people for himself as he brings about our sanctification. He longs to forgive and restore us, so that we might obediently trust in him, and testify to his marvelous grace. This marvelous grace is sometimes manifest in divine discipline, and we are to submit and embrace it with thanksgiving, for God is treating us as sons.

5

Divine Discipline and the Atonement

The Effects of the Cross of Christ on Divine Discipline as Manifested in the Church

IN OUR OPENING CHAPTERS, we discussed the nature and purpose of divine discipline as understood at various times and by different personalities throughout the history of the church. We have also taken a cursory look at how the Bible, with a particular emphasis on the Old Testament, helps us to develop a biblical theology of the nature and purpose of divine discipline as experienced by God's people (Israel) both on the individual and corporate levels. As a prominent part of the story of redemption, divine discipline is one of the ways that God as our heavenly Father expresses his covenant love to his people. Furthermore, we identified two main senses of this discipline in chapter 3. Depending upon context, it may have an instructional or a punitive sense, or at certain times, may possess a mixture of both. We also concluded that with regard to the punitive sense, the retributive element of the punishment was not fully realized for the remnant of God's people. Rather, they experienced a "stay of execution" as they would await a prophesied substitutionary sacrifice that would bear the full penalty or punishment (*mûsār*) for their iniquity (Isa 53:4–6).[1] Paul suggested that it was our Lord Jesus Christ who served

1. For more on the relation of the Servant of Isaiah 53 to the person and work of Jesus Christ, see the article by Otto Betz entitled "Jesus and Isaiah 53," in Bellinger and Farmer, *Jesus and the Suffering Servant*, 70–87. The extraordinary nature of this vicarious suffering and atonement pictured in Isaiah 53 and how it not only would quench God's wrath but also lay the ground for a "universal and permanent purification" for the sins of many is persuasively argued in J. Alan Groves, "Atonement in Isaiah 53," in Hill and James, *The*

as this "sacrifice of atonement" (i.e., *hilastērion,* "propitiation") in Romans 3:25–26 and our "sin offering" in Romans 8:3, as a demonstration of God's justice and judgment on sin.[2] According to the Apostle Peter, this judgment was poured out on Christ on the cross (1 Pet 2:24). Therefore, in light of the significance of the cross of Christ, it is this punitive sense that is worthy of theological reflection as we contemplate the role and nature of divine discipline as embodied in the church (the company of the redeemed) today. Specifically, we may ask whether there is room for any sense of retribution to the idea of church discipline in *light of the significance of the cross event* as the payment (or propitiation) for human sin.

In addition, this chapter will further reflect on the relationship of discipline to forgiveness and love. Just how exactly is divine discipline embodied in the church related to the idea of the church being a forgiven/forgiving and reconciled/reconciling community of believers who love one another from the heart? It will be my contention that church discipline is a significant means used by God to communicate love and forgiveness to one who, on account of his or her sin, has wandered away from fellowship with God and his people.

THE PENAL SUBSTITUTIONARY MODEL OF ATONEMENT

For centuries theologians have employed a variety of models and metaphors derived from the biblical writers of Scripture that seek to grasp in some measure the significance of the death of Christ for the Christian faith.[3] As a primary symbol of the faith and a central teaching of evangeli-

---

Glory of the Atonement, 61–89.

2. See Carson, "Atonement in Romans 3:21–26," in *The Glory of the Atonement,* 119–39. Douglas Moo rightly notes that in Romans 8:3, Paul highlights the fact that Christ came in the "form of sinful flesh" in order to show that "the Son possesses the necessary requirement to act as our substitute." Moo, *The Epistle to the Romans,* 479. Further, Moo argues rather emphatically that "the condemnation that our sins deserve has been poured out on Christ, our sin-bearer; that is why 'there is now no condemnation for those who are in Christ Jesus' (v.1)," a point we will discuss further later in this chapter (481). For an excellent summary of the role and purpose of offerings and sacrifices in the Bible, see VanGemeren's, "Offerings and Sacrifices in Bible Times," in Elwell, *Evangelical Dictionary of Theology,* 854–8.

3. Bruce Demarest does a fine job of presenting and explaining the variety of models of atonement that have been used throughout the history of the church. A few of the more prominent models include the following: the Moral Influence Theory (Abelardian or subjective view); the Classic or Ransom Theory, more commonly known today as *Christus Victor* (Gustaf Aulén); the Governmental Theory (Grotius and Arminians); the

cal theology, the message of the cross of Christ and his subsequent resurrection and ascension has been a transforming gospel and the source of hope for millions who have trusted in its saving power. Paul reminds the believers in Corinth:

> The message of the cross is foolishness to those who are perishing, but to those of us who are being saved *it is the power of God* (1 Cor 1:18 NIV, emphasis mine).

The strength of the multiplicity of the models of atonement is that each of them communicates elements of Christian truth about the cross in a many-sided fashion. Thus we are able to more fully comprehend from a variety of angles just what in fact the cross of Christ achieved for those who respond in faith to the saving message of the gospel. John Driver identifies ten different images or models of atonement and asserts:

> The plurality of images used to understand the work of Christ is essential. The apostolic community allowed all to stand in a complementary relationship rather than attempting to reduce them to a single theory or a dogmatic statement. *The value of any one of these images depends on allowing it to remain in relationship to all the rest. Insofar as they have been held together, they have communicated powerfully the meaning of the death and resurrection of Christ* (emphasis mine).[4]

Leon Morris asserts a similar conclusion with regard to the need for a multiplicity of models.

> The plight of sinful humans is disastrous, for the NT [New Testament] sees the sinner as lost, suffering hell, perishing, cast into darkness, and more. An atonement that rectifies all this must necessarily be complex. So we need all the vivid concepts: redemption, propitiation, justification, and all the rest. And we need all the theories. Each draws attention to an important aspect of our

---

Universal Reconciliation Theory (Barth); the Satisfaction or Juridical Theory (Anselmian or Latin view); and the Penal Substitutionary Theory (some early fathers and Reformed view), the latter of which is the subject of our discussion. For more on these historical interpretations of the atonement and a helpful summary of each, see Demarest, *The Cross and Salvation*, 149–66; and Morris, "Theories of Atonement," in *EDT*, 116–9.

4. Driver, *Understanding the Atonement for the Mission of the Church*, 18–9. Driver lists the following biblical images of atonement: the conflict-victory-liberation motif; vicarious suffering; archetypal images; martyr motif; sacrifice motif; expiation motif and the wrath of God; redemption-purchase motif; reconciliation; justification; and the adoption-family image.

salvation, and we dare not surrender any . . . [though] we should not expect that our theories will ever explain it fully. Even when we put them all together, we will no more than begin to comprehend a little of the vastness of God's saving deed.[5]

Although there are a variety of important models of atonement, a few of them have become more prominent or useful than others. In other words, they have the ability to capture the heart of the gospel message and kerygmatically communicate its wonderful truths in a succinct and understandable manner.[6] One of the more influential models held by many early church fathers (e.g., Clement of Rome, Cyril of Jerusalem, Athanasius, Augustine) as well as a large majority of the Reformers (e.g., Luther, Calvin, Zwingli, Knox) was that of the penal substitutionary view of atonement (hereafter referred to as PSA). Demarest concisely defines this view by explaining:

> On the cross Christ took our place [substitution] and bore the equivalent punishment [penalty] for our sins, thereby satisfying the just demands of the law and appeasing God's wrath. As repentant sinners appropriate Christ's vicarious sacrifice by faith, God forgives sins, imputes Christ's righteousness, and reconciles the estranged to himself.[7]

Wayne Grudem calls this model the "*orthodox* understanding of the atonement held by evangelical theologians" (emphasis mine).[8] Its draw

---

5. Morris, "Theories of Atonement," in *EDT*, 119.

6. I have in mind the *Christus Victor* model of atonement and the penal substitutionary view, two views often preached in contemporary evangelical circles today. The *Christus Victor* model of atonement portrays Jesus as securing a cosmic victory over sin, death, the devil, and accompanying forces of evil. Demarest notes that it comes in two different forms. In one form, the theory suggests that Christ's death paid the ransom payment (Mark 10:45) due the devil, who held the souls of humankind in his power, enslaving the sinner in sin. The second form of this theory suggests that God triumphed in battle over Satan (Col 2:15) and his ability to have a hold on sinners in sin and death. Therefore, Christ stripped Satan of his power and rescues or delivers those held captive by him. See Demarest, *The Cross and Salvation*, 149–50. The penal substitutionary view will be the subject of this section.

7. Demarest, *The Cross and Salvation*, 159. Demarest does an excellent job of tracing those early fathers who advocated PSA, though to be sure, the model was more fully developed by Luther, Calvin, and many of the other reformers. See ibid., 158–66. He further exposits and defends PSA (166–75) as the theory of atonement that "best accords with the considerable body of biblical data on the subject." Ibid., 166.

8. Grudem, *Systematic Theology*, 579. Though the church did not settle on a single

is that it puts more of the emphasis on the seriousness of human sin and God's response to it *and* remedy for it, rather than focusing on spiritual warfare and the now-defeated powers of the devil and his minions. The focus of PSA is

> . . . in contrast to other views that attempt to explain the atonement apart from the idea of the wrath of God or payment of the penalty for sin.[9]

In agreement with Grudem, the message of the cross has a primary emphasis on what has God has done to pay the penalty (through an eternal sacrifice) and overcome the problem of human *sin*. Consider the following verses where the issue of sin is emphasized.

> She will give birth to a son, and you are to give him the name Jesus, because he will save his people from their sins (Matt 1:21 NIV).

> God made him who had no sin to be sin for us, so that in him we might become the righteousness of God (2 Cor 5:21 NIV).[10]

> For this reason he had to be made like his brothers in every way, in order that he might become a merciful and faithful high priest

---

view of atonement in the way that they did other doctrines, like the two natures of Christ (see James, "The Atonement in Church History," in *The Glory of the Atonement*, 209), Grudem's use of the word "orthodox" may be better stated as one of the "mainstream or more prevalent views" held by evangelicals. This was confirmed in private conversation.

9. Ibid. Grudem further states that in Christ's obedience in meeting the requirements of the law and in his penal substitutionary death, "The primary emphasis and the primary influence of Christ's work of redemption is not on us, but on God the Father. Jesus obeyed the Father in our place and perfectly met the demands of the law. And he suffered in our place, receiving in himself the penalty that God the Father would have visited upon us. In both cases the atonement is viewed as objective; that is, something that has primary influence directly on God himself. Only secondarily does it have application to us, and this only because there was a definite event in the relationship between God the Father and God the Son that secured our salvation." Ibid., 570. The prominent theologian Jonathan Edwards held a similar view of Christ's atonement, seeing his active obedience and passive obedience as a part of the comprehensive satisfaction made to God in our stead for the righteous requirements of the law. "And so the word *satisfaction* is sometimes used, not only for his propitiation, but also for his meritorious obedience. For in some sense, not only suffering the penalty, but positively obeying, is needful to satisfy the law." Edwards, "A History of the Work of Redemption, 2.2.1" in *The Works of Jonathan Edwards*, 574.

10. This verse is a primary verse used in support of PSA, as it speaks of substitution, implied punishment, and imputed righteousness.

in service to God, *and that he might make atonement for the sins of the people* (Heb 2:17 NIV, emphasis mine).

Unlike the other high priests, he does not need to offer sacrifices day after day, first for his own sins, and then for the sins of the people. *He sacrificed for their sins once for all when he offered himself* (Heb 7:27 NIV, emphasis mine).

So Christ was sacrificed once *to take away the sins of many people*; and he will appear a second time, not to bear sin, but to bring salvation to those who are waiting for him (Heb 9:28 NIV, emphasis mine).[11]

He himself bore our sins in his body on the tree, so that we might die to sins and live for righteousness; by his wounds you have been healed. For you were like sheep going astray, but now you have returned to the Shepherd and Overseer of your souls (1 Pet 2:24–25).[12]

It would seem that the penal substitutionary view of atonement (PSA) holds pride of place as the model that "best accords with the considerable body of biblical data of the subject."[13] Therefore, if one model

11. This verse would also seem to support our contention in chapter 3, wherein we argued that destruction and a final, decisive judgment were stayed for the remnant of God's people who trusted in the Lord. This is in opposition to the wicked who did not believe and who received the fullness of punishment for sin. So Christ here in Hebrews is said to be the sacrifice for the sins of *many* (πολλων) people (i.e., the remnant and today's church). Cf. Romans 3:25, where Paul acknowledges that the sins committed prior to the cross remained unpunished and that God presented Christ as a sacrifice of atonement (or *as the one who would turn aside his wrath, taking away sin*, NIV text note) in order to fulfill justice for those who are declared just before God through faith. This is not to say that Christ's sacrifice was not sufficient for the sins of all humanity; it is simply to say that it is efficient only for those who respond to God in faith (both OT and NT saints), and so in this sense Christ died for *many*. See also Hebrews 9:15 where Christ died to ransom and set free from sin, "those who are called (οἱ κεκλημένοι)." It is my contention that this is specifically referring to an effectual call and not simply the general gospel call, lest we fall into universalism. So also Bruce, *Hebrews*, 221. For more on the distinction between the two types of "calls," see Grudem, *Systematic Theology*, 692–5.

12. An obvious allusion to Isaiah 53:12, here Peter asserts that our sins were vicariously placed on Christ, our substitute, who bore our punishment so that we can now live godly lives "for righteousness" with the knowledge that "by his wounds we are healed."

13. Demarest, *The Cross and Salvation*, 166. Other than in Demarest's text (171–5), fuller expositions and defenses of PSA can be found in modern standard works such as Morris's, *The Apostolic Preaching of the Cross*; Stott's, *The Cross of Christ*; McDonald's, *The Atonement of the Death of Christ*; the landmark essay by Packer entitled, "What Did the Cross Achieve? The Logic of Penal Substitution," 3–45; and Hill and James, *The Glory*

seems to communicate more fully the central message of the gospel than the others do it is the model of PSA. The Southern Baptist leader and theologian R. Albert Mohler Jr. argues that PSA was not simply a Latin theory; it was in fact the heart of the apostolic message. He maintains that Scripture demands that it is the primary model of atonement, and that without it, there "is no 'good news' for sinners . . . [and in fact,] there is no Christianity."[14] Robert Letham offers similar sentiments.

> Had it not been for the coming of Christ and God's gracious covenant, we should have had no option but to face the just wrath of

---

of the Atonement. John Driver is highly critical of the penal substitutionary view and charges that it inappropriately makes God the object, and not the agent of reconciliation. He further criticizes what he feels is PSA'a "overriding preoccupation with guilt," arguing that this preoccupation is not in the New Testament (56). Rather, the New Testament, according to Driver, bases its view of atonement on an Old Testament view of sacrifice that is more concerned with restoration and the harmony of relationships rather than the guilt. Even the Levitical priest who placed his hands on the sacrificial sheep (Lev 4:32–35) was "not placing his guilt on the sheep and having it sacrificed in his stead. Rather, he was identifying with the purity of his gift and offering himself to God" (57). In response, why then was it necessary for Christ to *die* if all that was necessary for atonement was that we identify with him and offer ourselves to God? We can only identify with him as our representative if he is first the propitiatory sacrifice for sin. Otherwise sin still separates us. (Cf. Isa 59:1–3). For a more thorough rebuttal of some of Driver's main critiques, see the essays entitled Peterson, *Where Wrath and Mercy Meet.*

14. Mohler, "The Glory of Christ as Mediator," in Armstrong, *The Glory of Christ,* 67. Gary Jenkins, in a very insightful booklet, gives a treatment of what he calls the "pastoral power" and spiritual impact of the model of PSA on the conscience and spiritual growth of the believer in Christ. He argues, "Substitution speaks particularly and powerfully to those who fell a profound sense of guilt and to those who feel a deep sense of worthlessness and lack of personal significance." Jenkins, *In My Place,* 8. Jenkins argues that the substitutionary death of Christ speaks to the issue of human guilt. He writes, "For the person overwhelmed by guilt, it is the knowledge that their sin and guilt has been carried by Christ on the cross that sets them free" (12). PSA also reveals to us how valuable we were to God. "To come to the cross and to see it in a substitutionary way is to experience the fullness of God's love and to know our true worth before Him" (19). It is profound to consider that Jesus Christ died for his people, of which I am a part. Thus, Paul could rightly and personally say that Christ gave of himself for *me* (Gal 2:20). Jenkins states that this is a powerful message to the believer in Christ. "It was for *me* that Jesus died. He died in *my* place and in doing so he showed not only how much he loved me but also how much I was truly worth. This is of profound pastoral significance in ministering to those who believe themselves to be worth nothing" (19). Finally, PSA inspires us to be filled with praise and thanksgiving to a God to whom we are indebted. It further inspires us to "sacrificial living and giving" (22). For as Jenkins argues, if Christ was willing to lay down his life for us, then we ought to be willing to love, serve, and worship in turn with our very lives.

God . . . apart from the provisions of God's grace in the substitutionary atonement of Christ *there is no salvation* (emphasis mine).[15]

In recent years there has been a resurgence of criticism of the penal
substitutionary view, and it has become one of the primary topics of theological debate within Western Christianity.[16] Many non-violent atonement advocates and feminist theologians object to using this model of
atonement, asserting that it reflects negatively on God as a violent, venge-
ful, wrathful deity who, like the pagan gods, simply needs to be appeased,
a mere punitive father of an innocent Jesus.[17] Feminists react strongly to
this notion of a father image who punishes an innocent victim who sup-
posedly is to receive the "abuse" passively.[18] However, keeping in mind the
unity of fellowship within the Trinity, Robert Letham argues:

15. Letham, *The Work of Christ*, 136.

16. See, for example, Green and Baker, *Recovering the Scandal of the Cross*, 146–50;
and Hoyles, *Punishment in the Bible*, 63–8. Green and Baker argue that "penal substitution . . . is unbiblical not just because it distorts or leaves out biblical concepts but also
because of its attempt at having one image or model serve as an all-encompassing theory,
the only correct and needed explanation of the atonement." Ibid., 148. Steve Wellum, in
a persuasive assessment and critique of Green and Baker's abandonment of PSA, argued
at a conference of the Evangelical Theological Society (2003) that in their text they de-
emphasize or dismiss some essential Scriptures that are needed in order to have a fuller
understanding of the atonement. Further, Green and Baker downplay or dismiss the
substitutionary aspects of sacrifice as well as the necessity of God's wrath as a response
toward human sin.

17. The critics of PSA object that this presents an inappropriate division within the
Trinity. They argue that PSA pits a wrathful God (the Father) against a loving Jesus. See,
for example, Gunton, *The Actuality of the Atonement*, 165. But this is not a proper representation of what PSA asserts. There is no division within the Trinity in the PSA model.
As John R. W. Stott has rightly noted, "Any notion of penal substitution in which three
independent actors play a role—the guilty party, the punitive judge and the innocent
victim—is to be repudiated with the utmost vehemence. It would not only be unjust in
itself but would also reflect a defective Christology. For Christ is not an independent
third person, but the eternal Son of the Father, who is one with the Father in his essential
being. What we see, then, in the drama of the cross is not three actors but two, ourselves
on the one hand and God on the other." Stott, *The Cross of Christ*, 158. Borrowing Stott's
terminology, Gary Jenkins has rightly called it "the self-substitution of God" and thus
the Father and Son cannot be ontologically independent of one another, as this would
collapse the orthodox view of the Trinity. See Jenkins, *In My Place*, 6.

18. For example, Rita Nakashima Brock criticizes PSA and laments that "such
doctrines of salvation reflect and support images of benign paternalism, the neglect
of children, or, at their worst, child abuse, making such behaviors acceptable as divine
behavior—cosmic paternalism, neglect, and child abuse as it were . . . the experience of
grace is lodged here, I believe, in a sense of relief at being relieved of punishment for

Rather than presenting a cruel and distorted picture of God, what penal substitution shows us is that God's love for us is such that *he* was prepared to pay the ultimate price that love can pay . . . it tells us that God has identified himself with us in our suffering, that no situation of grief through which we pass is outside his own experience or beyond his direct sympathy. When we remember the *unity of the Son with the Father in the triunity of the Godhead, the scene is transformed* (emphasis mine).[19]

Opponents of PSA also critique its supposed cultural and practical ramifications, arguing that this model of atonement has corrupted Western society in that it advocates judicial violence "all in the name of God" and that it further sanctions and "pumps retributivism into the legal bloodstream."[20] It is viewed as an outdated model of atonement that is cold, mechanical, impersonal, advocating a divinely sanctioned violence.[21] It will be worth our while now to briefly respond to some of these critiques.

---

one's inevitable failings and not in a clear sense of personal worth gained from an awareness of the unconditional nature of love. The shadow of the punitive father must always lurk behind atonement. He haunts images of forgiving grace." Brock, "And a Little Child Will Lead Us: Christology and Abuse," in Brown and Bihn, *Christianity, Patriarchy, and Abuse*, 52–53. Seemingly, what we have here then is a modern-day agenda that is hostile and suspicious toward any hint of patriarchy or hierarchy being projected back on to the PSA model.

19. Letham, *The Work of Christ*, 137. Bruce L. McCormack concurs, saying, "The moral charge against penal substitution cannot be sustained so long as we operate with a well-ordered Christology and an equally well-ordered doctrine of the Trinity. *We must know who it is that judges here, and who it is that is judged, if we are not to fall into error*" (emphasis mine). McCormack, "The Ontological Presuppositions of Barth's Doctrine of Atonement," in *The Glory of the Atonement*, 365. He further writes, "Surely forgiveness is not *elicited* from the Father (grudgingly?) by what Christ did on our behalf; it is rather *effected* from the Father in and through Christ's passion and death. So the picture of an angry God the Father and a gentle self-sacrificial Son who pays the ultimate price to effect an alteration in the Father's 'attitude' fails to hit the mark." Ibid., 366.

20. Gorringe, *God's Just Vengeance*, 224.

21. This latter view is the primary objection of J. Denny Weaver, who writes, "Satisfaction atonement *in any form* depends upon divinely sanctioned violence that follows from the assumption that doing justice means to punish." Weaver, *The Nonviolent Atonement*, 203. Thus, Weaver denies that the Christ's death on the cross was part of God's intentional plan. He is just merely the victim of the world's systemic evil. Weaver declares, "Neither did the Father send him [Christ] for the specific purpose of dying, nor was his mission about death, as is the case for both satisfaction and moral atonement models." Ibid., 132. Weaver states that Christ's primary purpose was not so much to die (contra the clear testimony of 1 John 4:10) as much as it was to make the reign of God

Henri Blocher, in a recent article responding to critics of PSA, has outlined many reasons why PSA has received such criticism in postmodern society. For starters, society has seemingly become increasingly secular in its mindset.

> The secular mindset seems to be the first and foremost factor. In a world which looks increasingly like a man-made world (for better and for worse), the sense of Numinous loses its edge; the awe of the sacred, the fear of the Lord, mean almost nothing. God's only excuse, if he/she is allowed to exist, is his/her usefulness in providing me with fulfillment.[22]

Additionally, similar to the secular mindset is the consumer mentality that pervades current thinking, and this is that society shops for products or lines of thought that appeal to one's own desires (or as Blocher says, "hedonistic tendencies"), that which satiates the appetite or appeals to personal preferences. PSA is not a preferred model of atonement, because it's seemingly too negative about the state of the human condition and its need to make amends with God or turn aside his angry wrath (never mind that this is the clear testimony of Scripture, e.g., Rom 1:18–32, Eph 2:1–3). Instead, the atonement models that appeal more with secular society are those that see God as empathetically identifying with us in our lowly human state (solidarity) or liberating from oppression.[23]

---

visible on the earth mainly through the resurrection. "While Jesus' mission for the reign of God made his death inevitable in narrative Christus Victor [the model he upholds], neither the purpose nor the culmination of the mission was to die. God did not send Jesus to die, but to live, to make visible and present the reign of God. It is obvious that for narrative Christus Victor, the agent of Jesus' death was not God but the powers of evil." Ibid., 74. But as David B. McWilliams has pointed out in his review of Weaver's book, the Scriptures would seem to emphatically refute such a notion that Christ did not come for the set purpose of dying for sin (e.g., John 6:51; Matt 16:21; Luke 22:37; Acts 2:23; Acts 4:27–28). See McWilliams, "Book Review: Non Violent Atonement," 217–20. A simple critique of Weaver's view might be this: yes indeed God reigns, but if Christ did not come to die for our sins, then we are still liable.

22. Blocher, "The Sacrifice of Jesus Christ: The Current Theological Situation," 28. Blocher is echoing a thought I have held for quite some time, and that is that this secular mindset that he describes has invaded the church to such an extent that we fail to realize how serious the offense of our sin is in the eyes of a holy God. It is obviously offensive enough that it warrants the punishment of exclusion from the blessed presence of God for eternity to those who refuse to repent and believe. Thus when the seriousness of sin is not taken into account, one is likely to overlook the necessity for a serious demand in response (the shedding of blood and death) to atone for the magnitude of the offense.

23. To be sure, the message of the gospel does not exclude these ideas, for Christ did

Blocher also identifies the individualistic nature of Western culture and with its humanistic, democratic (egalitarian) thought as another facet to the mindset that objects to PSA.[24] Objective standards of moral law become eroded and have fallen to the "god" of relativity.

> Moral law and judicial law, ultimately, stand or fall together. It is no surprise, therefore, if the rationale of judgment and penalty seem to decompose under our eyes. The whole judicial system undergoes a severe crisis . . . all this produces inimical reactions to the idea of objective guilt and guilt-transfer.[25]

Further, he adds that it is commonplace among artists and thinkers nowadays to rebel against "institutional norms, social and moral order." The result is that cultural forces "blow" against older Christian orthodox convictions.[26] In spite of all of these cultural forces that "blow" against

---

come in the likeness of sinful flesh (Rom 8:3), was made like us in every way (except for sin, Phil 2:7; Heb 2:14–17; 4:15), and is our deliverer from the oppression and bondage of sin (John 8:32; Rom 6:7, 18, 22; Gal 5:1; Heb 9:15; Rev 1:5). However, to emphasize these aspects to the exclusion of the issues involved in PSA (law, wrath, punishment, substitution, and imputed righteousness) robs the gospel of its primary illocutionary force. Jesus identified with us in order to pay the penalty for us, so that the righteous requirements of the law (active and passive obedience) could be met. And we are freed from the bondage of sin because it was he who secured the victory over it by appeasing and turning aside God's wrath upon the sin that so consumed and entangled us, held us in slavery, made us by nature objects of his wrath, and had rendered us at one time enemies of God.

24. David Peterson makes a similar comment. "I find myself wondering whether those who downplay or deny the theme of penal substitution are driven by personal or cultural agendas, rather than by biblical theology." Peterson, "Introduction," in *Where Wrath and Mercy Meet*, xiii.

25. Ibid., 28. In contrast to the current trend, however, objective guilt and guilt-transfer seem to be the primary issue at hand in Paul's "unfinished" excursus and comparison of the first and second Adam in Romans 5:12–21, for the reality of guilt and its transference is the basis on which Paul argues that those who lived prior to the giving of the law faced death in 5:14.

26. Blocher suggests that this is true of Michel Foucault, a philosopher who felt that Christianity held to its orthodox doctrines in such a way that it served its ability to maintain power over people and coerced them to conform through the threat of punishment, either in this life or the next. See Foucault's, *Discipline and Punish*. Blocher suggests that the root cause of this rebelliousness is not so much due to the inherent problems in Christian doctrine and practice, but rather stems from a "*resentment* of gifted people as they have seen that power was and remains in other hands, whom they despise (in ancient times, they had to flatter the princes and the wealthy, just to get their living; now it pays more to flatter the streak of rebelliousness in all individuals)." Blocher, 28–29.

holding to the view of PSA, Blocher asserts that the psychoanalytical attempts to deconstruct sacrifice in the Bible

> . . . did not pass without an answer on their own ground. If we sift "hard" facts and rigorous reasoning from matters of taste and ideology, we observe that there is little of weight left against penal-sacrificial views of atonement.[27]

Blocher unleashes a critique of critics of PSA who play word games with the concept of sacrifice.[28] He charges that opponents use vague language and invent words to describe the effects of Christ's work (e.g., Christ "absorbed" sin, according to Stephen Travis, commenting on 2 Cor 5:21.)[29] Blocher asks, "How did Christ 'absorb' sin? How did that supposed 'absorption' cancel the spiritual reality of sin?"[30] He then emphatically asserts that "absorption" is not even a biblical metaphor!

Blocher provides numerous biblical examples of how penal language and sacrificial terms are melded together (e.g., Deut 32). In addition, he argues affirmatively for a connection between retribution and wrath,[31] upholds the biblical idea that guilt transfer is intimately related

---

27. Ibid., 29. Blocher highlights Romans 3:24–26, where he points out that we find two, even three motifs "in the same verses, and it is difficult to disentangle them." For here Paul "mixes forensic language (just, justice, justify, leaving unpunished), ransom-language (redemption) and sacrificial language (means of propitiation, blood)" together. Ibid., 30. Blocher even shows how the biblical language of expiation and ransom are related to one another and how key phrases of the PSA view (i.e., bearing the sin/offense) are not even given recognition in the works of critics as punitive in nature in passages such as Isaiah 53 (he has in mind the series of articles contained in *Atonement Today*, edited by John Goldingay).

28. For example, John Goldingay prefers to use the word "stain" but not "guilt" with regard to what offerers are passing on to the victim of sacrifice in the OT. John Goldingay, "Old Testament Sacrifice and the Death of Christ," in Goldingay, *Atonement Today*, 10. Blocher then asks, "What *is* the spiritual stain if not their guilt before God?" Blocher, "The Sacrifice of Jesus Christ," 31.

29. He is referring to Stephen Travis's article entitled "Christ as the Bearer of Divine Judgment in Paul's Thought about the Atonement," in *Atonement Today*. Here Travis asserts that "the essential point is that Christ has experienced the sinner's estrangement from God, he has absorbed and thereby taken away sin, so that we might be brought into a relationship with God." As quoted by Blocher, "The Sacrifice of Jesus Christ," 31. Blocher's initial response is, "Why 'experience' when Paul says 'death' (v.14f)? Why 'estrangement' when Paul thinks in terms of 'imputation' (*logizomenos*, v.19)?" Ibid., 31.

30. Blocher, "The Sacrifice of Jesus Christ," 31.

31. "Scripture plainly 'translates' numinous wrath as just retribution." Ibid., 32.

to substitution,[32] and opposes the idea that what is legal or forensic is not personal.

> The basic antimony between the legal and the personal is also radically foreign to Scripture: there is nothing more personal than in-law relationships—marriage itself is first of all a legal reality (and the notion of *persona* is first juridical).[33]

On this latter point, Garry Williams has written a strong defense of the idea that PSA is a very personal model of atonement. He claims that PSA is derived from a view of the law where God is intimately involved in its outworking. After citing numerous scriptural examples that emphasize God's personal involvement in the giving of the law that is based on his holy character (e.g. Lev 11:44-45; 19:2; 20:26; 21:8), Williams argues:

> From this it emerges that the law, in its nature, role, and final purpose is intimately related to the being of God himself . . . for God to relate to his creatures by means of the law (and here we think more widely than the OT law) is not for him to become subject to an alien code which operates apart from his most intimate nature and concerns. It is for him to relate through a law which takes every aspect of its definition from who he himself is.[34]

Williams concludes that those who criticize PSA have not fully understood significant personal and relational features in the biblical understanding of divine law and punishment.

> Instead, they have attacked penal substitution on the basis that it is bound in a culture that we have that we have left behind and is mathematical or mechanistic. Against this, the close identifica-

---

32. "No distance may be created between the idea of transfer and that of substitution, abundantly witnessed to in Scripture: they are two sides of the same coin." Ibid. A more detailed biblical and theological defense that agrees with Blocher's assertions may be found in David Peterson's two definitive essays entitled "Atonement in the Old Testament" and "Atonement in the New Testament," as found in *Where Wrath and Mercy Meet*, 1–66.

33. Ibid. The objection by the critics is that PSA is merely a cold, mechanical, legal transaction and does not make salvation personal like the term "reconciliation" would imply. For an excellent rebuttal of this criticism of PSA, see Williams, "The Cross and Punishment of Sin," in *Where Wrath and Mercy Meet*, 81–98. Williams argues that it is modern understandings of cold, mechanistic law that are improperly imposed back on to the model of PSA.

34. Williams, "The Cross and Punishment of Sin," in *Where Wrath and Mercy Meet*, 86–87.

tion of God with the law and with the act of punishment made in
Scripture shows that he is thoroughly involved in both, and thus
proves that penal substitution, being formed by such categories, is
not a consequence impersonal or mechanistic.[35]

In his classic defense of PSA, John R. W. Stott vehemently defends
the "satisfaction through substitution" principle and the personal character of the atonement even with all of its legal, forensic elements.

> There is nothing even remotely immoral here, since the substitute
> for law-breakers is none other than the divine Law-maker himself.
> There is no mechanical transaction either, since the self-sacrifice
> of love is the most personal of all actions. And what is achieved
> through the cross is no merely external exchange of legal status,
> since those who see God's love there, and are united to Christ by his
> Spirit, become radically transformed in outlook and character.[36]

Robert Letham highlights the personal nature of PSA by nuancing
the *type of justice* we are seeing in it. He writes:

> The atonement stems from the love of God, and since God's love is
> *just* love and his justice is *loving* justice, the cross is a demonstration
> *par excellence* of that love in a way that is commensurate with his
> justice. Similarly, his just requirements are fully satisfied in a man-
> ner which displays the amazing grandeur of his love and grace.[37]

35 Ibid., 94. D. A. Carson likewise retorts, "It is far from clear that any biblical writer
thinks God's love is personal while his wrath is impersonal." Carson, "Atonement in
Romans 3:21–26," 132. See also Gaffin, "Atonement in the Pauline Corpus," in *The Glory
of the Atonement*, 140–62.

36. Stott, *The Cross of Christ*, 159. Stott further defends the magnificent wonder of the
gospel and the amazing significance of Christ's penal substitutionary atonement when
he remarks, "The concept of substitution may be said, then, to lie at the heart of both
sin and salvation. For in essence sin is substituting himself for God, while the essence of
salvation is God substituting himself for man. Man asserts himself against God and puts
himself only where God deserves to be; God sacrifices himself for man and puts himself
where only man deserves to be. Man claims prerogatives which belong to God alone;
God accepts penalties which belong to man alone." Ibid., 160. Here, then, the ground
of forgiveness is laid by the fact that the just demands of the law are satisfied and God's
wrath that was due to man is quenched.

37. Letham, *The Work of Christ*, 138. To be precise, we are dealing with *justice* in the
context of a *covenantal relationship*. As Kevin J. Vanhoozer writes, "We need some such
phrase as '*making right covenantal relationship*' to catch both the objective and subjective outcomes of Christ's atoning work. The atonement makes things 'right,' to be sure,
but this rightness is legal *and* interpersonal, objective *and* subjective." Vanhoozer, "The
Atonement in Postmodernity: Guilt, Goats, and Gifts," in *The Glory of the Atonement*,

THEOLOGICAL CONFUSION
AND THE ABANDONMENT OF PSA

It is beyond the scope of this work to unleash a full-fledged defense of PSA against all of its critics or a constructive formation of the model. I believe that others have already done this successfully.[38] Besides the personal and cultural agendas that are seemingly "blowing" against the model of PSA, there also seems to be some theological confusion surrounding key doctrines and attributes of God. For some, it would seem that any doctrine that would teach that God could ever be angry or full of wrath is incompatible with the idea of a loving God, as if the attributes must be mutually exclusive. Similar to what Blocher was arguing earlier, this is simply due to secular ideas that have crept into people's understanding of God.[39] It is furthermore a distortion of the biblical evidence, as argued and defended by Tony Lane.[40] He assertively writes:

---

381. Later, Vanhoozer will say it again emphatically. "The shed blood is a sign that God has proved this covenant faithfulness precisely by undergoing the sanctions, legal and relational, for covenant disobedience." Ibid., 398.

38. See footnote 13. I believe, however, that the series of essays edited by David Peterson entitled, *Where Wrath and Mercy Meet*, the essays edited by Charles E. Hill and Frank A. James entitled, *The Glory of the Atonement*, as well as the latest volume by J. I. Packer and Mark Dever entitled, *In My Place Condemned He Stood: Celebrating the Glory of the Atonement* are perhaps the best recent defenses that adequately deals with current critiques of PSA that have been raised in the last couple years. These texts build a solid biblical theology of PSA.

39. So also R. P. C. Hanson, who writes, "The contemporary rejection by Christians of the biblical doctrine of the wrath of God is a typical example of our allowing secular, non-Christian ideas to creep into our understanding of the Christian faith in such a way as to distort it." Hanson, *God*, 38; quoted in Lane, "The Wrath of God as an Aspect of the Love of God," in Vanhoozer, *Nothing Greater, Nothing Better*, 153.

40. See his aforementioned article, "The Wrath of God as an Aspect of the Love of God," 138–67. Lane also argues that the biblical concept of wrath cannot be understood in merely impersonal cause and effect terms. He defends it as "God's personal, vigorous opposition both to evil and evil people. This is a steady, unrelenting antagonism that arises from God's very nature, his holiness." Ibid., 154. In support of such a conclusion Leon Morris highlights 2 Thessalonians 1:7–9. He asks, "What are we to make of the revelation of the Lord Jesus from heaven with the angels of his power in flaming fire, rendering vengeance to them that know not God, and to them that obey not the gospel of our Lord Jesus: who shall suffer punishment, even eternal destruction from the face of the Lord and from the glory of his might? . . . Paul's vigorous language gives us rather a picture of a God who is personally active in dealing with sinners. As Hebrews 12:29 puts it, 'our God is a consuming fire.'" Morris, *The Apostolic Preaching of the Cross*, 183.

God's wrath should be seen as an aspect of his love, as a consequence of his love . . . there is no true love without wrath.[41]

In both the Old Testament (especially the Psalms) and the New Testament, the wrath of God is portrayed as flowing from his holy and righteous character, as a personal response to sin.[42] We have noted such a personal punitive discipline earlier in this work. The fullness of the love of God can only be rightly understood as one upholds and maintains the idea of God's displeasure and hatred of that which is contrary to his character and nature (and contrary to love itself), that which is in essence evil and sin.[43] Lane rightly recognizes that in Romans 12:9, "Paul's injunction that love be sincere is followed by the command to hate what is evil."[44] Therefore to hold to the idea that God is loving and yet at the same time can be wrathful, in particular against evil, is not an oxymoron.[45] To be

41. Lane, "The Wrath of God," 159. He continues by saying that, "failure to hate evil implies a deficiency in love" and so a "lack of wrath against wickedness is a lack of caring which is a lack of love . . ." Ibid., 160.

42. In 2 Chronicles 19:10, while appointing judges to settle disputes in the land, King Jehoshaphat of Judah declared to them, "In every case that comes before you from your fellow countrymen who live in the cities—whether bloodshed or other concerns of the law, commands, decrees, or ordinances—you are to warn them not to sin against the LORD, otherwise his wrath will come on you and your brothers." Personal vengeance is discouraged by Paul in Romans 12:19. Yet as a reminder, Paul reminds them that wickedness will not go unpunished but will incur the wrath of God, who will personally avenge and repay. Furthermore, the personal character of God's wrath is supposed in Romans 2 where Paul writes, "But because of your stubbornness and unrepentant heart, you are storing up wrath against yourself for the day of God's wrath, when his righteous judgment will be revealed . . . for those who are self-seeking and who reject the truth and follow evil, there will be wrath and anger" (Rom 2:5, 8, NIV). This is not a passive cause-effect judgment, but God is portrayed as actively condemning sin and evil via his wrath. Lane writes, "It is not enough to say that God's punishment is simply the sinner punishing himself. God's role in judgment is not passive." Lane, "The Wrath of God," 158.

43. James I. Packer defines God wrath as "a judicial expression of holiness repudiating unholiness, as it must. God's wrath is retribution re-establishing righteousness where unrighteousness was before, so vindicating God's goodness." Packer, "Anger," in Alexander, *NDBT*, 382.

44. Ibid., 160. He follows with the following example: "A husband who did not respond to his wife's infidelity with a jealous anger would thereby demonstrate his lack of care for her." Ibid.

45. Letham maintains, "Essentially, God's wrath is his settled antagonism towards sin. It is the form taken by his holiness against sinful rebellion in the creature. If he did not have wrath in this context, he would no longer be holy. He would no longer be against sin, and so would no longer be God." Letham, *The Work of Christ*, 141.

sure, it is the clear testimony of Scripture and the key to understanding the significance of the cross. By this we mean that it is the way in which those who advocate PSA can confidently say that God was expressing love to the world (John 3:16) by giving his Son, who would vicariously suffer God's wrath poured out on him as a propitiation for human sin (Rom 3:25–26).[46] In his first letter to the church, the Apostle John portrays the ultimate expression of the love of God as none other than the sending of his Son to die on the cross, incurring his wrath as a propitiatory sacrifice for God's people.

> This is love: not that we loved God, but that he loved us and sent his Son as an atoning sacrifice (*hilasmos*) for our sins. Dear friends, since God so loved us, we also ought to love one another (1 John 4:10–11 NIV).[47]

It is proper, then, to see the cross as the place where both love and wrath find their ultimate and climactic expression. To vicariously bear the full retribution of a believer's sin is one of the most loving acts one

---

46. Indeed, one of the most popular sections of the gospel of John (3:14–16) is not often given due attention to the fact that in love God was "lifting up" and "giving" his Son. The question then naturally arises: in what sense was Christ being lifted up and God giving his Son? D. A. Carson remarks, "The Greek verb for 'lifted up' (*hypsoō*) in its four occurrences in this Gospel (cf. 8:28; 12:32, 34) always combines the notions of being physically lifted up on the cross, with the notion of exaltation." Carson, *The Gospel According to John*, 201. Part of God lifting up Christ and giving his Son as an expression of his love has everything to with what took place on the "violent and wrath-filled" cross event, where one could say "wrath and mercy meet" (borrowing from David Peterson and others). Carson further remarks, "apart from God's love for the world, the very world that stands under his wrath, no one would be saved . . . because John 3:16 is sandwiched between vv. 14–15 and v. 17, the fact that God *gave* his one and only Son is tied both to the Son's incarnation (v. 17) and to his death (vv. 14–15). That is the immediate result of the love of God for the world: the mission of the Son." Ibid., 206.

47. Packer comments that the Greek word *hilasmos* used here and translated as "propitiation" is best defined as the "sacrificial death of Jesus Christ, God's incarnate Son, that quenches divine anger against sinners . . . Christ's death was a vicarious enduring of the penalty that was our due. The once popular view that expiation of sins is all this word group [referring to the noun *hilasmos*, the verb *hilaskomai*, the adjective *hilastērion*, and the noun *hilastērion*] signifies rested on the supposition that there is no wrath of God needing to be dealt with, rather than on linguistic or contextual considerations, and is largely now abandoned." Packer, "Anger," in *NDBT*, 383. It is more appropriate, then, to see PSA including "the ideas of both expiation (the removal of the guilt of sin) and propitiation (appeasing God's wrath). It is also helpful however, to recognize these elements as different albeit inseparable." Letham, *The Work of Christ*, 140.

could ever imagine. Paul echoes this sentiment as he expresses amazement when he considers the sacrificial nature of God's love in Romans 5.

> Very rarely will anyone die for a righteous man, though for a good man someone might possibly dare to die. But God demonstrates *his own love* for us in this: While we were still sinners, *Christ died for us* (Rom 5:7–8 NIV, emphasis mine).[48]

Our Lord surely had his atoning death in mind when he proclaimed the extent his love was willing to go in speaking to his disciples in John 15.

> Greater love has no one than this, that he lay his life down for his friends (John 15:13 NIV).[49]

Therefore, our understanding of the depth of God's love for us is actually increased (not decreased) and the profundity of the cross event is magnified all the more when we maintain the propitiatory idea of God's wrath being poured out on and appeased by Christ. He is the Son of God who died on the cross for our sins and was raised from the dead for our justification (Rom 4:25).[50] This is redemptive love reaching full expression, and to abandon God's wrath poured out on the cross would have devastating consequences. We would still be liable to God for our sins (even though we possessed the gift of faith), and his wrath would be unquenched and rightfully upon us. Our sins would remain unpunished (contra Rom 3:25), and God's righteousness would still need to be expressed since Christ's work would be fallible and thus rendered an incomplete expression of the justice of God (contra Rom 3:26). Our exoneration would be null and void, and we would no longer be justified or standing in a state of grace (Rom 5:1–2). Thus it is critical to maintain the truths held within the PSA atonement model so that the very gospel itself is preserved.

---

48. Love and Christ's vicarious atoning death are held in theological apposition here.

49. D. A. Carson remarks, "At one level, this axiom lays out the standard of love Jesus' disciples are to show to one another; at another, *it refers to Jesus' death on behalf of his friends*—even if the disciples could not have understood this point when they first heard the words" (emphasis mine). Carson, *The Gospel According to John*, 521.

50. Gaffin writes, "To conclude otherwise [that Christ's death was a penal substitution], short of also rejecting or ignoring what we have seen as essential aspects of his clear teaching about sin and God's wrath, would mean that those aspects remain unaddressed by Christ's death." Gaffin, "Atonement in the Pauline Corpus," 160.

IMPLICATIONS FOR OUR UNDERSTANDING
OF CHURCH DISCIPLINE

We may now turn our attention toward the significance of the model and doctrine of PSA, as it will have an effect on our understanding of the role and nature of divine discipline as it is embodied today in the church. If indeed God's complete wrath and retribution for the sins of his people was poured out once and for all on Jesus Christ through his death on the cross, it would then have significant ramifications for our constructive understanding of church discipline.[51] Specifically, this would mean that *church discipline should be seen as devoid of any punitive or retributive elements within its very nature and purpose.* Though this does not preclude the fact that church discipline at times could "feel" like punishment, it does, however, eliminate the possibility, theologically speaking, that there is any sense of retributive punishment inherent in the church practice itself. For if church discipline was to be seen as a *punitive* or *retributive* action of the church, then it would essentially be communicating to the Christian community that the atonement that Christ accomplished on the cross *was insufficient to atone fully for the sins of the God's chosen people.* What then would be the point of Christ's sacrificial death,[52] and how would it be any different than any of the Old Testament sacrifices, which were only a temporary expiation providing an outward cleansing for the sins of God's people (Heb 9:13)?

Yet it is the *complete sufficiency* of Christ's "once for all" atonement for sin that is the argument of Hebrews 10. The author argues that the blood of bulls and goats that were given in sacrifice were unable to take

51. The Holy Spirit, whose role is to testify to the finished work of Jesus Christ (John 16:14), is also the One who applies the significance of the atonement into the life of the church—not only on the personal level through regeneration, justification, and sanctification, but also at the corporate level in the practices of the church. Hütter argues, "Christ's saving presence cannot be separated from the Spirit's sanctifying mission as enacted through his particular works, the church's core practices." Hütter, "The Church," in Buckley and Yeago, *Knowing the Triune God*, 37.

52. That Jesus's death was regarded as a *sacrificial* death can be deduced from the following Scriptures. See Romans 3:25; Ephesians 5:2; Hebrews 9:26; 10:10, 12, 14; 1 John 2:2, 4:10. First John 4:10 teaches us that this was the primary purpose of his incarnation, having been "sent" for such a purpose. In commenting on the book of Hebrews, H. D. McDonald remarks, "The Epistle to the Hebrews makes the idea of sacrifice the master-key of its understanding of Christ's work. He fulfills, in his dying, all the functions of sacrifice. Everywhere, in fact, in the epistle, Christ's work is cast in the language of sacrifice." McDonald, *The New Testament Concept of Atonement*, 80.

away sins (v. 4). Though the law required it, it was merely a shadow of the ultimate sacrifice that was to come (v. 1). It could never make us perfect and completely exonerate us before God. But, the author states, when Christ came, his sacrifice was sufficient so that he set aside the sacrificial system (v. 9), establishing the new reality that by his own sacrifice he is able to completely cleanse us (make us holy) by taking away sins "once for all" (v. 10). As is written:

> We have been made holy through the sacrifice of the body of Jesus Christ once for all (Heb 10:10 NIV).[53]

There is a sense of finality to the sacrifice, which communicates to us that there is no longer any need for the sacrificial system to be operating, because complete atonement has been made and full retribution and punishment for the sins of God's people have been exacted. A climactic moment has occurred within redemption history. The cross of Christ serves as the pivotal point in God's plan of salvation from sin and death in that it nullifies the necessity of *continuing* punitive and retributive sacrifices for God's people. The writer of Hebrews gives us an overall glimpse of the sacrificial situation (if you will) throughout the various sections of redemption history, past and present, while profiling the death of Christ as the hinge on which redemption history turns. The author writes in this extended quote:

> Day after day every priest stands and performs his religious duties; again and again he offers the same sacrifices, which can never take away sins. But when *this priest* had offered for all time one sacrifice for sins, he sat down at the right hand of God. Since that time he waits for his enemies to be made his footstool, because by one sacrifice he has made perfect forever those who are being made holy . . . 'their sins and lawless acts I will remember no more.' And where these have been forgiven, there is no longer any sacrifice for sin. Therefore, brothers, since we have confidence to enter the Most Holy Place by the blood of Jesus, by a new and living way opened for us through the curtain, that is, his body, and since we have a great priest over the house of God, let us draw near to God with a sincere heart in full assurance of faith, having our hearts

---

53. With regard to holiness, verse 10 is speaking of a *positional* holiness, whereas we receive the perfect righteousness of Christ imputed through faith. This is our standing before God, though in terms of our progressive sanctification (practically speaking) we are still in the process of "being made holy" (v. 14).

sprinkled to cleanse us from a guilty conscience and having our
bodies washed with pure water (Heb 10:11–14, 17–22 NIV, emphasis mine).[54]

So in light of these biblical assertions about the sufficiency of Christ's
sacrifice, it is our conclusion that the retributive punishment for the sins
of God's people has been completely satisfied in the work of the God-man,
Jesus Christ. He was the one who paid our penalty in full and appeased
the wrath of God that was due our sin while on the cross. And he *is seated*
(communicating finality) at the right hand of God after completing his
work and once for all doing away with the need for the sacrificial system.
"There is therefore now no condemnation for those who are in Christ
Jesus" (Rom 8:1).[55]

In addition, the Old Testament remnant of believers whose punishment was temporarily stayed has finally seen divine justice fulfilled once
and for all with respect to its sin. It was God's forbearance (Rom 3:25) that
allowed for the delay of their full punishment (which was to be placed on
Christ, cf. Isa 53:5). This allows us to see the "heavy hand of God" (Job
23:2) that was upon them as simply a form of divine *discipline* rather than
a full retributive judgment for sin, as it was the case with those who were
not in faithful covenant relationship with Yahweh (see chapter 3). The
salvation of the believing remnant is now made complete in the *judicial*

---

54. The fact that our author mentions the fact that Christ "sat down" after offering
"for all time one sacrifice for sin" is especially significant in light of the argument of the
sufficiency of Christ's sacrifice as a full and final retributive punishment. F. F. Bruce comments, "The Aaronic priests never sat down in the sanctuary; they remained standing
throughout the whole performance of their sacred duties. In this our author sees a token
of the fact that their sacred duties were never done, that their sacrifices had always to be
repeated . . . the priests of the old order never sat down in the presence of God when a
sacrifice had been presented to him. But it was equally in keeping with the perfection of
Christ's sacrifice of himself that, when he had presented it to God, he sat down. No further sacrificial service can be required of the priest who appeared on earth in the fulness
of time to put away sin and sanctify his people once for all. *A seated priest is the guarantee
of a finished work and an accepted sacrifice*" (emphasis mine). Bruce, *Hebrews*, 245.

55. For those who are in spiritual union with Jesus through faith, that is (Rom 8:1
NIV). The word translated "condemnation" is κατάκριμα, a strong judicial term. Some
alternate translations could be "punishment or penalty." *BDAG* notes, "The use of the
term 'condemnation' does not denote merely a pronouncement of guilt, but the adjudica-
tion of punishment." Danker, *BDAG*, 518. Thus the church, in my mind, is spared from
anything related to the wrath of God, for this has to do with punishment. However God's
wrath is yet unquenched for those who are not in union with Christ, who are storing up
wrath against themselves (Rom 2:5).

sense.[56] Thus all of the Old Testament saints were saved through faith on the basis of Christ's future atoning work, which would become their perfect, full, and final sacrifice for sin. The new covenant through Christ that God has wrought to his people has fulfilled the promise of the completion of their redemption from sin. As Hebrews testifies:

> These [the OT saints listed in Hebrews 11] were all commended for their faith, yet none of them received what had been promised. God had planned something better for us *so that only together with us would they be made perfect* (Heb 11:40 NIV, emphasis mine).[57]

The community of God's people then has become a new creation, having achieved a newly justified status in light of the cross event.[58] This new status will in turn affect the way that God will deal with his people who are a part of the new covenant established through Christ. As Hays has rightly said concerning Paul's teaching in the New Testament, the community of faith is "being caught up in the story of God's remaking of the world through Jesus Christ."[59] They are the new work of God (thanks to Christ's work) who is building his kingdom here on earth.[60] With sin fully atoned for and retributive justice met, the church and its biblical practices, and in our particular case, church discipline, cannot be seen as embodying any sense

56. In other words, though they have not received their "full adoption as sons" in terms of receiving complete, glorified, resurrected bodies (Rom 8:23), they have now found their sin to be fully atoned for within the economy of divine justice. God has shown himself to be a just God (Rom 3:26), enabling him to be able to fully justify all those who trust in him (past, present, and future).

57. Bruce comments, "But now the promise has been fulfilled; the age of the new covenant has dawned; the Christ to whose day they looked forward has come and by his self-offering and his high-priestly ministry in the presence of God he has procured perfection for them—and for us . . . they and we together now enjoy unrestricted access to God through Christ, as fellow citizens of the heavenly Jerusalem." Bruce, *Hebrews*, 330.

58. For more on using the focal images of *community, cross,* and *new creation* as a paradigm for understanding how life is to be ethically lived out in the New Testament era today, see Hays's, *The Moral Vision of the New Testament.*

59. Hays, *Moral Vision*, 45.

60. So Vanhoozer asserts, "Jesus' seminal interpretation of his own death enables us to understand its saving significance as the inaugurating event of a newer and more wonderful covenant. Jesus' death on the cross is a new exodus, a new Passover supper, a new return from exile, an entry into a new kind of promised land, a building of a new and better temple." Vanhoozer, "The Atonement in Postmodernity: Guilt, Goats, and Gifts," 399. For more on the impact that a denial of PSA would have on the Christian life, see Packer, "The Atonement in the Life of the Christian," in *The Glory of the Atonement*, 420–5.

of punitive retribution. We can therefore confidently assert that insofar as church discipline is charged with dealing with sin and error in the church, *its nature and purpose is not punitive retribution, but is rather instructional, remedial, restorative, and reconciliatory.*[61] We are indebted to the cross of Christ as the pivotal hinge of redemption history that eliminates the idea of divine retribution from the practices of the church.

> Within the story, everything points to the death and resurrection of Jesus as the pivot-point of the ages; the old cosmos has met its end, and God's eschatological righteousness/justice has broken in upon the present, making everything new.[62]

DISCIPLINE IN THE NEW COMMUNITY

The cross of Christ has created, then, the grounds for a new community of faith (the church), embodied by the Holy Spirit, whereby believers are exonerated from divine punishment, forgiven for all sin, and freed from God's wrath. As we stated earlier, this has an effect on the nature of the practices of that community of faith, especially the practice of church discipline. The church, as a community of believers *forgiven by Christ* through faith on the basis of his vicarious suffering, death, and resurrection, should themselves seek to emulate their forgiving God by embodying forgiveness in all its practices.[63] As L. Gregory Jones has rightly noted:

> Those who are forgiven by Jesus are called to embody that forgiven-ness in new life signified by communion with Jesus and other disciples.[64]

61. Our next chapter will take a specific look at the biblical texts of the New Testament that warrant this conclusion, and the achievement of a biblical theology of church discipline will be one of our goals.

62. Hays, *Moral Vision*, 46.

63. As F. Leron Shults rightly notes, "The forgiveness manifested on the cross is related to the real dynamics of grace in community, wherein we are called to forgive others." Shults, "Faces of Forgiveness in Theology," in Shults and Sandage, *The Faces of Forgiveness*, 193. Shults also laments, "Too often . . . when forgiveness is discussed in North American churches, it is abstracted from the real concrete practices of shared life together in community. We need an understanding of divine grace and forgiveness that invades, permeates, and empowers the life of the church" (104). Vanhoozer connects the practices of forgiving and peace-keeping in the church to the gift of the promised Holy Spirit made possible by Christ's "horrific exodus." Vanhoozer, "The Atonement in Postmodernity: Guilt, Goats, and Gifts," 400.

64. Jones, *Embodying Forgiveness*, 121. In a similar vein, Colin Gunton remarks,

Therefore, such church practices as baptism and the Lord's Supper are a few practices (and in their case ordinances) of the church that embody or proclaim the message of God's forgiveness. Both testify to the person and work of Christ who has provided the means of redemption through a sacrificial substitutionary death on behalf of sinners. In the same way, church discipline, as a practice of the church, embodies and proclaims the message of forgiveness to a believer who has been grieving the Spirit of God through his or her continual and unrepentant sin. In fact, Jones includes the idea of church discipline as essentially part of what he calls the "practice of reconciling forgiveness." He argues that forgiveness and reconciliation are embodied in practices where sin is dealt with properly according to the principles of Matthew 18.

> We often shy away from confronting our brother or our sister be-
> cause of our fears, or perhaps even our experience, of how such
> confrontation exacerbates rather than resolves conflicted situa-
> tions. We sometimes refer to avoiding such confrontations as a
> form of "keeping the peace." But the logic of the passage, and of
> the gospel, suggests that we will be able to "keep the peace" only
> insofar as we foster practices of forgiveness and reconciliation in
> which sin is acknowledged and confronted.[65]

Thus the goal of Matthew 18:15–20, which is a passage we will look at extensively in our next chapter, is forgiveness and reconciliation, made possible by the cross.

Further, when the church enacts the procedures of church discipline derived from Jesus' teaching in Matthew 18, it becomes an expression of God's forgiveness *in action*, seeking to reach out to the unrepentant one in an effort to restore him or her from his or her sin.[66] Yet if the unrepentant

---

"Forgiveness is therefore about being placed in a position—in the life of a community—where the evil past can be acknowledged while at the same time being used as a basis for a new form of life; where it can be atoned because it has been atoned . . . to enter the church is therefore to enter a form of community in which the vicarious suffering of Jesus becomes the basis for a corresponding form of life, one in which the offense of others is borne rather than avenged." Gunton, *The Actuality of the Atonement*, 190.

65. Jones, *Embodying Forgiveness*, 192.

66. Jones remarks, "This pattern of binding and loosing describes communities where practices of discernment and forgiveness are central to their ongoing life, where the gospel of God's reconciliation shapes their struggle to live with one another as reconciled and reconciling people." Ibid., 193. So in binding and loosing, they are seeking to live out the gospel of God's reconciliation manifested in their midst.

refuses to acknowledge his or her need for forgiveness, then the church's action of excommunication (the final step) is not only the binding and loosing authorized and endorsed by God (v. 18), but is a recognition of the fact that the person has excluded him or herself from the community of faith committed to living in truth.

> In such situations, the way of forgiveness is truncated and the prospects for reconciliation are, if not temporarily eclipsed, at least not fully possible. If offenders persistently refuse to acknowledge their need for forgiveness as the extensive process of people talking with them described in this passage goes on . . . then they ought to be treated as "gentiles and tax collectors."[67]

The unrepentant one is turning his or her back on God's mercy, falling away from grace by not responding to God's forgiving hand reached out to him or her by means of the confrontation process outlined in Matthew 18.[68] He or she is rejecting *one of* God's means of grace that he has chosen to embody through this practice of the church.[69] So then, church discipline should be seen as a way in which God's forgiveness and love are being communicated as the Spirit works in the practices of the church.

In summary of our main argument of this chapter, it is in light of the penal substitutionary atonement of Christ for his people that all of what the church does in church discipline can be seen as the "practice of reconciling forgiveness." It was at the cross where retribution for the sins of God's people was carried out, thus exonerating them from retributive punishment in any way. Church discipline, then, is not "punishment" (as

67. Ibid., 194.

68. In saying that they are falling away from grace, I am not suggesting that a true believer could lose his or her salvation and the inheritance that can never perish, spoil, or fade, kept in heaven for him or her (1 Pet 1:4). Those who are regenerated and indwelled by the Spirit are sealed (Eph 1:14) and have their names written in the Book of Life. My point is that the unrepentant one is rejecting the blessing of the grace of God (cf. Gal 5:4), and in so doing is straining and grieving the fellowship he or she has with God.

69. Reinhard Hütter remarks, "Christ's saving presence cannot be separated from the Spirit's sanctifying mission as enacted through his particular works, the church's core practices." Hütter, "The Church," in Buckley and Yeago, *Knowing the Triune God*, 37. Thus when one refuses to repent and respond to church discipline, one is in essence rejecting Christ, whose saving presence and grace is being manifested by the power of the Holy Spirit at work in the actions of church discipline. The assertion that Christ is present with the church when they act on matters of church discipline is the clear teaching of the Lord himself, who declared, "For where two or three come together in my name, there I am with them" (Matt 18:20, NIV).

it is commonly misperceived) but should rather be seen as God's hand of grace extended for the purpose of restoration and reconciliation, a love that rescues, which we will investigate further next. In addition, the parameters and biblical mandate for the church to engage in the practice of church discipline will be the subject of our next chapter. There we will seek to develop a biblical theology of New Testament church discipline. It is to these tasks that we now turn.

6

Divine Discipline as Manifested in the Church

U P TO THIS POINT, we have been laying the groundwork for a construc- tive understanding of church discipline. Our goal is to understand its nature and purpose in light of the role of God's "fatherly" discipline on his people throughout redemption history and the significance of the cross of Christ as the penultimate moment of that history. For divine dis- cipline, as we have seen, is a unique way that God relates to his people, whom he has chosen for himself. Throughout the course of Israelite his- tory, God has employed discipline in multiple contexts using a variety of ways and means to accomplish his purposes. Whatever the purposes may be (e.g., instruction and training, punishment and judgment of the wicked, or temporal chastisement for sin), we have seen God's hand at work in direct or indirect ways in the execution of the discipline. Yahweh directly had a hand in disciplining Israel in the wilderness experience and used more indirect means when using the strength of foreign nations during the period of the exile.

Now as we turn our attention to the New Testament, following the ascension of Christ, we see that God primarily chooses to manifest himself, his redemptive purposes, and saving activity on earth in a new context, through the Spirit-embodied community of faith, or his church. We now see both Jews and gentiles with the gift of saving faith and the Spirit of God not simply in their presence but embodying their hearts. Further, in light of the significance of the cross of Christ, we also have a new paradigm for understanding the nature and purpose of that dis- cipline for God's people, as our last chapter has shown. Two significant developments are a part of this new paradigm.

First, as we concluded in our last chapter, divine discipline is now no longer to be qualified as retributive or punitive in nature for God's people, but is rather instructional, remedial, restorative, and reconciliatory. Second, another development we find is that divine discipline has a new medium through which it is executed—the practices of the church— where the Spirit of God is at work, specifically the practice of church discipline.[1] The discipline we are referring to has parameters and controls that are outlined in Scripture, which we will be looking at in detail now. It will be our task to develop a fuller understanding and biblical theology of church discipline, as God expresses his "fatherly" love and forgiveness *in action*, as we stated in our last chapter.

JESUS' MANDATE TO DISCIPLINE

Any discussion of church discipline in the New Testament must center in large part around Jesus' teaching on the matter to his disciples in Matthew 18:15–20. It reads as follows:

> If your brother sins against you, go and show him his fault, just between the two of you. If he listens to you, you have won your brother over. But if he will not listen, take one or two others along, so that "every matter may be established by the testimony of two or three witnesses. If he refuses to listen to them, tell it to the church; and if he refuses to listen even to the church, treat him as you would a pagan or a tax collector. I tell you the truth, whatever you bind on earth will be bound in heaven, and whatever you loose on earth will be loosed in heaven. Again, I tell you that if two of you on earth agree about anything you ask for, it will be done for you by my Father in heaven. For where two or three come together in my name, there am I with them (NIV).

The context of Jesus' teaching follows the parable of the lost sheep in verses 10–14 and precedes the parable of the merciful servant in verses 21–35. Therefore, the disciplinary instruction given to the disciples falls contextually between a parable that emphasizes restoration of that which has gone astray (vv. 10–14) and the canceling and forgiveness of an outstanding debt (vv. 21–35). This is an extremely significant contextual "sandwich," for the instructions to the disciples in verses 15–20 concerning disciplinary action and the authority to enact it has as its primary goal the forgiveness, restoration, and reconciliation of a brother or sister who

---

1. The Spirit of God is at work in the practices of the church insofar as he is at work in the lives of his people, leading and guiding them into all truth, causing them to bear fruit for God by glorifying God and building his kingdom, and by transforming hearts and minds through the word of God in keeping with their progressive sanctification.

through sin has gone astray. In this way, the teaching by Christ in verses 15–20 has thematic elements of that which precedes and follows it.[2] A debt (or sin) has incurred a breach of relationship, and forgiveness is needed. Therefore, a plan of action is instituted[3] for the purpose of "winning your brother over" (v. 15)—the goal being reconciliation. To "win over" someone is to reconcile the relationship. It must not be understood as a mere victory to an interpersonal battle, but the hope of bringing back an erring member of the church so that unity and fellowship can be restored and the road of discipleship maintained. As Stuart Murray has aptly noted:

> Your purpose is not to win an argument but to win a brother, not to make a complaint but to help a sister make progress as a disciple.[4]

In this way, then, the "reign of God" will be more faithfully displayed in a satisfactory way within the church.[5]

2. Jesus has further instructed and warned his followers against causing others to sin in verses 5–9, specifically the "little ones." And what he will outline in verses 15–20, when followed correctly, will help minimize the effects of sin on the whole community when genuine repentance takes place. David McClister has identified a rather large thematic chiasmus that perfectly fits Matthew 17:22—20:19, whereby the thematic climax is found in 18:18–20. He argues that this section ultimately deals with the death of Christ, personal discipleship, and the relationships between disciples. He further declares, "Discipleship demands that there must be a correspondence between heaven and earth in all things" as we learn what it means to live in union with Christ and each other. McClister, "Where Two or Three Are Gathered Together: Literary Structure as a Key to Meaning in Matt 17:22—20:19," 556. The themes of forgiveness and reconciliation within the context of discipleship spearhead this section as Jesus explains the reasons for his death.

3. Jones has rightly noted that whenever there is a breach in relationship, the aura of peace in the community is broken, and this demands action. As we quoted earlier, but now with renewed emphasis, "the logic of the passage [Matt 18:15–20], and of the gospel, suggests that we will be able to 'keep the peace' insofar as we foster practices of forgiveness and reconciliation in which *sin is acknowledged and confronted*" (emphasis mine). Jones, *Embodying Forgiveness*, 192.

4. Murray, *Explaining Church Discipline*, 24.

5. The singular aorist active form of the verb κερδήσω, translated "won over," is a figurative expression that carries with it the idea of placing someone within the sphere of the reign of God. See Danker, *BDAG*, 541. Paul used the same root term in reference to seeking to "win over" those who were not of the faith and were subsequently outside of the kingdom of God in 1 Corinthians 9:19–22, and Peter used the term in a similar fashion with respect to the behavior of believing wives whose actions may "win over" their non-believing husbands (1 Pet 3:1). The term in Matthew 18:15 is meaningful in that the idea of "winning over your brother" and seeing his attitude and actions return to the sphere of the reign of God is in contrast to the one who "refuses to listen" to the threefold admonition of the believing community. Those who refuse to listen qualify

The process that Jesus outlines for winning your brother or sister over if found in sin is to be initiated or begun outside of the public eye. The offended believer is commanded to go and show the offender the fault, "just between the two of you."[6] This should be done in great humility and love. The privacy of the matter allows for the sin to be reproved and confessed in the smallest possible community.[7] There are several advantages to this. As Carl Laney aptly points out, one benefit is that it allows for any misperceptions concerning the "alleged sin" to be corrected.[8] Thus, if the person doing the confrontation has misunderstood the situation or

---

and show themselves to be like those who are altogether outside of the kingdom, not submitting to the reign of God. For the Jewish audience that Jesus was speaking to, this idea could be captured well by telling the unrepentant to be treated like a "pagan or a tax collector" (v. 17).

6. A textual situation is noted here in that some manuscripts carry the words "against you" in verse 15 and others do not (notably ℵ, *Codex Sinaiticus*, fourth century; and B, *Codex Vaicanus*, fourth century). UBS (fourth rev. ed.) and Nestle-Aland (twenty-seventh ed.) express great uncertainty as to whether the words "against you" belong in the text. D. A. Carson notes, "If the words 'against you' are included, Jesus is looking at offenses within the Messianic community . . . from the viewpoint of the brother against whom the sin is committed. If 'against you' is omitted, Jesus is telling the community as a whole how to handle the situation when a brother sins [in general]." Carson, *Matthew 13–28*, 402. It would seem, however, that the approach that Jesus advocates would be applicable in either situation. J. Carl Laney's insights are helpful in that, "whether the words 'against you' are in the original text or not, it is clear from Gal 6:1 that believers have a responsibility to confront sin in general, not just when it is an offense against one's person." Laney, *A Guide to Church Discipline*, 49. Peter, however, seemingly personalizes Jesus' remarks in his response in verse 21. Thus, it is a distinct possibility that "against you" (v. 15) was in the original text due to context.

7. Jesus not only taught that the offended person should go immediately to resolve the situation in private, but he also taught earlier in Matthew 5:23–24 that the one who actually has done the offense should pursue reconciliation with the same sense of urgency if he or she have knowingly sinned against another party. "Therefore, if you are offering your gift at the altar and there remember that your brother has something against you, leave your gift there in front of the altar. First go and be reconciled to your brother, and then come and offer your gift" (Matt 5:23–24 NIV). As Jay Adams has noted, "Jesus pictures him as interrupting an act of worship to do so [be reconciled], thereby showing the high priority he places on good relations between Christians; cf. 1 Pet 3:7." Adams, *Handbook of Church Discipline*, 48.

8. Laney remarks, "In some situations the sin is very apparent and there is little to no doubt that the brother or sister has sinned. Usually, however, it is wise in the first confrontation to allow for the possibility that I am misjudging. Perhaps I misunderstand the situation or somehow have the facts wrong . . . I have sometimes found, after leaping to a conclusion, that I don't have the facts in order." Laney, *A Guide to Church Discipline*, 50.

does not have all the facts, then the one-to-one discussion prevents false information from spreading.

Another advantage of keeping things within the smallest possible community is that this helps prevent the sin and its effects from spreading to others.

> The author of Hebrews tells Christians to see to it that "no 'root of bitterness' spring up and cause trouble, and by it *the many become defiled*" (Heb 12:15). This means that if conflict between persons is not resolved quickly, the effects may spread to many others—something that sadly seems to be true in most cases of church division.[9]

The seriousness of allowing a sin to spread through the believing community was a deep concern of Jesus, as he warned the disciples many times against the hypocrisy of the Jewish elite (e.g., Matt 16:5; Mark 8:15; Luke 12:1).[10] The same was true for Paul as he reminded the church of the inherent danger of not disciplining the immoral brother in 1 Corinthians 5.

> Your boasting is not good. Don't you know that a little yeast works through the whole batch of dough? Get rid of the old yeast that you may be a new batch without yeast as you really are. For Christ, our Passover lamb has been sacrificed (1 Cor 5:6–7 NIV).

When the community is close knit, the possibility that one might be tempted to participate in the same sin is all the more real. Thus, even when one is involved in confronting the erring brother or sister, one must take heed.

> Brothers, if someone is caught in a sin, you who are spiritual should restore him gently. *But watch yourself, or you also may be tempted* (Gal 6:1 NIV, emphasis mine).

Not only was this true for the New Testament community, but it was also a serious concern for the Old Testament community of Israel. In Deuteronomy 13 the Israelites are warned against false prophets, close relations, or anyone who may have "arisen among you" who would lead

---

9. Grudem, *Systematic Theology*, 895. Thomas C. Oden, whose comment is influenced by the writings of the early theologian Cyprian, proclaims, "Like an astringent amid an epidemic, corrective love seeks to *resist the infectious process by which the pollution of one infects another* in the community. Uncensored sin threatens to exert contagious influence. If left unchallenged, sin gains momentum and license to spread into the healthy cells of the community of faith." Oden, *Corrective Love*, 84–5.

10. Thiselton, *The First Epistle to the Corinthians*, 400.

them astray to follow foreign gods. When sin is found within the covenant community, it must be dealt with accordingly, so that by its very presence it does not tempt or lead the rest of the community astray. Moses reiterated why such action is necessary when he reminded the Israelites:

> You are the children of the LORD your God . . . you are a people holy to the LORD your God. Out of all the peoples on the face of the earth, the LORD has chosen you to be his treasured possession (Deut 14:1a–2 NIV).

Therefore, according to Moses, the very identity (v. 1a), holiness (v. 2a), and reputation (v. 2b) of the covenant community was at stake, and his was a call to faithfulness. So the necessary response to sin or compromise found in the community was not to be indifference, but action, lest the yeast work its way through the whole batch of dough. Inaction would only bring judgment or the removal of the Yahweh's blessing, as was the case for Eli the priest and his two sons in the book of 1 Samuel, a story we will turn to at the end of this chapter.

In this initial stage of discipline, the seriousness of keeping the matter "just between the two of you" cannot be emphasized enough. To recap, unless the issue to be confronted is a gross public sin, privacy in confronting the matter will allow for misunderstandings to be straightened out and will keep the sin from spreading to others. Further, it shows respect for the one being confronted, so that his or her sins are not broadcast or subject to gossip throughout the community.[11] This may allow for him or her to maintain a good reputation and prevents others in the community from developing a critical spirit toward the offender. Laney remarks:

> If the one you have confronted heeds what you say and either clarifies the issue or recognizes the sin and repents of it, *that person is saved for usefulness in the body of Christ* (emphasis mine).[12]

11. Stuart Murray, in his brilliant little booklet on church discipline, writes, "There is a direct correlation in local church life between failure to exercise church discipline and the prevalence of gossip . . . if the process of church discipline is not understood and owned by church members, the probable outcome of such tensions will be disunity, back-biting, gossip, and broken relationships . . . church discipline protects a community from gossip and restores relationships." Murray, *Explaining Church Discipline*, 23. Further, confronting a brother or sister in private is another way of loving your neighbor as yourself (see Lev 19:17–19).

12. Laney, *A Guide to Church Discipline*, 51. Jay Adams stresses that even though privacy is essential at this level of confrontation, this does not mean that this is a promise of absolute confidentiality. For if repentance does not take place at this level, then

This is in keeping with the loving approach called for by James in his epistle to the church, who wrote:

> My brothers, if one of you should wander from the truth and someone should bring him back, remember this: Whoever turns a sinner from the error of his way will save him from death and cover over a multitude of sins (Jas 5:19–20 NIV).[13]

If this initial stage (stage 1) of confrontation is done in humility, love, and gentleness and with a caring attitude, there is a strong likelihood that the brother or sister will "listen to you," and thus respond positively in repentance.[14] Without such a virtuous approach, however, the situation may become destructive. A self-righteous, vindictive, or judgmental spirit on the part of the person confronting undermines the spirit of the process. The goal is to gently restore the brother or sister (Gal 6:1) so that peace will reign.[15] Many attempts at church discipline, even if they are done "by the book," have been unsuccessful and damaging simply because the attitudes and approaches of the person(s) confronting have been wanting.[16] Yet if done appropriately, the results can be marvelous.

---

an ever-widening circle of accountability may be necessary. See Adams, *Handbook of Church Discipline*, 30–33, 52. Further, there may be certain sins (such as sexual abuse) where confidentiality may not be legally permissible.

13. Here someone has strayed from the truth, or "the way of truth," as some alternative manuscripts read (p[74], ℵ, 3, 81 623), and a compassionate brother who helps bring him back to repentance will save his brother from (spiritual or perhaps physical) death and procure the forgiveness of God, blot out sins, and preserve peace (any of which could serve as the meaning of "cover over a multitude of sins," cf. Prov 10:12; 1 Pet 4:8). This may serve to prevent the "sinner" from getting further into a sinful lifestyle and help keep him or her walking on the "straight and narrow" path of righteousness, rendering him or her useful for service in the kingdom of God.

14. Or the matter may be further clarified and any misunderstandings may be resolved or cleared up. Adams labels this stage step 2, in keeping with his idea that self-discipline is step 1. Adams, *Handbook of Church Discipline*, 55.

15. Timothy George writes, "Paul [in Gal 6:1] was not here calling for the kind of leniency that overlooks the transgression committed or precludes any kind of penitential act on the part of the transgressor. But he was saying that the work of restoration should be done with sensitivity and consideration and with no hint of self-righteous superiority." George, *Galatians*, 411. To be sure, this approach should pervade each and every step of any disciplinary endeavor. The Greek word for "restore" (*katartizō*) literally means "to put in order," or "to restore to its former position," and this describes the nature and purpose of church discipline. Ibid.

16. Dietrich Bonhoeffer, in his timeless classic entitled *Life Together*, draws out the importance of introspection on the part of the one doing the restoration, so that sober-mindedness will prevail, and a judgmental and self-righteous spirit is more readily

However, if your brother or sister "refuses to listen to you" or acknowledge and repent of his or her sin after the initial one-on-one confrontation, then Jesus' instruction is that one or two additional people should go along, so that "every matter may be established by the testimony of two or three witnesses" (v. 16). This idea, derived from the Old Testament law (Deut 19:15), is a judiciary principle that held that a person could not be convicted of a crime on the testimony of just one person. The idea in this context would have several different purposes.

First, it could be that the witnesses (who need not have witnessed the sin themselves) would serve as those who could bear testimony that the confrontation has occurred appropriately if in fact the matter is later by necessity brought before the whole church.[17] Second, it could send a message to the unrepentant that this is a serious matter not to be taken lightly and that sin unchecked affects more than just the person but a whole community. Third, as John Calvin has noted, it could "give greater weight and impressiveness to the admonition."[18] But primarily, these witnesses serve as those who will help aid in this reconciliation process, and they may bring an additional element of objectivity to the situation.[19] There are no qualifications put on these witnesses (such as the need to be

---

avoided. He writes, "For when does sin ever occur in the community that he [the restorer] must not examine and blame himself for his own unfaithfulness in prayer and intercession, his lack of brotherly service, of fraternal reproof and encouragement, indeed, for his own personal sin and spiritual laxity, by which he has done injury to himself, the fellowship, and the brethren?" Bonhoeffer, *Life Together*, 103.

17. Though Laney believes that these witnesses may indeed be observers of the actual sin, I do not see where this is a necessary conclusion. As Adams has rightly noted, this would make the sin a more public matter, whereby step 1 would not be a "private matter" since there were witnesses. Adams, *Handbook of Church Discipline*, 59–60.

18. John Calvin, "Commentary on a Harmony of the Evangelists, Matthew, Mark, and Luke, vol. 2," in Pringle, *Calvin's Commentaries, Vol. 16*, 355. Calvin continues, "Alluding to that law [Deut 19:15], Christ says that, when two or three witnesses shall rise up to condemn the obstinacy of the man, the case will be clear, at least till the church be prepared to take cognizance of it; for he who refuses to hear two or three witnesses will have no reason to complain that he is dragged forth to light." Ibid.

19. Adams notes that these "witnesses" may actually serve as counselors, mediators, or those who actually participate in the reconciliation process, and he offers a very helpful step-by-step and practical guide to bringing these witnesses into the situation in his text. Adams, *Handbook of Church Discipline*, 60–5. With regard to the character of these witnesses, Murray remarks, "If concern for the person who has sinned is foremost, rather than self-justification, you will opt for wise and trusted persons rather than those you expect to back you up regardless." Murray, *Explaining Church Discipline*, 25.

church officers), but they certainly should be spiritually mature believers, since we are dealing with such sensitive matters.

If reconciliation is achieved, then all those involved should agree to keep the matter private, promising not to bring it up again in any other context. This perhaps may be an additional way to understand the proverbial "overlooking of an offense" (Prov 19:11). Putting the matter to rest is part of the essence of forgiveness and is in keeping with life in God's eschatological kingdom.[20] In addition, the parties involved should be willing to meet more than once if necessary, because one need not rush the process if meaningful progress toward reconciliation is being made.[21] Jesus gives assurance that as they go through this judicial process, his presence to bless is with those who are pursuing righteousness and reconciliation, "for where two or three come together in my name, there I am with them" (Matt 18:20 NIV).[22]

However, if it is apparent that the unrepentant still refuses to reconcile, then Jesus prescribes a third step in this ever-expanding circle of accountability. He continues and says, "If he refuses to listen to them, tell it to the church" (Matt 18:17a). This now becomes a very solemn step, for the information regarding the transgression of the unrepentant is now to become public knowledge. That which was informal has become more formal in character.[23]

20. The church should embrace this "already not yet" principle (cf. Isa 65:17; Jer 31:34; Heb 8:12; 10:17) in practice today in keeping with our ministry of reconciliation (2 Cor 5:18, 19). Jones captures the idea well when he says, "Practicing forgiveness in Christian community—that eschatological community called into being by the Father, identified by the Son, and sustained, judged, and guided by the Spirit—enables us to be sustained for our hope for a new humanity, for the New Heaven and the New Earth to appear in its fullness . . ." Jones, *Embodying Forgiveness*, 165.

21. To be sure, more than one effort toward reconciliation may be necessary at any of the steps that Jesus has outlined. Only if there seems to be an impasse should the next level of accountability be introduced.

22. Unfortunately, verses 19–20 have been widely taken out of context today, whereby many use them as promises applicable to specific prayer meetings rather than seeing them as specific to church discipline proceedings. D. A. Carson does a fine job of summarizing. "These two verses should not in this setting be taken as a promise regarding any prayer on which two or three believers agree (v. 20). Scripture is rich in prayer promises (21:22; John 14:13–14; 15:7–8, 16); but if this passage deals with prayer at all, it is restricted by the context and by the phrase *peri pantos pragmatos* (NIV, 'about anything'), which should here be rendered "about any judicial matter": the word *pragma* often has that sense (cf. 1 Cor 6:1; BAGD, s. v.), a sense nicely fitting the argument of Matthew 18." Carson, *The Expositor's Bible Commentary, Matthew 13–28*, 403.

23. Murray's insight into how this will affect a church is enlightening. "From this

Churches with differing models of church government and traditions may vary on how this step is carried out, yet the principle of widening the web of accountability remains the same. As Adams has noted, *how* to "tell it to the church" is not spelled out in specific detail, so drawing from other biblical principles and Scriptures will be necessary to put this into motion.[24] Since the circle of confrontation is widening in this process, perhaps the best place to start informing the church would be to present the matter to the church leadership (pastors, elders, or deacons). Grudem remarks:

> After a private meeting and a small group meeting, Jesus does not specify that the elders or the officers of the church are next to be consulted as a group, but certainly this intermediate step seems to be appropriate, because Jesus may simply be summarizing the process without necessarily mentioning every possible step in it. In fact there are several examples of small group admonition in the New Testament which are carried out by elders and other church officers (see 1 Thess 5:12; 2 Tim 4:2; Titus 1:13; 2:15; 3:10; James 5:19–20). Moreover, the principle of keeping the knowledge of the sin to the smallest group possible would certainly encourage this intermediate step as well.[25]

Since the elders and leaders of the church are given charge over the flock and its care (Acts 20:28; 1 Pet 5:2), they should be the first to engage the situation at this broader level. This intermediate step may be labeled as step 3A, and all parties that have been involved up to this point should be included in this appeal to the one being confronted. With the inclusion of the leadership of the church to this situation, a deeper level of spiritual maturity and experience is brought to the matter, which may aid in the reconciliation process.

However, if attempts to bring restoration and reconciliation have ultimately failed here, then the leadership is obligated to bring the situation before the whole body of believers. We may label this step 3B. It is at this point that Christ's mandate to tell it to the church is fulfilled in its fullest

---

point the matter becomes public knowledge within the church, and it is now that the maturity of the church, its understanding of the principles of church discipline, and its commitment to the process will be tested." Murray, *Explaining Church Discipline*, 27.

24. Adams, *Handbook of Church Discipline*, 68. Laney remarks that there needs to be some flexibility here as to how it is presented to the church. See Laney, *A Guide to Church Discipline*, 54.

25. Grudem, *Systematic Theology*, 897.

sense.[26] Once the church has been made aware of the situation and the facts by the leadership, they in turn now have the opportunity to reach out to the unrepentant in an attempt to urge him or her to repentance.[27]

26. How this is done should be up to the discretion of the leadership. This may be done via a congregational letter, though Adams argues that if it is done that way, the letter should be destroyed after it has been read so that it would not fall into the hands of non-members. Adams, Handbook of Church Discipline, 69. Some may advocate a specially called congregational meeting consisting of members only, thus avoiding a worship ser-vice setting, which may consist of both believers and nonbelievers. It is most appropriate that this is dealt with by believers in the congregation who have committed themselves to mutual accountability. John White and Ken Blue argue that large churches (where not ev-eryone knows everyone) should avoid a widespread announcement of the charges against an unrepentant sinner for fear that it would become a beacon for gossip. They argue that the church in the first century was primarily made of small house churches where people would have been quite familiar with one another. "In such a setting a disciplinary matter that is resisted is de facto a community matter. Therefore it would seem best to interpret Christ's words 'to the church' to refer to the particular subgroup with which the offender associates most, if such a group exists." White and Blue, Church Discipline That Heals, 128. Yet they do say that if it is a situation that is already being gossiped about, it may actually do well to announce the charges in the widest sense in order to preserve church purity and to present a clear statement of truth, hopefully "taking the spice" out of gos-sip that may be circulating. Though it is true that large mega churches are a more of a modern-day phenomenon, I believe the principle of sharing the charges to the entire body for the purpose of a more comprehensive accountability still remains at the heart of Jesus' teaching, no matter how large that community of believers might be.

27. Some churches may short-circuit this step by simply presenting the facts to the congregation and then calling immediately for the next step, which is excommunication. The logic behind such action is that some view the elders and leadership of the church as representatives of the entire congregation, and thus the view is that one has officially "told it to the church" when the leadership has heard the facts of the case and has made attempts to bring it toward reconciliation. Though it is true that many elder- or deacon-led congregations make many decisions on behalf of the entire church (such as business matters, policies, spiritual direction, etc.), I do not believe that church discipline matters should operate this way. This is also the contention of Stuart Murray, who writes, "It is important that church leaders do not usurp the role of the community. The focus in Matthew 18 is on church discipline, community accountability, rather than on church leaders taking responsibility for exercising discipline." Murray, Explaining Church Discipline, 27. Laney holds to a similar emphasis, saying, "After the church leaders *and congregation* unsuccessfully have *made every effort* to bring the sinner to repentance, they must ostracize the offender from the church fellowship" (emphasis mine). Laney, A Guide to Church Discipline, 56. It would seem, then, that the purpose of "telling it to the church" is that this allows the corporate body time to draw upon the relationships within the church in their attempts to reach out to the fallen brother or sister and call him or her back to repentance. Thus we have allowed time for personal (step 1), small group (step 2), and corporate accountability (step 3) to be utilized before we proceed to the final, somber act of excommunication (step 4). This is the most natural reading of the text in Matthew

With restoration and reconciliation as the goal, the laity can express the genuine love of the Christian community seen through the act of admonishment. This captures the essence of Paul's instruction to the church in Colossians 3.

> Let the word of Christ dwell in you richly as you teach and admonish one another with all wisdom . . . (Col 3:16a NIV).[28]

In this way, the love and mercy of Christ flows through the redeemed people of God as they embrace what it means to be a *forgiven* and *forgiving* community.[29] And even more than this, this is what it means to be a *reconciled* and *reconciling* community.[30] The church serves as representatives

---

18, especially since the beginning clause in verse 17b (as we will soon see), implies that the church has already been told and has had ample time to reach out and call one to repentance before they exercise the authority to "bind and loose" (v.18). Additionally, the church can then have the assurance that all means have been exhausted to restore the sinner before we proceed to the somber event of excommunication. This writer observed a well-known pastor from California bring a church discipline matter before the congregation right before the church celebrated communion together. He read a letter from the elders that stated the name of the offender, what he was alleged to have done, the steps that had been taken to call him to repentance (with the Matt 18 progression), and then stated that it was now the church's responsibility to draw upon their relationships with the offender in attempt to reach out and call their brother back to repentance so excommunication would be unnecessary. I believe that it was an excellent example of what it means to "tell it to the church." Luther condemns anything different than involving the whole church when he criticizes the Catholic church by saying, "I call it a devil's and not God's ban, contrary to Christ's command, when people are cursed with the ban sacrilegiously, before they have been convicted in the presence of the assembled congregation." Luther, "The Keys," in Brgendoff, *Luther's Works*, 371.

28. Notice that at the heart of disciplinary issues and admonishment is the theme of wisdom. Surely church discipline is an exercise in discernment for the local body.

29. Thus Bonhoeffer writes, "When God was merciful to us, we learned to be merciful with our brethren. When we received forgiveness instead of judgment, we, too, were made ready to forgive our brethren. What God did to us, we then owed to others . . . thus God Himself taught us to meet one another as God has met us in Christ." Bonhoeffer, *Life Together*, 25. According to L. Gregory Jones, when the church acts this way, it embarks on the process of learning and unlearning. He writes, "The practice of forgiveness entails unlearning all those things that divide and destroy communion and learning to see and live as forgiven and forgiving people. The goal of this unlearning and learning is the holiness of communion–with God, with others, and with the whole Creation. We are called to do this most specifically, though by no means exclusively, among those who seek to live in truthful communion with God and with one another in Christian community." Jones, *Embodying Forgiveness*, 164.

30. Jim Van Yperen writes, "Forgiveness is not reconciliation; it is barely the first step to being restored. Reconciliation is living together in the light of our confession and

and ambassadors of Christ, who is making his appeal to the unrepentant through this process (2 Cor 5:20). We may say that it is through this disciplinary process that the community of faith embodies the "fatherly" love of God, a point we will return to later.

This is a very challenging step, to be sure, as Murray explains:

> This is a tremendously demanding process, for the church as well as for the person concerned. There is plenty of scope for division, gossip, wrong attitudes, and confusion. It is not surprising that church leaders sometimes prefer to restrict this stage to themselves. *But the impact of the whole church expressing its concern for the person in this way can be tremendous. Nothing should be done that would dilute this* (emphasis mine).[31]

Yet if the appeal of the church to the unrepentant goes unheeded, then the church has no choice but to proceed to step 4. For Jesus says, "And if he refuses to listen even to the church, treat him as you would a pagan or a tax collector" (Matt 18:17b NIV). At this point the unrepentant has "refused to listen,"[32] and it is assumed that all measures to win the brother or sister back have been exhausted. The unrepentant has in fact hardened his or her heart to the loving reach of the Christian community. Jesus' prescription for dealing with such a person is that he or she should be treated as a "pagan or a tax collector." To the Hebrew mind, the pagans and tax collectors would be "widely considered . . . outside the circle of God's immediate blessing."[33] They would not be considered as a part of the covenant community, but rather are "cut off."[34] In Paul's command

---

forgiveness. Reconciliation is a commitment to transformation . . . for reconciliation to fully restore the sinner to fellowship, it must change our character as well as forgive our sin." Van Yperen, *Making Peace*, 245.

31. Murray, *Explaining Church Discipline*, 28. He further adds, "This stage not only gives the brother or sister another chance to repent, it also acts as a deterrent to others and as a spur to discipleship." Ibid.

32. The Greek is παρακούσῃ, a strong term meaning "to refuse to listen to" or "disobey." See Danker, BDAG, 767. This is obviously a stronger term than simply the μὴ ἀκούσῃ, "he will not listen," that we see in v. 16. So also Murray, *Explaining Church Discipline*, 29.

33. Mounce, *Matthew*, 176. The pagans were not considered as the partakers of the covenant, and tax collectors were despised due to their affiliation with corruption and the oppressive Roman government. Since Matthew, the gospel writer, was once a tax collector, he would know fully the forcefulness of Jesus' words. For more on the significance of being a pagan or a tax collector, see Laney, *A Guide to Church Discipline*, 56.

34. Blomberg notes the Old Testament precedent for such treatment in Genesis 17:14;

to expel the offending brother in 1 Corinthians 5, he parallels the man's removal with the idea of *putting someone out of the scope of the community where God's blessing resides*, a "handing of the man over to Satan" (1 Cor 5:5), which we will look at in more detail later in this chapter.

This disfellowshiping or excommunication from the community means that the unrepentant would no longer be allowed to have membership in or normal fellowship with the community of faith. He or she would also be unable to participate in such important church practices such as the Lord's Supper.[35] He or she would essentially be regarded as an unbeliever, in need of repentance and faith. Members of the church should be instructed to refrain from intimate contact with the unrepentant, and any contact that is made ought to be for the strict purpose of restoration. As Blomberg rightly notes, the purpose of this "drastic action remains rehabilitative rather than retributive in design."[36]

In the epistles there several warnings to the church about fellowshipping with a believer who refuses to repent and receive forgiveness for his or her sins. Below are examples of such stern warnings, many from Paul.

> I have written you in my letter not to associate with sexually immoral people—not at all meaning the people of this world who are immoral, or the greedy and swindlers, or idolaters. In that case you would have to leave this world. But now I am writing you that you must not associate *with anyone who calls himself a brother* but is sexually immoral or greedy, an idolater or a slanderer, a drunk-

Exodus 12:15, 19; and 30:33, 38. Blomberg, *Matthew*, 279.

35. Grudem notes, "The person would not be allowed to take Communion, since partaking in the Lord's Supper is a sign of partaking in the unity of the church (1 Cor 10:17: 'Because there is one bread, we who are many are one body, *for we all partake of the one bread*')." Grudem, *Systematic Theology*, 898.

36. Blomberg, *Matthew*, 279. Laney concurs, saying, "Even this most severe step in church discipline should be motivated out of love and fulfilled in a way that encourages repentance and restoration. Excommunication should communicate the message, 'We find your present conduct unacceptable to God and this congregation. Our love for you therefore demands that we take action, which, though painful, we hope by God's grace will result in your repentance and restoration to us.'" Laney, *A Guide to Church Discipline*, 56–7. In the same way Marshall writes, "The goal of every type of church discipline, whether it is admonition, public rebuke, or social ostracism, is not merely the maintenance of group boundaries, though this is essential for the survival and flourishing of any community committed to a distinctive way of life; the ultimate goal is always repentance and restoration of the offender to fellowship." Marshall, *Beyond Retribution*, 161. Adams provides some helpful examples of what a refusal to have normal fellowship with someone under discipline might look like. See Adams, *Handbook of Church Discipline*, 73–4.

ard or a swindler. With such a man do not even eat (1 Cor 5:9–11 NIV, emphasis mine).[37]

In the name of the Lord Jesus Christ, we command you, brothers, to keep away from every brother who is idle and does not live according to the teaching you received from us . . . if anyone does not obey our instruction in this letter, take special note of him. Do not associate with him, in order that he may feel ashamed. Yet do not regard him as an enemy, but warn him as a brother (2 Thess 3:6, 14–15).[38]

But avoid foolish controversies and genealogies and arguments and quarrels about the law, because these are unprofitable and useless. Warn a divisive person once, and then warn him a second time. After that, have nothing to do with him. You may be sure that such a man is warped and sinful; he is self-condemned (Titus 3:9:11 NIV).[39]

Anyone who runs ahead and does not continue in the teaching of Christ does not have God; whoever continues in the teaching has both the Father and the Son. If anyone comes to you and does not bring this teaching, do not take him into your house or welcome him. Anyone who welcomes him shares in his wicked work (2 John 9–11 NIV).[40]

37. The removal of table fellowship was a serious matter in Hebrew culture.

38. With the goal being restoration, the offender must not be regarded as "an enemy." Richard B. Hays remarks, "To say that the expelled sinner must be 'as a gentile or tax collector' cannot mean that the person becomes a pariah to be shunned by the church; it means, rather, that the person becomes an object of the community's missionary efforts." Hays, *The Moral Vision of the New Testament*, 102. Similarly, Marshall writes, "The offender once again becomes a candidate for the gospel, a recipient of the call to discipleship, a lost sheep awaiting restoration (cf. 18:10–14)." Marshall, *Beyond Retribution*, 159.

39. It is possible that this divisiveness may be due to the teaching of false doctrines. See Kitchens, "Perimeters of Corrective Church Discipline," 208–10. Unrepentance on the part of a believer would in fact cause one to question whether the person was truly saved to begin with. Thus even excommunication may be a tool that would assist in discerning the true church. Adams writes, "What this means is that those who leave the church, renouncing Christ, make it evident that though at one time they were part of the visible body, they were never saved; they never belonged to the invisible church." Adams, *Handbook of Church Discipline*, 78.

40. Here John teaches that fellowship is to be withheld from someone who does not teach sound doctrine, or who is a false teacher. Coupled with Titus 3:9–11, it would seem, then, that another purpose of church discipline is to not only purify the church morally, but theologically as well.

It is worth repeating that the attitude that members of the church take when disfellowshiping or excommunicating an individual is essential to its effectiveness and its ability to communicate Christ-like love. It is a loving, gentle, yet firm exclusion from fellowship couched in humility.[41] The church is making a "judgment" on sin in the church, taking a stand for righteous living and purity, but they are not inappropriately or hypocritically judging someone in a manner that even Jesus himself opposed earlier in Matthew (see Matt 7:1–5).[42] In that context, those who were judging were doing the very same things they were judging others for. Further, their attitude was anything but humble but was rather arrogant and rude. But here, in church discipline, the church has gone through a four-step process before they actually make a judgment on a person's sins. The process is a solemn one and is not done in a hypocritical fashion but is rather done according to biblical principles in keeping with the living

41. Interestingly, Adams distinguishes between "excommunication'"" and "removal from the midst," claiming that excommunication actually begins after the offense has been "told to the church," (our step 3B) but before expulsion. However, as Laney has pointed out, the term "excommunicate" comes "from the Latin ex ('out') and communico ('share, communicate'). It refers to the cutting off of a person from church membership, fellowship, or communion." Laney, A Guide to Church Discipline, 56. It would seem that this "cutting off" of a brother or sister is not to be carried out until every effort to reconcile has been made and his or her "refusal to listen" to the church has been established. How could one "cut off" someone while there is an ongoing attempt of the entire Christian community to bring him or her back to reconciliation? It would seem to be a natural reading of the text in Matthew 18:17 that "excommunication" from the church (or as the text says, treatment like "a pagan or tax collector") does not take place in any way until the church has exhausted its efforts. It is then that Christ says that they should be treated like a "pagan or tax collector," the idea of exclusion from the covenant community. Marshall looks at excommunication not only as the church's formal action in discipline, but also as the "symbolic enactment" of the self-punishment inherent to the sin itself. "For this reason, excommunication can be seen as a kind of self-judgment, or more accurately as an external, symbolic enactment by the church of what the offender has already done at a moral and spiritual level—separate himself or herself from the sanctity of the community." He further adds, "It might also function as a forewarning of future divine punishment on those that have done so (cf. 1 Cor 11:31). But the immediate goal of the procedure . . . is redemptive." Marshall, Beyond Retribution, 158.

42. Yet even in taking a stand for righteous living and purity in the church, we cannot forget that we are equally *concerned about the sinner*. To forget this would be to misunderstand the primary motive behind discipline. As John Howard Yoder writes, "Concern may move from the offender to the 'standards' . . . the brother is then less important to the church than its identity and reputation and standards or even than the power of its leaders that is threatened by the offender's not conforming." Yoder, "Binding and Loosing," in *The Royal Priesthood*, 343.

out of the truth. Mark Dever argues persuasively for the church's biblical mandate to make judgments concerning sin.

> Remember that God Himself is a Judge, and, in a lesser sense, God intends others to judge as well. He has given the state the responsibility to judge (Rom 13:1–7). In various places we are told to judge ourselves (1 Cor 11:28; 2 Cor 13:5; Heb 4; 2 Pet 1:5–10). We are specifically told to judge one another within the church (though not in the final way that God judges); Jesus' words in Matthew 18, Paul's in 1 Corinthians 5–6, and other passages clearly show that the church is to exercise judgment within itself. If you think about it, it is not really surprising that a church should be instructed to judge. *After all, if we cannot say how a Christian should not live, how can we say how a Christian should live* (emphasis mine)?[43]

As Dever has noted, Paul himself rebuked the church in Corinth for their refusal to make a judgment on sin in the church, saying:

> What business is it of mine to judge those outside the church? Are you not to judge those inside? God will judge those outside. "Expel the wicked man from among you" (1 Cor 5:12–13 NIV).

Paul assumes their spiritual maturity and biblical authority to handle situations, calling on them to make a proper judgment. Noting their authority and obligation to make judgments on sin, Paul reminded the church that this is just the first of an even greater responsibility that the church will have in God's eschatological kingdom.

> Do you not know that the saints will judge the world? And if you are to judge the world, are you not competent to judge trivial cases? Do you not know that we will judge angels? How much more the things of this life (1 Cor 6:2–3 NIV)![44]

This authority given to the church to carry out the process of church discipline is given by Christ himself as he unfolds and teaches the disciples this four-step process found in Matthew 18. Furthermore, Jesus solidifies the church's responsibility and authority to enact church discipline when he states in verse 18:

---

43. Dever, "Biblical Church Discipline," 29.

44. Paul is rebuking the church for their willingness to take disputes between believers before secular authorities rather than handling these situations themselves as those competent to make a sound and wise judgment.

I tell you the truth, whatever you bind on earth will be bound in
heaven, and whatever you loose on earth will be loosed in heaven
(Matt 18:18 NIV).[45]

Jesus describes the church's authority to discipline as the power to
"bind and loose," and this peculiar idea is worthy of our investigation.

THE AUTHORITY TO BIND AND LOOSE

Just what did Jesus mean when he gave the church the power "to bind and
loose"? Earlier in Matthew 16, Jesus made a similar statement to Peter and
the disciples. Peter had just finished confessing that Jesus was the Christ,
something that had been revealed to him from the Father. And it was to
be on that confession of faith in the gospel that Jesus was going to build
his church.

And I tell you that you are Peter, and on this rock I will build my
church, and the gates of Hades will not overcome it. I will give you
the keys of the kingdom of heaven; whatever you bind on earth
will be bound in heaven, and whatever you loose on earth will be
loosed in heaven (Matt 16:18–19 NIV).[46]

45. John Howard Yoder, in this noteworthy quote on Jesus' prerogative to grant the
church authority to "bind and loose" in Matthew 18, remarks, "It gives more authority to
the church than does Rome, trusts more to the Holy Spirit than does Pentecostalism, has
more respect for the individual than humanism, makes moral standards more binding
than Puritanism, is more open to the given situation than the 'new morality.' If practiced
it would change the life of churches more fundamentally than has yet been suggested by
the perennially popular discussions of changing church structures." Yoder, "Binding and
Loosing," 325.

46. The Greek syntax in this verse is quite unique and even complicated. With both
the binding and the loosing, we have future periphrastic perfect participles, which may
be translated as "shall/will have been bound" and "shall/will have been loosed" (NASB).
The idea here is that when Peter proclaims the gospel and the binding and loosing
of the kingdom takes place, it is assured that these actions are in sync with what has
been already declared or pronounced concerning the gospel from heaven. Thus Carson
remarks, "Whatever he binds or looses will have been bound or loosed, so long as he
adheres to that divinely disclosed gospel. He has no direct pipeline to heaven, still less
do his decisions force heaven to comply; but he may be authoritative in binding and
loosing because heaven has acted first (cf. Acts 18:9–10). Those he ushers in or excludes
have already been bound or loosed by God according to the gospel already revealed
and which Peter, by confessing Jesus as the Messiah, has most clearly grasped." Carson,
Matthew 13–28, 373.

Thus Peter was to be one of the primary persons whom God will use to bring the gospel to the earth. When people hear the gospel proclamation (from Peter and subsequently the rest of the disciples), their hearts will either be open and accept it, thus entering the kingdom, or their hearts may be hardened to it, thus closing the doors of the kingdom to their soul. So Peter was given the "keys" to the kingdom of heaven (v. 19) insofar as he is one who proclaims the gospel, which has both drawing and repulsing power, the ability to gain or withhold access into the kingdom.[47] It would seem, then, that Jesus' statement about binding and loosing would have everything to do with holding the key that opens the door to the kingdom of heaven, where forgiveness is received upon repentance and faith.[48] And this has application not just for Peter and the original disciples but to the entire believing community, who is charged to proclaim the gospel (which is the consistent testimony of the New Testament). So Blomberg remarks:

> One should pursue the imagery of keys that close and open, lock and unlock (based on Isa 22:22) and take the binding and loosing as referring to Christians' making entrance to God's kingdom available or unavailable to people through their witness, preaching, and ministry.[49]

Now as we return back to our passage in Matthew 18, we see that Jesus uses *the same statement about binding and loosing* in verse 18 to

---

47. Carson writes, "By this means the Lord added to the church those who were being saved ([Acts] 2:45), or, otherwise put, Jesus was building his church (Matt 16:18). But the same gospel proclamation alienates and excludes men; so we also find Peter shutting up the kingdom from men" (Acts 4:11–12; 8:20–23). Ibid. Indeed, it was Peter who preached the first evangelistic sermon after Pentecost, fulfilling his role as the one who initially was given the keys to the kingdom. The Apostle Paul expounded on the gospel's two-fold power in 2 Corinthians 2, where he says, "But thanks be to God, who always leads us in triumphal procession in Christ and through us spreads everywhere the fragrance of the knowledge of him. For we are to God the aroma of Christ among those who are being saved and those who are perishing. To the one we are the smell of death; to the other, the fragrance of life" (2 Cor 2:14–16 NIV).

48. We must be careful, however, to note that holding the keys to the kingdom, where forgiveness and reconciliation are found, does not mean that Peter or even the church has the authority for proclaiming the forgiveness of sins in the absolute sense, as Roman Catholic doctrine asserts. As Grudem notes, "It is clear that that can only be done by God himself (Isa 43:25; 55:7; Mark 2:7, 10; Ps 103:3; 1 John 1:9)." Grudem, *Systematic Theology*, 891.

49. Blomberg, *Matthew*, 254.

authenticate the authority he is giving the disciples (and subsequently to "the church," as in 18:17) in matters of church discipline. This may help us understand why the term "keys" in Matthew 16:19 is plural. As Grudem has rightly noted:

> The plural "keys" suggests authority over more than one door. Thus, more than simply entrance into the kingdom is implied; some authority *within* the kingdom is also suggested.[50]

The same future periphrastic perfect participles are used in 18:18 ("shall have been bound" or "shall have been loosed") as they were in 16:19.[51] And the context of 18:18 tells us that the plural neuter ὅσα, translated as "whatever" (in "whatever you loose") is clearly talking about persons.[52] So when this authority to bind and loose is further applied to matters of church discipline, it communicates the idea that *when the church acts in concert with the truth on any judicial matter, they can rest assured that their actions are in sync with what has been already declared or pronounced on the matter from heaven.*[53] The church's disciplinary action, based on truth, "shall have been bound" or "shall have been loosed" in heaven. Wayne Grudem describes it the following way in this extended quote:

> Jesus is teaching that church discipline will have heavenly sanction. But it is not as if the church must wait for God to endorse its ac-

---

50. Grudem, *Systematic Theology*, 890.

51. Carson remarks, "If the church, Messiah's eschatological people already gathered now, has to exercise the ministry of the keys, if it must bind and loose, then clearly one aspect of that will be the discipline of those who profess to constitute it. Thus the two passages are tightly joined: 18:18 is a special application of 16:19." Carson, *Matthew 13–28*, 374. A helpful discussion of the complicated Greek syntax (future perfect participles) and how it applies to Matthew 18:18 (our disciplinary text) can be found in Daniel Parmelee, "An Exegetical Study of Ecclesiastical Discipline: Comparing Paul's Application with Christ's Principles," 15–24. For more on the issues surrounding Matthew 18:18, see Duling, "Binding and Loosing," 3–31.

52. Though Grudem argues that it encompasses more than just persons, but more generally to "*situations* and *relationships* that come up within the church." Grudem, *Systematic Theology*, 890. However, it is not clear how certain situations and relationships would not by default include *persons*.

53. John White and Ken Blue do an excellent job of defining what this means in disciplinary terms. They write, "*To bind* means to withhold fellowship, to recognize formally the state of alienation which has come about. *To loose* means to forgive, to open one's arms wide to someone who is being reconciled. *To bind* can also mean to forbid, to declare that certain actions are prohibited. *To loose* thus also means to permit, to declare that other actions are acceptable." White and Blue, *Healing the Wounded*, 98.

tions after the actions have occurred. Rather, whenever the church *enacts discipline* [bind] it can be confident that God has already begun the process spiritually. Whenever it *releases from discipline* [loose], forgives the sinner, and restores personal relationships, the church can be confident that God has already begun the restoration spiritually (cf. John 20:23). In this way Jesus promises that the spiritual relationship between God and the person subject to discipline will be immediately affected in ways consistent with the direction of the church's disciplinary action. Legitimate church discipline, therefore, involves the awesome certainty that corresponding heavenly discipline has already begun.[54]

In light of this profound connection between the church's actions in discipline and the heavenly sanction of God, one can fully conclude that the church has the necessary authority (and mandate) to carry out biblical church discipline. In fact, as Yoder eloquently states, "The authority given the church is parallel to the authority of Christ himself (John 20:19–23)."[55] This authority is further authenticated in the epistles, as we mentioned earlier, where Paul expects and commands the church to act in matters of church discipline. Perhaps the clearest Pauline application of Christ's disciplinary mandate is found in his letters to the Corinthians, where we see a gross public sin addressed as well as the goal of church discipline realized, that being forgiveness and restoration.

54. Grudem, *Systematic Theology*, 891. So Martin Luther, in describing this from God's perspective, remarks, "But he speaks in this fashion, if you bind and loose on earth, I will also bind and loose right along with you in heaven. When you use the keys, I will also . . . it shall be one single action, mine and yours, not a twofold one. It shall be one and the same key, mine and yours, not a twofold one. While you do your work, mine is already done. When you bind and loose, I have already bound and loosed. He binds and joins himself to our work." Luther, "The Keys," 365.

55. Yoder, "Binding and Loosing," 330. See also Luther, who writes, "Here we have the true significance of the keys. They are an office, a power or command given by God through Christ to all Christendom for the retaining and remitting of the sins of men." Luther, "The Keys," 366. He further declares, "And when such a judgment is pronounced, it is a judgment of Christ himself." Ibid., 372. Jonathan Edwards, the great pastor and theologian, agrees, saying, "When it is regularly and duly inflicted, it is to be looked upon as done by *Christ* himself. That is imported in the definition, that it is *according to his will*, and to the directions of his word. And therefore, he is to be looked upon as *principal* in it, and we ought to esteem it as really and truly from him, as if he were on earth personally inflicting it." Jonathan Edwards, "The Nature and End of Excommunication," in *The Works of Jonathan Edwards*, 120. We must emphasize that the authority pertains to biblical church discipline based on truth and is not a blank check for the church to have heavenly sanction in all its decisions.

We will be turning to that episode briefly, but before we leave Matthew 18, we must understand that Jesus' mandate to discipline and the brother/sister language that is a part of our passage reminds us that this is how life is to be conducted *within the family of God.* As Dietrich Bonhoeffer would say, this is a necessary component of "life together." Up to and until excommunication, church discipline assumes that we are dealing with a fellow member of God's family. Using the power of the keys is not simply a cold, mechanical, institutional exercise of power, as someone like Foucault may argue. To the contrary, the power to bind and loose is given to a covenant community, a family of believers, the children of God, a people who live in communion and fellowship with each other and their merciful God as those who have been redeemed by his grace. Those periphrastic future perfect participles in Matthew 16 and 18 link our disciplinary actions with the loving hand of a Heavenly Father who longs to "lavish" his reconciling love on his children (1 John 3:1).[56] And our actions in discipline are to be the actions of caring brothers and sisters who together are operating under the authority of the One we mutually call our Heavenly Father, whose sanction has been given. As Jesus has stated:

> Again, I tell you that if two of you on earth agree about anything you ask for, it will be done for you *by my Father in heaven.* For where two or three come together in my name, there am I with them (Matt 18:19–20 NIV, emphasis mine).[57]

Therefore, as Marianne Meye Thompson has rightly stated:

> It is precisely the fact that the community knows and calls upon God as "our Father in heaven" that obligates them in turn to treat each other with familial love and care. In this light, the traditional understanding of Matthew 18 as a chapter on "church discipline" would be better viewed as a chapter that seeks to show how brothers and sisters in a family are to treat each other and to make sure that their life together functions as the heavenly Father desires.

56. This strange grammatical construction in the Greek (Matt 18:18) provides dynamic support for our thesis that *the Church, as an embodiment of Christ empowered by the Holy Spirit, is authorized and obliged to exercise discipline as an expression of God's "fatherly" love toward the company of his redeemed children.* Thus when we act, God simultaneously acts, or perhaps saying it more appropriately, God is acting through the disciplinary practices of the church.

57. Hays asks, "How can so much spiritual power [authority] be entrusted to the *ekklēsia*? The answer lies in the remarkable promise of Jesus' continuing presence in and with the gathered praying community." Hays, *Moral Vision*, 120.

Again, the Father's own actions provide warrant for the life of the community. No one is to despise "the little ones," because "it is not the will of your Father in heaven that one of these little ones should be lost" (Matt 18:14; cf. 18:11).[58]

Within the family, the "lost sheep" who has wandered off should be recovered. The "prodigal son" needs to be forgiven and welcomed home. And God as our Father is seeking to reclaim, restore, and reconcile one of his children through the means of the church's disciplinary actions, for this is one of the ways the Father prunes his children so that they will bear much fruit (John 15:2).[59]

PUBLIC SIN AND RESTORATION IN CORINTH

The Apostle Paul's love and concern for the church is readily attestable throughout his letters to the churches. Forasmuch as he was confident in the church's ability to stand as the "pillar and foundation of truth" (1 Tim 3:15), he also prayed "night and day" (1 Thess 3:10) for the spiritual health, vitality, and ministry of God's chosen bride. So when Paul learned of a public and grossly sinful situation that was happening in the church in Corinth, a church that he himself helped to establish as recorded in Acts 18, he was despondent.

It is actually reported that there is sexual immorality among you, and of a kind that does not occur even among pagans: A man has his father's wife. And you are proud! Shouldn't you rather have been filled with grief and have put out of your fellowship the man who did this (1 Cor 5:1–2 NIV)?[60]

It would seem that even in spite of the church's giftedness (1:4–7), it was still spiritually immature, divided, weak, and ensnared by sin. The church's toleration for and even approval of sexual immorality in its midst

58. Thompson, *The Promise of the Father*, 110.

59. So Knuteson, *Calling the Church to Discipline*, 59–62.

60. The sin apparently was that a man had been sexually active with his stepmother. This sort of incest was not even common in the larger Roman society, and so it would have truly shamed the church "even among the pagans." It was certainly condemned among God's people (cf. Deut 27:20; Lev 18:8; 20:11). The stepmother apparently was not a member of the church, or else Paul would have called for action against her as well. Maria Pascuzzi argues, "The judgment of the Corinthians was impaired by a Stoically influenced concept of freedom skewed by individualism" in the Corinthian culture. Pascuzzi, *Ethics, Ecclesiology, and Church Discipline*, 185.

was despicable. It made a mockery of the gospel of God's grace, publicly shamed the name of Christ, and brought reproach to the church. Rather than bring the church grief, it became their source of boasting and pride, an abuse of their freedom in Christ.[61]

The principle of keeping the circle of confrontation to the smallest possible number of people (according to the rule of Christ in Matthew 18) had been broken due to the gross *public nature* of the sin. This should have advanced the process of church discipline to its latter stages, where the corporate church should have been confronting and perhaps should have gone as far as excommunicating the unrepentant and unashamed sinner. But the church had somehow rationalized the sin and failed to see the need for discipline, and so Paul decided to act, drawing upon his apostolic authority to activate spiritual discipline on the erring brother.

> Even though I am not physically present, I am with you in spirit. And I have already passed judgment on the one who did this, just as if I were present. When you are assembled in the name of our Lord Jesus and I am with you in spirit, and the power of our Lord Jesus is present, hand this man over to Satan, so that the sinful nature may be destroyed and his spirit saved on the day of the Lord (1 Cor 5:3–5 NIV).

Paul "passed judgment" on the unrepentant brother. Yet, in keeping with the rule of Christ in Matthew 18, this would not be sufficient. For the discipline to be enacted properly and fully in accordance with Jesus' teaching, the formal assembly of the church, along with its communal power and

---

61. Even though Paul was indeed concerned about the soul of the offending brother (1 Cor 5:5), he seems to be more enraged at the church as a whole for their arrogant and tolerant disposition toward the sin. For this sinful "yeast" may bring destruction to "the whole batch of dough" (v. 6). As Richard B. Hays writes, "Paul insists that the community has moral responsibility for the conduct of its members and that the conduct of the individual members (even private conduct between 'consenting adults') affects the life of the whole community." Hays, First Corinthians, 82. There are many parallels between the spiritually weak church of today and the situation in Corinth. It is likely that the church in Corinth did not confront the sin because they may have wrongly seen value and Christian love in "tolerance." Though tolerance is indeed a virtuous disposition in the church, it cannot be given at the cost of moral or biblical compromise. Notice that it was the "tolerance" of certain cultural sins that brought the church in Thyatira a rebuke from Jesus (Rev 2:20–25). Further, the Corinthians may also have dismissed the sin due to their misunderstanding of Christian liberty or freedom in Christ. Paul, in another epistle, would warn or correct the church in Galatia for this attitude, saying, "You, my brothers, were called to be free. But do not use your freedom to indulge the sinful nature" (Gal 5:13 NIV).

authority to bind and loose, must be formally instigated. This, as we noted earlier, is where heaven's sanction and the "power of Christ" cooperates with the assembled, gathered church who excommunicates the unrepentant, pronouncing divine discipline and judgment on sin (Matt 18:17).

It is interesting to note that Paul describes excommunication or expulsion from the church as a "handing over to Satan" (v. 5). Paul used similar language in 1 Timothy, where he told the young pastor that he delivered Hymenaeus and Alexander over to Satan, so that they would "be taught not to blaspheme" (1:20). Paul does not have an attitude of vengeance in either case. Rather, in both contexts the purpose of the "handing over" is remedial, correctional, or restorative, so that they may be "saved" in the end. It would seem that to "hand someone over to Satan" is to place him or her outside of the covenant community, outside of the sphere of God's protection and blessing, so that the trials and tribulation that may come from such an excommunication may "destroy the self-sufficient, carnal attitude of the unrepentant offender."[62] This is likely what Paul means when he infers that being placed into Satan's domain as that which will literally bring about a "destruction of the flesh."[63] Physical

---

62. Laney, A Guide to Church Discipline, 69. Hays remarks, "The best explanation of the 'handing over to Satan' is suggested by the Passover metaphor (vv. 6–8). By excluding the incestuous man from the community, the church places him outside the sphere of God's redemptive protection. He is no longer inside the house (cf. 3:9, 'God's building') whose doorposts are covered by the blood of Jesus. He is therefore hung out to dry in the realm of Satan ('the god of this world,' 2 Cor 4:4), exposed to the destructive powers of the world" (cf. the reference to "the destroyer" in Exod 12:23). Hays, First Corinthians, 85.

63. There are translation differences and interpretive difficulties to verse 5. The Greek literally says, "Hand him over to Satan for the destruction of the flesh, in order that the spirit might be saved on the Day of the Lord." See Fee, 1 Corinthians, 210. The challenge is to understand what Paul means by "the destruction of the flesh," a phrase that the NIV has interpreted (instead of translated) as "so that the *sinful nature* may be destroyed" (emphasis mine). There are *at least* two ways to understand the word *sarx* (translated "flesh") in the epistles. It could mean the flesh of the physical body (as in 1 Cor 15:39), or it could mean the carnal, sinfulness of humanity that Paul often calls the flesh (see esp. 1 Cor 3:1–3). A helpful summary of the issues and interpretive challenges surrounding Paul's use of *sarx* may be found in Ladd, A Theology of the New Testament, 509–20. We may indeed have a play on words here, whereby the consequences of handing someone over to Satan may allow for the physical suffering of the flesh where God's protection has been removed (as in the case of Job, though his suffering was not on account of sin but as a test). Yet it may also be this kind of physical suffering that may have a purifying effect from evil, "fleshly" desires, echoing the truth that Peter stated when he said, "He who has suffered in his body is done with sin. As a result, he does not live the rest of his earthly life for evil human desires, but rather for the will of God" (1 Pet 4:1, 2 NIV; see also Gal 5:24).

death is not the goal here (though physical suffering that could lead to death may possibly be involved), but rather the purpose or goal seems to be the removal of the man's carnality so that he may experience salvation from sin.[64] Even if the man's removal did lead to physical suffering, the brother should rightly see such suffering as a form of God's fatherly discipline, since the goal of such discipline is so that he may share in God's holiness (Heb 12:10). Interestingly, for this situation in Corinth, excommunication may not only be a destructive force with regard to *the man's* carnality, but it may also be that which destroys *the community's* pride over this sin. As Anthony Thiselton writes:

> What is to be destroyed is arguably not primarily the physical body of the offender (although this may or may not be secondarily entailed) but the 'fleshly' *stance of self-sufficiency* of which Paul accuses *primarily the community* but surely *also the man* . . . if consigning to Satan means excluding him from the community, this spells the end of self-congratulation about their association with such a distinguished patron; while for the offender himself sudden removal from a platform of adulation to total isolation from the community would have a sobering if not devastating effect.[65]

This is more likely the idea, since the discipline seems to have a restorative and salvific purpose. Fee's comments are insightful concerning the destructive power of Satan. He writes, "In contrast to the gathered community of believers who experience the Spirit and power of the Lord Jesus in edifying gifts and loving concern for one another, this man is to be put back out into the world, where Satan and his 'principalities and powers' still hold sway over people's lives to destroy them." Fee, *1 Corinthians*, 209. Christopher Marshall places emphasis on the *consequences of the sin* after God's protection has been lifted, saying, "This 'turning over' is a matter of withdrawal of God's protective hand (here the fellowship of believers) so that unrepentant malefactors experience the full consequences of the choice they have already made to 'abandon themselves' to sin (cf. *heautous paredokan*, Eph 4:19)." Marshall, *Beyond Retribution*, 155.

64. Fee reminds us of salvation's "already not yet" reality when he remarks, "Paul does not intend that he must wait until the final Day to be saved. Rather this is one of Paul's ordinary ways of expressing salvation. Salvation is primarily an eschatological reality, experienced in the present to be sure, but to be fully realized at the Day of the Lord." Fee, *1 Corinthians*, 213. For an excellent argument in favor of exclusion of the man from the community rather than complete destruction and death, see South, "A Critique of the 'Curse/Death' Interpretation of 1 Corinthians 5:1–8," 539–61.

65. Thiselton, *The First Epistle to the Corinthians*, 396. Therefore, as Thiselton writes, "The salvific purposes embrace both the community and the man." Ibid., 397.

We are not told how this "destruction of the flesh" will take place.[66] Could it be financial trials, sickness, or the removal of certain material and spiritual blessings? Could it be the pain of losing the fellowship of cherished relationships? We simply do not know. But there are several things that are clear. To be "handed over" to Satan entails that one is "put out of fellowship" (5:2), consigned to disassociation (5:9), under discipline or judgment (5:12), and expelled from the community of faith (5:13). The goal of such action, as we stated earlier from the text, is for the man to experience the reality of salvation from sin (both now and in the future), and not to experience death.[67] If there is any notion of death here it is most likely a wish for the man to "die to his sin" (cf. Rom 6:2).

So here in 1 Corinthians 5 we see a profound example of how the church should respond in instances of gross public sin. The latter principles of step 3 and step 4 in Matthew 18 are in play.[68] Due to the pub-

66. One may also ask why Satan would work against his own purposes by afflicting a man whom he has already ensnared. Fee remarks, "Perhaps we have been too quick to assume that Paul looked on Satan and his hosts as directly involved in the 'destruction.' More likely, whatever kind of buffeting from satanic forces he may experience 'out there,' the actual separation from the fellowship of the people of God, God's 'Spirit people,' who are living out the life of the future while they await the consummation, would in itself lead to his putting aside his sins so that he might once more join the community. The text itself does not say this, but the rest of Pauline theology certainly supports such a view" (emphasis mine). Ibid.

67. Someone may recall here the fact that Ananias and Sapphira were put to death by God due to their disobedience and deceit in Acts 5:1–10 during a critical time in the life of the early church. It is true that direct and sudden divine chastening for sin or the natural consequences of it (e.g., a sexually transmitted disease) may cause physical death (but not spiritual death or final judgment for the true believer, as even our text here would support), for we see in 1 Corinthians 11 (a passage we will look at soon) and in 1 John 5:16 that certain sins may weaken one and lead to physical death. However, there are no biblical examples of church discipline (where the church itself is acting) in keeping with the rule of Christ in Matthew 18 whereby the goal was anything but remedial, reconciliatory, or restorative. As Fee rightly notes, the fact that the church was not to associate with the incestuous man "implies that no immediate death is in purview." Fee, 1 Corinthians, 212. See his convincing arguments as to why the goal here is not total destruction and death but restoration in ibid., 210–3. Witherington writes, "[Paul] hopes that this shock therapy, expulsion of this man, might douse his sinful inclinations and shame him, which in the Greco-Roman culture was often thought of as a fate worse than death. There were no other ekklēsiae in Corinth, so this action would be effective if the man wanted to remain a Christian." Witherington, Conflict and Community in Corinth, 158–9.

68. Brian Rosner has pointed out the similarities between Matthew 18:15–20 and 1 Corinthians 5, saying, "In both passages, the whole church is involved in the process of excommunication (1 Cor 5:4; Matt 18:17). Secondly, in both cases, the Lord Jesus is

lic nature of the sin, the principle of keeping it to the smallest possible number of people would serve little purpose, and neither would private confession have an impact on what is known publicly.[69] For a *public* sin to be *publicly* forgiven, it will require a *public* confession and a *public* restoration (more on this later). Paul's concern was just as much or even more so for the corporate church as it was for the offending brother.

> Don't you know that a little yeast works through the whole batch of dough? Get rid of the old yeast that you may be a new batch without yeast—as you really are (1 Cor 5:6–7 NIV).[70]

The moral purity and public witness of the church as a redeemed community was at stake, and the offending brother was trapped in an immoral lifestyle and needed to be disciplined, restored, and reconciled.[71]

---

the real agent in the judgment . . . [and] in the third place, both 1 Corinthians 5 and Matthew 18:15–20 share a concern for the welfare of the sinner." Rosner, *Paul, Scripture, and Ethics*, 89.

69. Ken and Joy Gage argue, "The Corinthian believers were never told to follow the procedure outlined in Matthew [at least the earlier steps]. The man to be censured was not to be given an opportunity for private repentance for a public act of immorality . . . we believe we may safely assume that only one action should stop *the disciplinary process outlined in 1 Corinthians 5*—a public acknowledgement of repentance by the one to be censured. Once that is made, certainly the exclusion process would be interrupted. It should *not* be interrupted on the basis of a private confession as outlined in Matthew 18." Gage, *Restoring Fellowship*, 35–6.

70. Paul uses the illustration of the leaven forbidden from bread in the Passover feast to compare how sin in the church should be expunged so that it does not pervade and saturate the whole body like yeast does bread. He calls them to experientially become what they already are positionally in God's sight—holy, set apart, and made new thanks to the sacrifice of our Passover Lamb, Jesus Christ (v. 7b).

71. This comprises Grudem's three main reasons for the purpose of church discipline, which are: (a) the restoration and reconciliation of the believer who is going astray; (b) to keep the sin from spreading to others; (c) to protect the purity of the church and the honor of Christ. Grudem, *Systematic Theology*, 894–6. See also Adams, *Handbook of Church* Discipline, 13–9; Davis, "Whatever Happened to Church Discipline?," 352–61; Dever, "Biblical Church Discipline," 38–42; Edwards, "The Nature and End of Excommunication," 121; Knuteson, *Calling the Church to* Discipline, 43–63; Laney, *A Guide to Church Discipline*, 79–89. Stuart Murray has a similar but more nuanced list: (a) restoration of the sinner to a life of discipleship; (b) purifying the church; (c) maintaining the testimony of the church; (d) deterring others; (e) and deflecting God's judgment. Murray, *Explaining Church Discipline*, 43–6. He further adds, "Occasionally in the New Testament, church discipline is referred to as 'passing judgment' (e.g. 1 Cor 5:3) or as 'punishment' (e.g. 2 Corinthians 2:6–7), although it is clear in these passages that the intention is always remedial. *But these aspects are given relatively little attention in the New Testament compared to the main agenda which is to help one another continue as disciples*

Thus when the church acts it is not only seeking to restore the unrepentant sinner, but it also is in essence restoring itself, since sin does damage to a community as well as an individual.

Later in the passage, Paul lists not only sexual immorality, but also a number of other sins that may be happening in the church in Corinth that would be worthy of church discipline. He distinguishes between non-believers outside the church, whom we ought not to expect to act like Christians, with those who are inside the church who call themselves "brothers," whom we are to hold accountable. In the passage cited earlier, Paul writes:

> I have written you in my letter not to associate with sexually im-
> moral people—not at all meaning the people of this world who are
> immoral, or the greedy and swindlers, or idolaters. In that case you
> would have to leave this world. But now I am writing you that you
> must not associate with anyone who calls himself a brother but is
> sexually immoral or *greedy, an idolater or a slanderer, a drunkard
> or a swindler*. With such a man do not even eat (1 Cor 5:9–11 NIV,
> emphasis mine).[72]

This may cause us to naturally pause and ask: what sins, according to the Scriptures, are worthy of church discipline? Though we do have lists of sins and vices in the New Testament (e.g., Rom 1:29–31; 1 Cor 6:9–11; Gal 5:19–21; 1 Tim 6:3–5), Wayne Grudem reminds us:

> There does not seem to any explicit limitation specified for the
> kinds of sin that should be subject to church discipline . . . none-
> theless, a definite principle appears to be at work: all sins that were
> explicitly disciplined in the New Testament were publicly known
> or outwardly evident sins [the exception in Acts 5:1–11] and many
> of them had continued over a period of time. The fact that sins
> were publicly known meant that reproach was being brought on
> the church, Christ was being dishonored, and there was a very real

---

of Christ" (emphasis mine). Ibid., 46–7. Martin Jeschke argues that church discipline is intimately tied to and is a form of evangelism. He writes, "Congregational discipline belongs to the essence of the church as much as evangelism does because both are inescapable implications of the gospel. It makes no sense to declare the good news of liberation from sin to people outside the church and then refuse to declare it to Christians within the church." Jeschke, *Disciplining in the Church*, 109.

72. Fee writes, "It should be noted that all three of these sins—sexual immorality, idolatry, and greed—were particularly prevalent in Corinth of the mid-fifties A.D." Fee, *1 Corinthians*, 224.

possibility that others would be encouraged to follow the wrongful patterns of life that were being publicly tolerated. There is always the need, however, for mature judgment in the exercise of church discipline, because there is lack of complete sanctification in all our lives.[73]

He further points out that divisiveness, incest, laziness or refusal to work, disobedience, blasphemy, and teaching heresy were some of the diverse examples of the kinds of things that were subject to church discipline in the New Testament, adding:

> We should also remember that where there are issues of conduct on which Christians legitimately disagree, Paul encourages a wide degree of tolerance (Rom 14:1–23).[74]

It would seem, then, that church discipline should not be carried out unless there is a real public flavor and a truly unrepentant attitude toward the sin.[75] This is not to say that private sins that become known to

73. Grudem, *Systematic Theology*, 896–7.

74. Ibid., 896–7. Ted Kitchens remarks that the New Testament teaching suggests four major categories of sins that call for church discipline. He lists: (a) private and personal offenses that violate Christian life; (b) divisiveness and factions that destroy Christian unity; (c) moral and ethical deviations that break Christian standards; and (d) teaching false doctrine. Kitchens, "Perimeters of Corrective Church Discipline," 211–2.

75. Christopher Marshall remarks, "It is not the case that certain sins in themselves are thought to merit excommunication; it is persistent impenitence on the part of offenders that attracts the penalty." Marshall, *Beyond Retribution*, 158. Interestingly, there should always be a public nature to the discipline of *elders*, according to Paul's teaching in 1 Timothy 5, where the apostle writes, "Do not admit a charge against an elder except on the evidence of two or three witnesses. As for those who persist in sin, rebuke them in the presence of all, so that the rest may stand in fear. In the presence of God and of Christ Jesus and of the elect angels I charge you to keep these rules without prejudging, doing nothing from partiality" (1 Tim 5:19–21, ESV). Due to the public nature of an elder's leadership and service, he is to be above reproach (1 Tim 3:2) in the eyes of everyone. However, holding such positions of public leadership naturally lends itself to closer public "scrutiny, criticism, and rumors." Knight, *The Pastoral Epistles*, 235. Therefore, in order to protect an elder from unfair allegations and criticisms that leaders may often deal with, Paul adds that two or three witnesses are required in order for an accusation of sin to be entertained or brought against an elder. If the accusation is verified and true, then the elder is to be rebuked publicly (much like Paul did Peter in Gal 2:11–14). As Knute Larson writes, "The rebuke is intended to produce repentance in the sinner and to emphasize to the congregation the seriousness of all sin. *It is also a statement regarding the influence of a leader and how his actions affect those under his care.*" Larson, *1 and 2 Thessalonians, 1 and 2 Timothy, Titus, and Philemon*, 227. Larson's latter comment describes why this kind of rebuke falls into a special category, as the maintenance of trust

someone should never be addressed, but it should challenge us to be slow in initializing formal discipline. We should be gracious with one another as believers who still battle the sinful flesh that has yet to be fully eradicated. Ben Mitchell, in a published forum on church discipline, reminds us, "Corrective church discipline should be reserved for rebellion against clear commands of God revealed in Scripture."[76] He further cautions the church against abuse of the practice that has been seen in the church's history due to "arbitrary or extrabiblical rationales for discipline," whereby "legalism sometimes dictated the reasons for discipline rather than the biblical witness."[77] In our consideration of enacting church discipline, discernment, wisdom, and mature judgment must rule the day as "you who are spiritual" (Gal 6:1) seek to restore and encourage others to live and walk according to the truth (2 Thess 3:6). The call for formal action is not always necessary in every circumstance. However, for the unrepentant brother of 1 Corinthians 5, the church was indeed called to and in need of formal action, and Paul commanded the church with stern words to "expel the wicked man from among you!" (1 Cor 5:13 NIV).[78] His sin was a contaminating sin.

---

in church leadership is essential to the spiritual life of the flock. For more, see Grudem, *Systematic Theology*, 898–9.

76. Mitchell, as interviewed in the forum found in "The *SBJT* Forum: Perspectives on Church Discipline," 91. This should include not only rebellion against clear moral commands, but also orthodox Christian doctrine.

77. Ibid., 90–1. Yet, as George B. Davis writes, "Abuse in the past, however, can never justify neglect in the present. As M. Jeschke has succinctly stated, 'the answer to bad church discipline is good church discipline, not no church discipline.'" Davis, "Whatever Happened to Church Discipline?," 349.

78. Maria Pascuzzi writes, "The Christian community cannot be a partner to moral relativism nor can it adopt a posture of non-interference. To do so would be to abdicate responsibility for the spiritual well-being of both the offender and the community. To prevent this, Paul intervened to *rouse the community to assume its responsibility*" (emphasis mine). Pascuzzi, *Ethics, Ecclesiology, and Church Discipline*, 196. Brian Rosner notes the connection between Paul's theology of expulsion in 1 Corinthians 5 with the exclusion motifs of the Pentateuch (specifically such community exclusion texts like Deut 13:5; 17:7; 19:19; 21:21; and 24:7). He argues convincingly that it is more than just a few coincidental allusions to Old Testament terms or even to the quotation of Deuteronomy in 1 Corinthians 5:13b that links 1 Corinthians 5 with Jewish Scriptures. He traces theological motifs as well, such as the covenant motif (where people may be excluded for covenant disloyalty), the corporate responsibility motif (where the people as a whole are held responsible for the sin in their midst), and the holiness motif (where the emphasis is on ridding God's people from the contamination of sin that would defile them from being holy as God is holy). He notes how all these theological motifs (which are also found

We are not told whether the man actually publicly repented of his sin and was restored to fellowship, though some may believe that the restoration of the sorrowful brother in 2 Corinthians 2 may actually be the expelled man of 1 Corinthians 5. The apostle writes in 2 Corinthians:

> If anyone has caused grief, he has not so much grieved me as he has grieved all of you, to some extent—not to put it too severely. The punishment inflicted on him by the majority is sufficient for him. Now instead, you ought to forgive and comfort him, so that he will not be overwhelmed by excessive sorrow. I urge you, therefore, to reaffirm your love for him. The reason I wrote you was to see if you would stand the test and be obedient in everything. If you forgive anyone, I also forgive him. And what I have forgiven—if there was anything to forgive—I have forgiven in the sight of Christ for your sake, in order that Satan might not outwit us. For we are not unaware of his schemes (2 Cor 2:5–11 NIV).[79]

Paul refers to the disciplinary measure as "the punishment inflicted on him by the majority." If indeed there was a lot of pride over the incestuous man's sin in Corinth, any sort of congregational action might not be unanimous (though it should have). This may explain why the "punishment" (or reproof) was done only by a majority.[80] But this is still

---

in Ezra 7–10) are found in 1 Corinthians 5. Both Ezra and Paul utilize these motifs in their own respective contexts, showing their "indebtedness to Pentateuchal teaching on exclusion." Rosner, *Paul, Scripture, and Ethics*, 80 In the end, "1 Cor 5:1–3 is an instance where an interrelated complex of Scriptural ideas converge to profound effect." Ibid., 91. His entire argument is found in ibid., 61–93. For more on the corporate responsibility motif, see ibid., "Corporate Responsibility in 1 Corinthians 5," 470–3.

79. Notice the Apostle Paul's gentleness in not naming the details of the sin but simply saying, "if anyone has caused grief." David Garland remarks, "Naming names and specifying crimes and punishment would only unleash more grief by bringing more shame on the one who has now repented and has been sufficiently punished." Garland, *2 Corinthians*, 117. See also Garland's footnote (154) about how Paul delicately and vaguely refers to the sin of Onesimus in the book of Philemon. Ibid.

80. The NIV's "inflicted" is not in the original. Further, C. K. Barrett argues that the word ἐπιτιμία (translated "punishment") would be best translated as "reproof," citing the verbal forms of it that are found in the New Testament twenty-nine times, where the idea is more a rebuke or reproof than a punishment (the exception being in Jude 9). See Barrett, *The Second Epistle to the Corinthians*, 90. Even if one does translate it as "punishment," the context is abundantly clear that Paul and the church were not seeking retribution, but rather restoration and reconciliation. Due to the *retributive overtones* of the English word "punishment," Barrett's assertion to translate it as "reproof" may be preferable. Our argument from the previous chapter that the believer's retributive "punishment" was poured out on Christ once and for all would seem to support this idea,

all speculation. Scholars have mixed conclusions on whether this is the man of 1 Corinthians 5.[81] Yet even after conjecturing that this is indeed the incestuous offender that is being restored (with some persuasive arguments), commentator David Garland remarks that "while a case can be made for the incestuous man as Paul's nemesis, final certainty eludes us."[82] Nonetheless, the passage cited above is about forgiveness and restoration of *someone* who has been disciplined by the church. Hays writes:

> Even if 2 Corinthians 2:5–11 refers to a case different from that of the incestuous man, it demonstrates Paul's belief that stern community discipline can lead to transformation and reintegration into the life of the community . . . likewise, the other major New Testament passages on community discipline envision forgiveness and reconciliation as the ultimate goal of the community's action . . . it is clear that forgiveness *does not take the place of* discipline; rather it *follows* clear community discipline and authentic repentance.[83]

Paul clearly indicates in his letter that the disciplined man has repented of his sin and is "sorrowful." The goal of the disciplinary action has been realized, and just as the church had once "bound" the man, so should they now "loose" him. There should be no delay. The church that once acted resolutely in *discipline* should now act with just as much ur-

---

especially in light of how we often understand "punishment" today. John Milbank argues, "The trial and punishment of Jesus itself, condemns, in some measure, all other forms of alien discipline . . . the only finally tolerable, and non-sinful punishment, for Christians, must be the self-punishment inherent in sin." Milbank, *Theology and Social Theory*, 421. Though Milbank properly disposes of the need for Christian church "punishment" in a retributive sense, we cannot as a church simply take a passive stance concerning sin and hope that the inherent "self-punishment" or consequences of it will bring the person back to his or her senses. When one understands that church discipline is not retributive punishment, then this form of "alien discipline" is truly acceptable.

81. See David Garland, who does an excellent job of summarizing that various scholarly opinions in *2 Corinthians*, 117–25. Though most ancient commentators hold that this is the man of 1 Corinthians 5, the majority of commentators today say it is not. Laney is convinced that it is the same man. See Laney, *A Guide to Church Discipline*, 92, n. 1. Colin Kruse makes an intriguing case that this may indeed be the same man, arguing that after the letter of 1 Corinthians, the man challenged Paul's authority, which could possibly explain why Paul refers to a suggested personal attack in 2 Corinthians 2:5 and 7:7, 8, 12. See Kruse, "The Offender and the Offense in 2 Corinthians 2:5 and 7:12," 129–39. However, Maria Pascuzzi has written a convincing argument that "Paul's severe response to the immoral situation described in 1 Corinthians 5 was motivated primarily by his Christological, ecclesiological, and ethical concerns and not by a polemic about his apostolic authority." Pascuzzi, *Ethics, Ecclesiology, and Church* Discipline, 12.

82. Ibid., 123.

83. Hays, *First Corinthians*, 86.

gency and swiftness in *forgiving* and *restoring* him. Paul insists that the church "forgive and comfort" the repentant man, so that he will not be "overwhelmed by excessive sorrow" (v. 7). He calls their needed response to the man a "reaffirmation of love" (v. 8), that which appropriately describes the true nature of forgiveness, whereby the church no longer holds the man in contempt for his sin.[84]

We must remember that the principle of "binding and loosing" teaches us that when the church appropriately acts in matters of discipline and restoration, God is acting along with them and through them. Therefore, in this situation in Corinth, God is acting through the church's discipline to reveal his claim on the man as a legitimate son (Heb 12:7–8). The goal was to get the man out of sin so that he may share in God's holiness (Heb 12:10), so that a "harvest of righteousness and peace" (Heb 12:11) will be seen not only in the man's life, but in the church as well. God is not simply acting in *discipline* through the church, but he is also using the church's restorative actions to communicate his *forgiveness* and *love*. For as Jesus said in the gospel of John, "If you forgive anyone his sins, they are forgiven; if you do not forgive them, they are not forgiven" (John 20:23 NIV).[85]

It would seem plausible that due to the fact that excommunication was such a public event, so also should there be a public recognition of forgiveness, restoration, and reconciliation once repentance has taken place. This is what Paul is calling for here in 2 Corinthians 2, and this is in keeping with the words of Jesus in Luke 17, where Christ says:

84. See Laney, *A Guide to Church* Discipline, 94. In his pastoral commentary on 2 Corinthians, the popular Pastor John MacArthur lists seven motives that emerge from this passage that help develop the New Testament's theology of forgiveness. He derives from this passage that "believers are to forgive to deflect pride, show mercy, restore joy, affirm love, prove obedience, restore fellowship, and thwart Satan." MacArthur, *2 Corinthians*, 53. The aorist active infinitive verb κυρῶσαι (from the root κυρόω) translated here in verse 8 as "reaffirm" is a challenge from Paul to make a cognitive and intentional decision to express love to the man. This is not simply a moment of pardon (though the legal overtones of the word are certainly there, cf. Gal 3:15), but an opportunity to express Christ-like love, a love that is proactive and expressive in nature (cf. 1 John 4:10). Martin Jeschke has a helpful section on what it means to authentically forgive someone in the church in Jeschke, *Discipling in the Church*, 64–8.

85. Though the context in John has more to do with the evangelistic efforts of the disciples rather than church discipline, it would seem that the principle of forgiveness is applicable here. The same cooperative action resides here that resides in the principle of binding and loosing. But as we said earlier in footnote 48, this does not mean that the church has the market on proclaiming forgiveness of sins in any absolute sense, since that belongs to God alone.

> If your brother sins, rebuke him, and if he repents, forgive him. If
> he sins against you seven times in a day, and seven times comes
> back to you and says, "I repent," forgive him (Luke 17:3–4 NIV).[86]

The godly sorrow of the man under discipline has produced repentance (2 Cor 7:10), and it is now the responsibility of the community to
restore him, for the sake of both the man and the church.[87] In the story of
the prodigal son (Luke 15:11–32), the father was just as eager to restore
the son as the son was eager to be received home.[88] In practical terms
today, perhaps a special service of celebration could be convened; but in
any instance, the restoration "should be full and final, with the person
welcomed back into church membership."[89] As Adams has noted, the
matter should be completely closed and should not be raised again once

---

86. Barrett notes, however, "Paul shows no awareness that he is putting into practice
the words of Jesus . . . instead of citing authority he gives a reason for the course of action
he recommends: lest he be swallowed up in excessive sorrow." Barrett, *The Second Epistle
to the Corinthians*, 92.

87. So Marshall, *Beyond Retribution*, 157.

88. This parable of Christ is one of the most profound examples of forgiveness and
restoration in all of Scripture, and ought to serve as a paradigm for how the church
should respond in times of reconciliation. Laney tells the story of a man who had been
under discipline for five years. Being excommunicated from the church wore heavily
on his heart, and "after five years of heartache, misery and resisting God, Ralph wrote a
letter of confession and repentance which was read to the church. The church board then
met with him and discerned that his repentance was genuine. Rejoicing, they literally
gave him a new sport coat, had a gold ring made for his finger, and celebrated with him
over a veal dinner! Ralph has walked with God ever since." Laney, *A Guide to Church
Discipline*, 91.

89. Murray, *Explaining Church Discipline*, 35. Murray has many helpful ideas about
the process of restoration in the church. He lists several issues that should be understood
regarding the process of restoration, including (a) the restoration process should be as
public as the disciplinary process; (b) restoration must follow a clear change of heart and
a renewed commitment to discipleship, and a small group may need to meet with the repentant over time to access this commitment so as to encourage him/her; (c) restoration
may involve certain steps that may be implemented that express repentance which may
help the individual work through difficulties that resulted from the process of discipline
being implemented. Murray insists this must not be seen as "some kind of penance but
as an expression of the person's freedom and renewed commitment to discipleship and of
support of the church." Ibid., 34.; (d) there may be a place for confession or a public testimony by the repentant focusing on the present and future rather than the past, which
would be a "joyful affirmation" of what God has done through the disciplinary process;
(e) a symbolic act of restoration through things like the laying on of hands and prayer, or
other creative expressions of acceptance and love. Ibid., 32–6. For more on the value of
confession, see White and Blue, *Healing the Wounded*, 181–8.

forgiveness and restoration is accomplished, perhaps even putting a statement of closure in the church records.[90] This period of restoration should be a joyful and profound experience for a church and may strengthen the church's commitment to implementing church discipline in the future.

Therefore, when church discipline is appropriately enacted and results in restoration and reconciliation as we see here, Satan, the god of this age (4:4), is thwarted. His schemes that seek to destroy the church from within are undermined (v. 11).[91] However, when the church *does not* act and the word of God is *not* honored, the damage that Satan can do can be much greater, and this will cause the church to become weak, perhaps even forcing God to act on their behalf toward the man *and also toward the church.*[92] I am convinced that this is why so much of the church in America is weak, because even the very idea of church discipline is reproachable to those who have completely misunderstood its nature, purpose, and connection with the actions of a loving heavenly Father. God will not bring spiritual blessing to a congregation that refuses to obey his explicit commands, especially concerning sin. And obedience to the word of God through Paul was an issue at stake here in Corinth. For Paul wrote in verse 9, "The reason I wrote you was to see if you would stand the test and be obedient in everything." Therefore, we may emphatically say that the exercise of biblical church discipline in the church is a matter of corporate obedience to the will of God. The consequences of disobedience may altogether destroy a church and cause God to act to protect the honor of his name, something that has biblical precedent, as we will now see.

90. See Adams, *Handbook of Church Discipline*, 92–4. Adams further exclaims, "Any within the body who fail to forgive should be warned of the fact that to persist in such failure would place *them* in jeopardy of church discipline." Ibid., 94. However, it is this writer's contention that we should never *threaten* church discipline lest we continue to drive home the impression that it is a punitive whip that is waved around by the church. The manner in which one would admonish someone who refuses to forgive would be critical to how church discipline is perceived throughout the church.

91. Garland writes, "This passage and 1 Cor 5:1–5 reveal how important it is for the Christian community to balance the exercise of firm discipline with compassionate charity toward those who repent. Failure to do either plays into the hands of Satan. In this passage Paul reveals that showing forgiveness is one way for the church to close the door on Satan's evil designs to destroy it." Garland, *2 Corinthians*, 131.

92. The Lord did discipline the church in Corinth for their inaction concerning the abuses surrounding the Lord's Supper in 1 Corinthians 11, and we will briefly look at this next.

WHEN THE COMMUNITY REFUSES TO ACT

Due to the mandate given by Christ for the community to enact the process of discipline outlined in Matthew 18, and the command for the church to act by Paul in 1 Corinthians 5, the church is obliged to enact church discipline when unrepentant sin is discovered in the body of Christ.[93] When the church does indeed act, they are embodying God's reconciling love through the practice of the church. However, if the church should refuse to act or decides to turn the other way over blatant sin, then the body of Christ is being disobedient to God. The consequences of this may be that God may not only directly discipline the offending believer (without using the means of the church), but *he may also discipline the offending church.* There is precedent for such actions by the Lord in both the Old Testament covenant community and the New Testament church.

In the book of 1 Samuel, the priestly ruling family of the Israelite nation, led by Eli the high priest, had become corrupt during the time of the judges. Eli's sons, Hophni and Phinehas, who themselves were priests at Shiloh, were deemed wicked men or "sons of Belial" in 1 Samuel 2:12, having no regard for or knowledge of Yahweh.[94] Their wickedness stemmed from improper worship practices (1 Sam 2:13–17) and fornication with Israelite women who were serving at the entrance to the Tent of Meeting (1 Sam 2:22).[95] The sanctuary of the Lord's presence was being desecrated and profaned, and "they were treating the Lord's offering with contempt" (1 Sam 2:17 NIV). And further, their continual public sin would "make the LORD's people transgress" (1 Sam 2:24 NKJV).

When Eli, the high priest, learned of his sons' behavior (1 Sam 2:22), he rightly rebuked them. But with an unwillingness to repent, and with

---

93. By saying that the church is obligated to enact church discipline, I do not mean to imply that all of the steps of the disciplinary process from Matthew 18 will automatically be carried out. The process of church discipline begins first with self-discipline, then one-to-one admonition, and on up the line to a more public rebuke that may possibly lead to excommunication. As a reminder, the disciplinary process may be trumped at any level when confession, repentance, and reconciliation have occurred.

94. The differences between Samuel and the two sons of Eli are weaved throughout the opening chapters of 1 Samuel, and in contrast to these two evil young men who "did not know the LORD" (v. 12), Samuel gains knowledge of Yahweh through divine revelation. See 1 Samuel 3:7ff.

95. We are not told what these women are doing or why they are there, though their service at the entrance to the Tent of Meeting is attested to in Exodus 38:8. But such sexual immorality at the holy place is reminiscent of cultic Canaanite temple prostitution.

hardened hearts that will bring forth the judgment of God (v. 25), the sons refused to listen to their father. And Eli, the high priest, refused to do anything further. He simply told them they were wrong, but was rather indifferent in taking further action. As Bill Arnold has aptly noted, "Eli is either unwilling or unable to control his wayward sons."[96] This lack of action or passive allowance of the sins of the sons would result in the coming of a prophet, or "man of God," who declared that Eli was honoring his sons more than God (v. 29). It is here where the prophet pronounced judgment not simply upon the sons (who will both die on the same day, v. 34) for their active disobedience, but on Eli as well, for his inaction as the high priest. Eli was held accountable for his refusal to act in the situation, and this would have dire consequences to his priestly line.

The promise given to Eli, that his house and his father's house would minister before the Lord forever (v. 30), was revoked.[97] The corporate sentence is further seen in the fact that all those in Eli's house would die before they reached old age (vv. 31–33); the priesthood responsibilities would be given away to another, more faithful family line (v. 35)[98]; and poverty and hunger would consume Eli's lineage.[99]

The lesson to be learned in all of this is that God expects us in the covenant community to hold one another accountable and to take action when sin is discovered. Eli was unwilling to hold his sons accountable, and let their sins continue unchecked. This profaned the name of Yahweh and the place of his presence and violated the purity of others in the community, especially the women who were serving. Therefore Yahweh directly disciplined the two apostate sons who had violated the law and desecrated the holy place with their licentious sexual behavior. And in addition to this, God directly disciplined Eli and his family line for Eli's *refusal to act* when the sins were brought to light. It is clear that

---

96. Arnold, *1 and 2 Samuel*, 72.

97. A conditional promise based on faithfulness.

98. This comes to fruition when Zadok and his family assume the priestly duties during the reign of king Solomon, who removed Abiathar, a descendant of Eli, from the priesthood, "fulfilling the word the LORD had spoken at Shiloh about the house of Eli" (1 Kgs 2:27 NIV).

99. The "poetic justice" here is hard to miss, for the sons sinned by indulging themselves on the select meat before the fat, which was meant to be an offering to the Lord in keeping with the law (cf. Lev 7:31), was actually burned up. The consequences of such a sin would be realized in a future family line that would be begging for food (v. 36).

the removal of God's blessing from this family and community of priests was a consequence of inaction.

As we turn our attention to the New Testament, we also see precedent for God to directly intervene in discipline when his chosen vehicle, the church, *has refused* to do so. As we have seen earlier, in the Corinthian church, inaction over a number of sins in the church brought a series of rebukes from the Apostle Paul, who called for action. However, in one instance, the unchecked sin of the community was so grievous that it necessitated a direct act of divine discipline from the hand of God himself.

In 1 Corinthians 11, the Apostle Paul is chastising the church for their blatant abuse of the celebration of the Lord's Supper. It was common that when the church "gathered together" as a community to celebrate the bread and the cup (the Eucharist) in remembrance of Christ's sacrifice, there was also an accompanying fellowship meal.[100] The abuses were apparently occurring during these fellowship meals, and they were bringing reproach and disrepute to the practice of the ordinance. Sparing no words, Paul is direct in his agitated tone of condemnation of the sins that are occurring at the Lord's Supper.

> In the following directives I have no praise for you, for your meetings do more harm than good. In the first place, I hear that when you come together as a church, there are divisions among you, and to some extent I believe it. No doubt there have to be differences among you to show which of you have God's approval. When you come together, it is not the Lord's Supper you eat, for as you eat, each of you goes ahead without waiting for anybody else. One remains hungry, another gets drunk. Don't you have homes to eat and drink in? Or do you despise the church of God and humiliate those who have nothing? What shall I say to you? Shall I praise you for this? Certainly not (1 Cor 11:17–22 NIV)!

The abuses seemingly revolve around the divided hearts of the assembly that manifested itself in raucous and factious behavior. Paul earlier addressed divisions within this church in 1 Corinthians 1:10–13, and the

---

100. In fact, a hard distinction between an agape feast and the Eucharist would have seemed artificial in the early church, since they both occurred at that which was known as the Lord's Supper. As Richard B. Hays points out, "Evidently, the sharing of the symbolic bread and cup of the Lord's Supper occurred as a part of a common meal; otherwise the passage makes no sense. Christians accustomed to experiencing the Lord's Supper only as a ritual 'in church,' removed from a meal setting, will need to discipline their imaginations to keep this original setting in mind." Hays, *First Corinthians*, 193.

divisions that are seemingly occurring at "the Lord's Supper" are related and are specific in nature.[101] Apparently certain groups (perhaps more wealthy folks) were eating their "own private meals," even "devouring" their meals in front of those who had nothing, in an act of selfishness (where they refused to share food) and perhaps even fiscal exploitation.[102] Further, as if this was a high-class Roman dinner party, the celebration of these individuals escalated to the point where some were actually getting drunk (v. 21). Yet as Gordon Fee has noted:

> Paul is not so concerned about "drunkenness" per se. What he has done is to take from both parts of a meal, eating and drinking, and express them in their extremes. The one extreme is to receive nothing to eat, thus to "be hungry"; the other extreme is to be gorged on food and wine, thus to "be drunk." As the following sentence makes clear, Paul's concern is not with the drunkenness of the one (in other contexts he will condemn that as well), but

101. My use of quotation marks here is due to the fact that Paul remarks that what is supposed to be "the Lord's Supper" (used only here in the NT) is in fact anything but. He states, "When you come together, it is not the Lord's Supper you eat . . ." (1 Cor 11:20 NIV). The likely idea here is that the unity of fellowship and worship of Christ that ought to surround this sacred ordinance was being usurped and desecrated by the selfish splurging of individuals whose gluttonous and excessive behavior set them apart from others. So rather than being a *united* body, which is what the sacrifice of Christ has intended to bring to the church, the church was fractured in its relationships, which is an affront to the unity that ought to characterize "the Lord's Supper." So rather than being united in their focus on Christ, members of the church were more focused on themselves. Thiselton eloquently summarizes, "Just as in 1:10–12, the groupings caused splits by generating an ethos which came to give the peer group or subgroup more prominence than the 'one' Body (cf. 10:16, 17) of the whole church, so the dynamics of the celebrations of the Lord's Supper in house groups in all probability generated the same spirit of focusing on a patron or host to a group rather than exclusively on Christ." Thiselton, *The First Epistle to the Corinthians*, 850.

102. Ibid., 863. See also Fee, *1 Corinthians*, 540–1, Hays, *First Corinthians*, 195–7, and especially Winter, "The Lord's Supper at Corinth: An Alternative Reconstruction," 73–82. Fee also points to verse 22's first rhetorical question of whether the abusers have homes to eat and drink in to suggest that "this implies ownership [as opposed to 'those who have nothing'], not simply a place where meals may be eaten," thus inferring that Paul may be addressing those who are wealthy. Fee, *1 Corinthians*, 543. Hays writes, "This scenario no doubt seems strange to most readers of our time. It is hard for us to imagine how the wealthier Corinthians could possibly suppose such overt snubbing of the poor to be justified. In the context of first century Greco-Roman culture, however, the Corinthians probably understood their actions as entirely normal." Hays, *First Corinthians*, 195–6.

with the hunger of the other—especially in a context where fellow believers have more than enough to eat and drink.[103]

Thus, it is the excess of some without regard for the neediness of others that has made a mockery out of the Lord's Supper. That which was intended to be a celebration by the *whole* (united) family of God around the significance of the cross has now been tainted.[104] By their despicable actions, they "show contempt for God's church and humiliate (or shame) those who have nothing" (1 Cor 11:22).[105] They have failed to remember Christ's sacrifice (v. 25) and failed to proclaim and value the significance of it (v. 26).

> By showing contempt for those who have nothing, they are acting as though his death had not decisively changed the conditions of their relationship with one another.[106]

Therefore they were partaking of the Lord's Table in an "unworthy manner," and were "guilty of sinning against the body and blood of the Lord," (v. 27) or more specifically, Christ himself (as opposed to the elements themselves).[107]

And apparently the church was doing nothing to stop such abuses. Rather than commending someone who is attempting to put an end to

---

103. Fee, *1 Corinthians*, 543. Paul does address drunkenness in the church earlier in the letter where his instruction was never to have table fellowship or eat with anyone who calls himself a brother but who is known for indulging in this sinful practice (cf. 1 Cor 5:11).

104. "No 'church' can long endure as the people of God for the new age in which the old distinctions between bond and free (or Jew or Greek, or male and female) are allowed to persist. Especially so at the Table, where Christ, who has made us one, has ordained that we should visibly proclaim that unity." Ibid., 544.

105. My translation. The Greek word for "contempt" here is καταφρονέω, a strong word meaning, "to despise or treat with contempt." Coupled with καταισχύνω ("to put to shame, humiliate, or disgrace"), Paul drives home that fact that their actions are grossly unbecoming of God's redeemed people, in opposition to the secular mindset of the wealthy Corinthian culture.

106. Hays, *First Corinthians*, 199.

107. G. W. H. Lampe writes, "This suggests that to violate the solemn fellowship of Christ's people, as had been done by the scandalous selfishness of some participants in the Corinthian Eucharist, is to become implicated in responsibility for the death of Christ, just as for the baptized person to commit apostasy is, according to the writer of Hebrews, to crucify the Son of God." Lampe, "Church Discipline and the Interpretation of the Epistles to the Corinthians," in Farmer, Moule, and Niebuhr, *Christian History and Interpretation*, 346.

this behavior (which we do not see anywhere in the text), Paul holds the church collectively responsible for their passive allowance of the fiasco. For in verse 17 and in verse 22, he says:

> In the following directives I have no praise for you, for your meetings do more harm than good . . . What shall I say to you? Shall I praise you for this? Certainly not (1 Cor 11:17, 22b NIV)!

The striking element in all of this, which aids our understanding in this study, is that as a response to the inaction of the church, God has chosen to directly discipline some of the guilty parties.

> For anyone who eats and drinks without recognizing the body of the Lord eats and drinks judgment on himself. That is why many of you are weak and sick, and a number of you have fallen asleep (1 Cor 11:29–30 NIV).[108]

Paul, in prophetic fashion, is announcing that the direct hand of God is carrying out judgment (κρίμα) on those who are guilty of these abuses. A person essentially "sentences himself" to the Lord's direct discipline and the Lord has caused some to become physically weak and sick, and others have actually died (the euphemism is, "to fall asleep").[109]

---

108. Much ink has been spilled on the precise of meaning of μὴ διακίνων τὸ σῶμα, translated as "without recognizing the body." Thiselton does a nice job of tracing and identifying the various traditions of interpretation in an excurses (see Thiselton, *1 Corinthians*, 891–4.) This writer prefers the interpretation of Gordon Fee, who argues that we are not talking about the literal body of Jesus here in the same way we were in verse 27 where they were sinning against "the body" *and* "the blood" of the Lord. Rather, what Paul may be saying is that when one does not recognize (διακρίνω, "to recognize or discern") the body, one is essentially ignoring the corporate or communal concept of unity and harmony in the church, the "body of Christ," where there is to be no division or abusive relationship seen between the rich and poor. In creative fashion, Fee states, "The Corinthians are missing the meaning of the 'body' given in death; but Paul's present concern is with the furthest sense, the church as that body." Fee, *1 Corinthians*, 564. Other commentators, such as Witherington, *Conflict and Community in Corinth*, 252; Blomberg, *1 Corinthians*, 231; and Hays, *1 Corinthians*, 200, hold a similar view. Note as well, some reliable early Greek texts (i.e., p46; א*; A; B; C*; 33, and others) do not include the NIV's "of the Lord" after the word "body" in verse 29. The longer text may simply be an explanatory inclusion so that it sounds much like verse 27. Yet this may mislead the interpreter into thinking that we are referring to the literal body of Christ figuratively portrayed in the bread that Jesus was instituting earlier in Paul's recollection of the received tradition, and as Hays remarks, "This would be a complete non sequitur in the argument." Hays, *First Corinthians*, 200. Therefore, the shorter reading is preferred.

109. At first glance it may seem that the reflexive pronoun, "to eat and drink judgment *upon oneself*" (κρίμα ἑαυτῷ) would make God sound like a passive participant

This divine judgment or "discipline," as it is termed in verse 32 (παιδεύω, meaning "to train, discipline, or correct"), is not to be seen as a *final judgment* of an apostate people (like that seen of the unbelieving Israelites in the wilderness). Rather it is the temporal chastisement of the covenant community for the purpose of correcting and restoring the community to a right response (rather than passive allowance of sin). For Paul makes it clear that the purpose of the discipline is so that "we will not be condemned (or judged) along with the world" (v. 32) in the full and final sense. Yet in a few situations, the elect brethren actually have become physically weak to the point where it has led to death.[110] Seemingly, a sin that has involved abuse affiliated with physical eating and drinking is being disciplined by God in a physical manner. The refusal of the church to act, then, is the warrant for this supernatural act of divine discipline that is being directly dealt from the hand of God. And as the writer of the book of Hebrews has profoundly noted, "It is a dreadful thing to fall into the hands of the living God" (Heb 10:31 NIV).

But this is not to say that the church has sealed its fate. While Paul has prophetically declared that discipline has fallen on the church for their sins, he at the same time admonishes them toward the necessary action needed in order to avoid such corrective discipline both now and in the

---

in the judgment that occurs, as if the judgment is merely a natural consequence of the action. But the context makes this understanding impossible, since it is clear that in verse 32 that the judgment is "by the Lord." Concerning the necessity of God's actions in discipline, Davis remarks, "Church discipline, then, is designed to reclaim a wayward believer[s] before divine discipline becomes necessary." Davis, "Whatever Happened to Church Discipline?," 359.

110. This is not to say that every situation where weakness, illness, or death occurs is a direct result of divine discipline for sin. Surely this was not the case with regard to the weakness Paul had as described in 2 Corinthians 12, where he describes his "thorn in the flesh" that made him weak, causing him to rely on the sufficient grace of God. However, what it does say is that in certain situations, there may actually be a cause and effect relationship between certain sins and how God chooses to deal with us to correct us, and in this case his discipline is manifested in a physical manner. It is not likely that we are simply referring to a spiritual weakness, a spiritual illness, or a spiritual death (see the discussion in Thiselton, *1 Corinthians*, 894). Such an understanding would seem to contradict verse 32, where if it were actually a "spiritual death" Paul is referring to, this would be in contrast to the stated purposes of God for the discipline, which is to *keep us from being condemned* along with the world. The direct divine discipline here imposed upon the guilty is not meant to be an eternal condemnation like it would be for an apostate or non-believing individual. The bigger picture must be kept in mind here. One of the overall purposes of this discipline was that it be a remedial lesson for the Corinthian community.

future. Paul emphatically declares in a play on words that, "If we judged ourselves, we would not come under judgment" (v. 31). The principle of self-examination and discernment that Paul emphasized earlier in verses 28 and 29 is a necessary part of the self-discipline that the Christians in Corinth ought to be exercising. This ought to be the practice at both the individual and corporate levels. If the individual Christian would practice self-discipline and act accordingly, and if the church community would discipline its own erring members and seek to mend its divisions, then God's direct intervention would be altogether unnecessary. Paul then calls for corrective action and proper behavior that honors the Lord's Table (vv. 33, 34), so that the disciplining hand of God would be lifted from the church.

So summarizing, in both situations, with Eli and his sons and here in the Corinthian church, we see where a refusal act obediently in the correction of known sin(s) resulted in the divine judgment of individuals and the removal of God's blessing from the covenant community. Therefore, for the church today, we can conclude that the blessings that may abound (e.g., forgiveness, restoration, peace, renewed fellowship with God, and love) as a result of enacting biblical church discipline far outweigh the negative consequences of inaction that may come directly from the chastening hand of God. Apathy in the church on necessary disciplinary issues can be destructive for the unrepentant involved and may also result in forfeiture of specific blessings that were meant for the community as well. The church then would do well to choose the path of blessing that comes from obedient action that seeks to correct and embody forgiveness rather than subject themselves to the judgment of God.

As we conclude this chapter, it has been our aim to build a biblical theology of church discipline from the primary texts where it is found in the New Testament, with special emphasis on Matthew 18 and 1 Corinthians 5. With forgiveness, restoration, and reconciliation as its goal, church discipline seeks to call sinners back to a life of faithful discipleship, hold sin in check, maintain the public witness, unity, and purity of the church (both morally and theologically), protect the honor of the name of Christ, and defray the potential judgment of God on his people. There are clear procedures set in place that establish parameters for discipline, and the authority and mandate to carry it out is clearly given by God to the church.[111] Much discretion, wisdom, and care should be exercised upon its implementation. And when the church acts in accordance with the will of God, it is our understanding that God, as our loving heavenly Father, is acting along with and through us in seeking to rescue the lost sheep that has gone astray. We are essentially acting as "God's agent in the world."[112] As we wrap up our study, we would do well to summarize our findings and arguments and take note of an example of how church discipline embodies the "fatherly" love of God in the church today.

111. Kitchens notes, "Jesus desired self-discipline from His followers (Matt 5:22–23; Mark 7:14–23), but when self-discipline fails, then the Christian community is responsible to exercise discipline lovingly." Kitchens, "Perimeters of Corrective Church Discipline," 212. Indeed, self-discipline should be seen as a form of informal church discipline, or as we might say, a formative discipline. For more on the role of formative discipline, see Cox, "The Forgotten Side of Church Discipline," 44–58; and Jeschke, *Discipling in the Church*, 105ff. Cox defines formative discipline as "that structure through which the church helps believers become fruit-bearing disciples. It is a ministry of teaching and training within the community of believers whereby Christians are aided in the maturation process. The church has a responsibility to provide the structure and environment for this to happen, and the believer has the obligation to submit to it." Cox, "The Forgotten Side of Church Discipline," 53, n. 2.

112. Hays, Moral Vision, 102.

7

Conclusion: Summary and Implications of This Study

THE FOCUS OF THIS study has been to take a redemptive historical look at the nature and purpose of divine discipline, with specific emphasis on God's actions through the practice of New Testament church discipline. The following stood as our primary thesis and argument: *The church, as an embodiment of Christ empowered by the Holy Spirit, is authorized and obliged to exercise discipline as an expression of God's fatherly love toward the company of his redeemed children.* When the church fails to do so, it is withholding one of God's prescribed actions for the church whereby he embodies his forgiveness, grace, and love.

HISTORICAL CONSIDERATIONS

Our journey began with a look at how church discipline has been understood by significant figures or movements in the history of the church, especially those who spent much time discussing the nature and purpose of church discipline. It was necessary for us to be selective in this process, and thus Augustine, the Anabaptists, John Calvin, and a liberal theologian by the name of Friedrich Schleiermacher gave us a broad perspective from church history. Except for Schleiermacher, the proponents we looked at for the most part derived their understanding of church discipline from the Scriptures. It is apparent that the theology and applications of church discipline that many of these figures and movements embraced were heavily nuanced in light of their *Sitz im Leben* ("life setting"). The areas of distinguishable difference were found in how discipline was to be *carried out* (e.g., by the state, both church and state, or by the church alone) and the *severity* in which it was applied (ranging from gentle admonishment to banishment to even persecution).

The lessons gleaned from such a historical look demand that we remember to be cognizant of past triumphs and mistakes (avoiding extremes) and to be fully aware of some of our cultural, intellectual, and spiritual biases that we bring to the difficult task of interpretation and implementation of church discipline. In essence, it calls for a heart full of wisdom guided by the Holy Spirit. It further calls us to operate out of a fully developed biblical theology of church discipline that is faithful to the text and consistent with the life of discipleship as it is lived out in the context of a reconciled, forgiven, and committed covenant community. Lest the church be indistinguishable from the world, moral and doctrinal boundaries were essential in keeping with the truth of Scripture, the nature and mission of the church, and its witness to the gospel. For the most part, our historical figures saw *the necessity* of ecclesial discipline, not simply for practical and pragmatic purposes, but also because it was mandated by the Savior as a testimony to his person and work and as a measure of obedience to his teachings. They held to a genuine and healthy fear of the Lord, along with a commitment to community building. Though their story is locked in history, the timeless principles they lived out are not, and we would do well to learn from those who have gone before us who have passed on the legacy of faith that we now hold so dear.

DISCIPLINE IN REDEMPTION HISTORY: THE OLD TESTAMENT

Our biblical survey of divine discipline and its nature and purpose commenced with a look at its complexity in the Old Testament. Keeping in mind the appropriate contexts and biblical genres, we universally saw that divine discipline is executed by God within the context of a *covenant relationship*. This was true for God's relationship with Israel as a nation, King David and his line, as well as individual Israelites. This *covenant relationship* is a *key factor* in understanding discipline's nature and purpose, and this is true throughout all of redemption history (even today). Though at times there was a certain mystery in the mind of the covenant believer who longed to see its resolution (which would come later at the cross), divine discipline became a regular part of the history of God's chosen people as Yahweh revealed his character and love, revealed his plan of redemption and command for obedience, and appropriately dealt with the problem of human sin.

As we stated at the end of chapter 3, discipline in the Old Testament is depicted both as a medium for instruction and training as well as a punitive chastisement and judgment upon sinfulness. This complexity *cannot be overlooked*, and one must pay diligent attention to context in order to discern discipline's purpose.

As *instruction*, discipline teaches Israel about the character and sufficiency of Yahweh, the nature of their covenant relationship (which includes his steadfast love and favor), and stimulates them to love and obey Yahweh and his law while walking in his ways. His correction and rebuke (with punitive undertones) is his loving concern for their well being and the way in which he imparts wisdom, so that they might experience and know God and the fullness of his promises for blessing, protection, an inheritance, and mighty salvation. This type of discipline was especially prevalent in the exodus account (perhaps a definitive identity-shaping event for Israel) as well as in Wisdom literature.

As *punishment*, discipline is part of God's redemptive plan as he executes judgment and retribution on sin. On one hand, for the *believing remnant*, this can rightly be seen as a temporal chastisement and an experience of suffering that separates the faithful from the unfaithful (e.g., the wilderness and exile). Further, it can have a cleansing and restorative effect and serves as a deterrent from sin. Their stay of execution anticipates a future atonement in redemption history that will pay their debt in full as judgment for sin is poured out on their substitute sacrifice on the cross, who experiences the penalty they rightly deserve. This aspect of discipline stems from Yahweh's promise to the patriarchs, Israel's forefathers, and King David to redeem and restore a people for himself and establish his rule upon the earth, a rule characterized by justice, righteousness, and peace. This type of discipline is part of the way Yahweh expresses his everlasting love, assurance, and acceptance of his chosen people in spite of their sin. It is a way in which he instructs and calls them to persevere in purity and holiness, so as to rid sin from their midst. It is a restorative act of grace. To joyfully receive it like a growing child is to understand it rightly, as it is a sign of God's fatherly care and adoption as his children. To be sure, it is not often understood this way, even by the believing Israelites themselves, as the Psalms testify.

Yet on the other hand, punitive discipline can connote judgment that will fall on the *unbelieving nations* and *apostate Israelites,* and it will be the source of their demise as they are cut off and destroyed from the presence and promises of Yahweh. It is his just wrath on those who have turned away and have refused to repent of their evil and wicked ways. It is a decisive judgment and holds no hope for restoration. This is an altogether different aspect of discipline than that issued to the believing remnant, and it legitimately comes directly out of Yahweh's just and righteous rule of the earth. So then, there are two slightly different categories that fall under the heading of discipline as punishment. For the *remnant*, it is a temporal chastisement that anticipates complete retribution for sin to be fulfilled upon the cross, and for the *apostate* and *unbelieving pagans,* it is more of a final and decisive judgment with no hope of restoration. They are blown away like chaff. The difference between the two has everything to do with whether one is standing or living in *covenant relationship* with Yahweh.

THE "FATHERLY" COMPONENT

We have noted that for *believers* the idea of discipline is a valuable part of the covenant relationship between a holy God and sinful humanity. As we surveyed various texts, we saw different ways in which the intimacy of this relationship is expressed (e.g., the ownership idea of the covenant formula that exclaims, "They will be my people and I will be their God"). We also discovered an extremely powerful metaphor that is occasionally employed (sometimes explicitly, other times implicitly) to qualify the intimacy of the relationship within the context of divine discipline. Though it may not be overly prevalent due to the Canaanite background in which the Old Testament was written (though truly a part of Israelite piety), God is nevertheless portrayed as a "father" to Israel, especially in how he relates to them as their Creator, Redeemer, and the One to whom they should pay tribute and obey. He is further portrayed in the New Testament as the heavenly Father who disciplines us believers "for our own good," affirming our position as those who are loved and adopted by God and are "treated as sons," a point that is deepened and intensified in the new covenant age. The covenant language of fatherhood, the idea of discipline, and God's eschatological and restorative purposes are woven together in such a fashion that it informs the recipient about the nature and purpose of divine discipline. When God's people recognize and receive his discipline as a "fatherly" discipline, the metaphor becomes a powerful cognitive instrument that is a source of hope and assurance of the covenant relationship and inheritance with God. It teaches us that

God has our best interests at heart, as the Father who longs to give good gifts to his children and who is worthy of our trust. In this way it is an affirmation that we have life in him and that he wishes us to live "the life that is truly life" even in the here and now. His desire is that we be pure and holy before him, and his "fatherly" discipline helps to accomplish that.

After seeking to counter the critiques of those with modern-day agendas against the thought of seeing God as a "father" (even though this is the language of Scripture), we further noted that the fatherhood of God also serves as a conceptual bridge throughout redemption history. God is a Father to Israel, to Jesus Christ (though in a decidedly different and unique way within the context of the Trinity), and to the New Testament believer whose adoption and spiritual union are the grounds for our intimate cry of "*Abba*, Father" from within. Thompson called this the "eschatological trajectory of God's fatherhood." The conceptual bridge of fatherhood within discipline serves as a reminder that God's adopted people are to submit, trust, obey, and believe in the one whose plan of salvation and sanctification for us is further aided by such discipline. It then becomes a privilege for us to submit to God's "fatherly" discipline even when we suffer (Heb 12), and we should embrace it with thanksgiving, for our full adoption awaits.

DISCIPLINE AND THE ATONEMENT SECURED
BY THE CROSS

Having established that God's fatherhood in the disciplinary context serves as a conceptual bridge in God's redemptive purposes for his people, we then turned to the most significant moment of redemption history and the impact this has on our understanding of divine discipline. The biblical witness suggests that the sacrifice of Jesus Christ on the cross serves as the penal substitutionary atonement for all of God's people in redemption history. It is the fulfillment and resolution to the cry of the OT saint whose understanding of discipline was not yet fully understood or developed and whose punishment was temporarily stayed in the economy of divine justice. The punitive elements of discipline are fully satisfied in the retributive wrath that was poured out on Christ, and thus our understanding of discipline in the new covenant community is transformed and stripped of any retributive elements. The atonement for sin has been made, and therefore we can confidently assert that insofar as church discipline is charged with dealing with sin and error in the church, its nature and purpose is not punitive retribution, but is rather instructional, remedial, restorative, and reconciliatory. These elements of continuity remain, whereas the retributive aspects are satisfied and are thus discontinuous.

The death of Christ and his subsequent resurrection become the grounds of our justification, and therefore, there is no longer any condemnation for those who are in Christ. Therefore, as God now works out his redemptive plan through the Spirit-embodied church, his discipline can now be seen in the practice of church discipline (a new medium), where his forgiveness and love are expressed to his adopted children living in covenant relationship by means of a communicative action. Church discipline now serves as a testimony to the saving work of Christ, who rescued us from sin and whose will is that we walk as obedient disciples who are charged with teaching, guarding, embracing, and living the truth.

A BIBLICAL THEOLOGY OF CHURCH DISCIPLINE

In our final chapter, our goal was to build a biblical theology of church discipline. We sought to understand its nature and purpose in light of the role of God's "fatherly" discipline on his people throughout redemption history and the significance of the cross of Christ as the penultimate moment of that history. With God working his redemptive purposes out by means of the church's "ministry of reconciliation," the New Testament lays the foundation for how this discipline is to be understood and carried out. Sandwiched between parables that emphasize the restoration of that which has gone astray and the canceling and forgiveness of an outstanding debt, Jesus teaches and mandates the procedures for this new understanding of divine discipline that needs to be gently but obediently carried out through the actions of the church.

Not only does he outline the procedures for "winning *your brother* over" (note the covenant community language), he also delegates the authority necessary to act, proclaiming that when the church acts in accordance with the truth on any judicial matter, God is also acting along with them in keeping with the ministry of "binding and loosing" sin within the kingdom and family of God. This may be exercised in matters concerning moral purity or doctrinal integrity, where the truth of God has been clearly compromised. The Father in heaven is not willing that any of these "little ones" be lost (Matt 18:14), and so the church acts in order to reclaim a believer who needs once again to experience forgiveness and reconciliation on account of his or her current unrepentant pattern of sin. With the Father eager to see the "prodigal son" return home, God uses the church's disciplinary actions as a means to express his desire to see the sinner return to his or her senses and come home.

The Apostle Paul echoed and applied the Savior's mandate when he called the church to action on account of their failure to address the incestuous sin of a Christian brother. The gross public nature of the sin called for an immediate public response, and the purpose of Paul's command for the church to excommunicate was so that both the man and the church community would be purged of the sin so that the reality of salvation would be manifest among all involved. Though the primary goal of church discipline is reconciliation and restoration, in keeping with God's overarching goals of divine discipline, the action also maintains the testimony and purity of the covenant community, deters others from sin, defrays the removal of God's blessings and subsequent judgment, and honors the name of Christ by once again proclaiming the message of living a life in keeping with repentance and faith (the gospel). Church discipline communicates once again what it means to live life as a faithful disciple.

Our study further revealed Paul's expectation of the church's response of forgiveness and restoration when the goal of church discipline is realized and someone placed under discipline comes to repentance. In the same way that God works through the church to discipline the sinner, so he also works through the church's restorative actions to communicate his forgiveness, acceptance, and love. At the heart of all of these actions is the motivation to maintain the integrity and sanctity of the covenant relationship both individually and corporately. Having been bought and redeemed at a price, the church, as God's agent and ambassador of reconciliation to a dying world, must remain faithful to its nature and mission. For the Triune God has chosen to entrust the gospel and express his redemptive plan and purposes through the obedient actions of his chosen bride. And church discipline is an essential element to the ministry of reconciliation we are called to enact as God's holy people who have been called out of darkness into his wonderful light.

We concluded with two examples from both the Old and New Testaments of what happens when the covenant community refuses to act in discipline, whereby the removal of God's blessings and his temporal judgment falls upon his people who have failed to keep his precepts. Due to the apparent misunderstanding of the nature and purposes of church discipline today, we suggested that God may be acting in this manner today due to the prevalent weakness and lack of fruit that is being borne in many contemporary churches.

IMPLICATIONS OF OUR STUDY

We are now in a position to talk about some of the implications of this study for theology and the church. This book is essentially a theological reflection on the nature and purpose of divine discipline, especially as it relates to the practice of church discipline. I will assert two primary implications and then briefly touch on three minor insights.

From a theological standpoint, the church must understand that our union with the Triune God is not a static relationship but is rather an ongoing participation in the redemptive plan and purposes that God is implementing in the world today. *Based on the foundation of the person and finished work of Jesus Christ, the Father now enacts his covenantal (fatherly) discipline through the actions of the Spirit-embodied community (the church), so that his redemptive purposes might be manifested on earth through his disciples, who are called to glorify God, build his kingdom, and live by the truth.* Therefore, it is indeed true that the Triune God manifests himself in the life and through the practices of the church. Therefore, if we fail to practice biblical church discipline, *then we fail to understand the nature and character of our Triune God* and how he chooses to work his redemptive plan and purposes out in the world today. We must remember that our spiritual union is with a God who is our Creator, Redeemer, and Lord. And this dynamic covenant relationship calls us to identify and participate with who he is and what he is doing in redemption history. To be sure, it is a privilege to be in covenant relationship with this loving, forgiving, and reconciling God. And our lives ought to reflect our knowledge of and union with him by exemplifying his character and purposes in the loving, forgiving, reconciling act of church discipline.

Similarly (and second), as we stated in our introduction, the neglect of church discipline in many of today's churches reveals a fundamental misunderstanding *of the church's* nature and purpose as God's chosen vehicle for the gospel message. In Paul's second letter to the Corinthians, Paul reminds the church that God has entrusted us with his ministry and message of reconciliation (2 Cor 5:17–20). He calls us "Christ's ambassadors, as *though God were making his appeal* through us" (v. 20). If, as we have argued, church discipline is an communicative act of reconciliation and restoration, then this biblical practice becomes an essential part of the church's nature and purpose as a community committed to a ministry of reconciliation and the proclamation of the gospel. *Church discipline is therefore God's appeal* (through the church) to one of his sheep who has gone astray. We are the manner and means through which God has chosen to extend his grace. It would make little sense, then, to say that we are committed to spreading the gospel (the message of reconciliation) to a dying world but are unwilling to remain committed to it in the totality of life inside the church. As someone has rightly said, our charge is not to make converts but disciples. Church discipline, then, is an essential mark of a church committed to making disciples. It is not retributive punishment, and it is not hypocritical judging. It is part and parcel to the church's nature and mission and is a re-proclamation of the gospel message of repentance and faith in the one who has paid the ultimate price to deliver us from our sin. Therefore, this study is warranted and applicable for understanding something that is so key and pertinent to the church's nature and mission.

In a more positive light, the church that does practice church discipline is assured of God's presence with them (Matt 18:20) in their community building and ministry of reconciliation, and with God's presence there is always blessing. Despite the challenges, uncomfortableness, and awkwardness sometimes felt in holding one another accountable to a life of discipleship, the benefits and blessings of the fruit that is borne from it will have a profound and transforming effect on the individual, the church, and the world. J. Carl Laney provides a helpful example of what this looks like as he shares the following story.

> Ralph, a single man, was a church leader and an active discipler, a faithful attender at the weekly men's prayer breakfast and a lover of theological discussion. His life, from all appearances, was above reproach. Therefore the pastor was quite surprised when he read in the Saturday paper that Ralph had been arrested for propositioning a police "decoy." The pastor and a church elder visited Ralph in jail. At that time Ralph insisted he had only "wanted to talk to" the woman; he hadn't intended to have sexual relations with her. He neither acknowledged nor confessed any real sin. After

Ralph's release the matter of his conduct was brought before the church board. Ralph's roommate revealed that Ralph's arrest was not a one-time occurrence. Ralph had been involved in numerous incidents of immorality. The steps of Matt 18:15–17 were carefully followed, giving ample time for repentance and change after each stage. When the matter was lovingly and grievingly shared with the congregation, the brother left the church rather than confess and repent of his wrong. Five years passed. During that time God worked on Ralph's heart. After five years of heartache, misery, and resisting God, Ralph wrote a letter of confession and repentance which was read to the church. The church board then met with him and discerned that his repentance was genuine. *Rejoicing, they literally gave him a sport coat, had a gold ring made for his finger, and celebrated with him over a veal dinner* [echoes of the parable of the prodigal son]! Ralph has walked with God ever since (emphasis mine).[1]

The spiritual benefits of church discipline may actually transform *an entire community*. Consider the following hypothetical example and scenario of how this might be true.

Todd and Amy both came from broken families, where divorce was prevalent in their family upbringing. In light of their inherent fears of divorce, this young Christian couple decided it would be appropriate to try living together first to see if they were compatible partners for a marriage. When a few members of the church discovered that Todd and Amy were "living in sin," a spiritually mature deacon visited them in their home and gently confronted them. The deacon was aware of and sensitive to the family history of divorce and lovingly from the Scriptures showed them what a biblical marriage looks like and how their sinful start to a potential long-term relationship may actually be counterproductive, since statistics show that couples who live together prior to marriage are more likely to end in divorce than those who do not. The deacon (along with his wife) offered to house Amy in their home and serve as mentors for this young couple as they both committed themselves to pre-marital counseling with a local Christian counselor. After some initial hesitation, Todd and Amy confessed their fears about marriage and their sinful decision to cohabitate to God and agreed to separate and follow the deacon's plan.

After several months of counseling and private biblical study with the deacon and his wife, Todd and Amy took the step of uniting them-

1. Laney, *A Guide to Church Discipline*, 90–91.

selves in marriage (with the deacon and his wife as members of the wedding party) and subsequently offered up their testimony before the entire church about how the Lord had sent this deacon couple into their lives to help restore them on the path for marriage that God intends. Amazingly, this couple's testimony had such an impact on the church that many couples who were struggling in their marriage began coming to the deacon and his wife for counsel. Inevitably, this led the elders and pastors of the church to hold a marriage seminar (bringing in guest speakers), and an entire new ministry of the church geared toward strengthening marriages was formulated in the congregation. What began as simply an obedient step of church discipline on a young Christian couple evolved into a huge blessing for the entire congregation, whereby marriages were strengthened and a genuine openness and intimacy developed within the congregation. Such is the spiritual blessing that may come to an entire flock due to one obedient act of church discipline in accordance with Matthew 18.

Could it be that the church might experience revival and renewal in a new and fresh way as it commits itself to recovering a biblical understanding and implementation of the practice of church discipline? Oh, the depth and riches of knowing the God of grace and his purposes within church discipline in such a way that we might find our ministry of the gospel more effective and the transformation of lives more commonplace as we are committed to this path of discipleship.

In a practical manner, the church of today must be proactively teaching about the nature and purpose of church discipline, perhaps long before it needs to be implemented.[2] We further must be intentionally developing and training disciples and instructing new members, even before corrective church discipline is necessary.[3] As pastors, teachers, and lay leaders, we must foster and develop a culture of accountability to God

2. In a "sue-happy" culture, churches would do well to protect themselves by clearly defining the commitment to church discipline and the expectations of their members to submit to this biblical practice in their by-laws.

3. Don Cox writes, "As a matter of observation, I believe that most churches will have to begin by reinstating formative discipline before they can begin again to utilize corrective discipline." Cox, "The Forgotten Side of Church Discipline," 57, n. 37. Along the same lines, Kitchens reminds us of the task that lies ahead. He writes, "The church of the future may have a more complicated struggle than even the churches today. Without disciplinary boundaries that are clear yet pliable, the church cannot become a covenant community, separate from the world and not a captive of the culture." Kitchens, "Perimeters of Corrective Church Discipline," 213.

and one another, all the while seasoning the atmosphere with a dynamic attitude and presence of forgiveness and grace so that the church is a safe place for us to grow. We are to be a reconciling community of reconciled people *in action*. Each case of discipline is unique, and great wisdom and care must be used lest we fall into abuse (and with abuse will come the inevitable pendulum swing of the cessation of the practice). But in an age where moral and doctrinal compromise (relativity) is running rampant in the secular world as well as in the church, the church committed to church discipline assures itself of a healthy, God-glorifying, nurturing spiritual environment and secure identity as the people of God who will receive his blessings in this age and in the age to come.

Many people fear that drawing boundaries and enforcing church discipline might actually stifle church growth or simply cause the church to lose people to the church down the street.[4] As Roy Knuteson has aptly said, "Fearing the loss of members and a possible church split, it [the church] neglects the very thing that will cure its ills."[5] But in actuality, the drawing of ethical and doctrinal boundaries and the implementation of formative discipline may cause God's blessings to be poured out on the ministry committed to biblical principles, and this may actually lead to church growth.[6]

The following represents a few more minor theological implications that may be drawn from our study.

(A) Critics of the penal substitutionary model of atonement have not fully considered the consequences of abandoning this doctrine. If Christ did not fully pay the penalty for human sin on the cross, then we are still liable before a holy God, and the sacrifice of Christ is insufficient for us to confidently say that there is therefore now no condemnation for those who are in Christ Jesus. Further, the abandonment of the penal substitutionary atonement model may have an impact on the practice of

---

4. Jay Adams has a helpful chapter on how to carry out discipline between churches that are not related denominationally, as well as how to handle church-hoppers, divisive persons, and people who come from liberal churches. See Adams, *Handbook of Church Discipline*, 99–110.

5. Knuteson, *Calling the Church to Discipline*, 122.

6. Stanley Hauerwas writes, "Churches characterized by compassion and care no longer are able to retain membership, particularly that of their own children, whereas conservative churches that make moral conformity and/or discipline their primary focus continue to grow." Hauerwas, "Discipleship as a Craft, Church as a Disciplined Community," 882.

church discipline, whereby it may necessitate it being a form of retributive justice, contrary to the biblical witness. And if it did become retributive in nature, then we would be forced to see it as a spiritual atonement for our own sins, and this may threaten the evangelical doctrine of salvation by grace through faith alone.

(B) The intimacy of the covenant relationship between God and the believer is often couched in metaphorical language that is suggestive of a father-son relationship, especially in the context of discipline. This fatherly language and the designation of sonship became a powerful source of assurance and an affirmation of the covenant relationship that called Israel to a willing, obedient, and beneficial submission to the discipline of God. Therefore, if the language of sonship is stripped from away from the text under the auspices of a gender neutral translation, this circumvents this critical covenant language that became a part of Israel's identity and history and a part of the eschatological trajectory of God's fatherhood that is so critically weaved into the redemptive language of salvation history.[7]

(C) Theologians would do well to pay close attention to the individual nuances specific to the context of the passage they are considering in the development of their overall biblical and systematic theology.[8] For example, we discovered the richness and complexity of divine discipline throughout redemption history by avoiding the collapse of the idea of discipline into a single concept. This actually helped us capture a richer understanding of God's purposes in discipline and aided in our understanding of what is continuous and discontinuous in light of the shadow of the cross. Further, the redemptive historical approach shows much promise for the future of systematic theology, as it helps us learn how to better place ourselves in God's overarching redemptive plan (and in a community) while achieving a more comprehensive view of the nature, character, and purposes of God, who has clearly revealed himself in history.

I offer this study as an aid not simply to academia, but primarily to the glory of God and to his church, so that we may begin to live biblically

---

7. We specifically noted how the sonship language found in Hebrews 12 may have had a comforting effect and would have served as a powerful source of hope and assurance for the Jewish Christians who were suffering, but who needed to be encouraged to see the suffering as a form of divine discipline. See chapter 4, n. 89.

8. See the important article and contribution by Shultz, "Integrating Old Testament Theology and Exegesis: Literary, Thematic, and Canonical Issues," in VanGemeren, A Guide to Old Testament Theology and Exegesis, 182–202.

and think theologically about whose and who we are and what we are called to do as God's chosen people. If we are to be a church committed to a ministry of reconciliation, glorifying God, and building his kingdom, then it is imperative that a proper understanding and faithful implementation of biblical church discipline take place. We must be a church that proclaims a gospel of power over sin. Indeed, we must proclaim and embody the love of God that rescues us from that sin. In this way, we may confidently look forward to the chorus:

> Hallelujah! For our Lord God Almighty reigns. Let us rejoice and be glad and give him glory! For the wedding of the Lamb has come, and *his bride has made herself ready* (Rev 19:6b–7 NIV, emphasis mine).

Bibliography

Achtemeier, Elizabeth. "God the Father or God the Mother?" *Mission and Ministry* 8 (1990): 18–30.

Ackroyd, Peter R. *2 Samuel*. Cambridge Bible Commentary. Cambridge: Cambridge University, 1977.

Adams, Jay. *Handbook of Church Discipline*. Grand Rapids, MI: Zondervan, 1986.

Allen, Leslie C. "זכר." In *New International Dictionary of Old Testament Theology and Exegesis*. Vol. 1, ed. Willem A. VanGemeren, 1100–1106. Grand Rapids, MI: Zondervan, 1997.

Alston, William P. "Literal Talk of God: Its Possibility and Function." In *This Is My Name Forever: The Trinity and Gender Language for God*, ed. Alvin F. Kimel Jr., 136–60. Downers Grove, IL: InterVarsity, 2001.

Anderson, Francis I. *Job: Introduction and Commentary*. Tyndale Old Testament Commentaries, no. 13. Downers Grove, IL: InterVarsity, 1976.

Armstrong, John. "The Trinity: What and Why?" *Reformation and Revival Journal* 10, no. 3 (2001): 7–14.

Arnold, Bill T. *1 and 2 Samuel*. The NIV Application Commentary. Grand Rapids, MI: Zondervan, 2003.

Augustine, St. "Answer to the Letter of Petilian, Bishop of Cirta." In *Nicene and Post-Nicene Fathers of the Christian Church*, vol. 4, ed. Philip Schaff, 519–628. Grand Rapids, MI: Eerdmans, 1956.

———. *The Works of Saint Augustine: A Translation for the Twenty-first Century, Sermons 94A-147A on the New Testament*. Part 3, vol.4. Translated by Edmund Hill, ed. John E. Rotelle. Brooklyn, NY: New City Press, 1990.

———. *The Works of Saint Augustine: A Translation for the Twenty-first Century, Letters 1–99*. Part 2, vol. 1. Translated by Roland Teske, ed. John E. Rotelle. Hyde Park, NY: New City Press, 2001.

Baber, Harriet. "Abba, Father: Inclusive Language and Theological Silence." *Faith and Philosophy* 16, no. 3 (1999): 423–32.

Badcock, Gary. "Whatever Happened to God the Father?" *Crux* 36, no. 3 (2000): 2–12.

Baker, David W. "Aspects of Grace in the Pentateuch." *Ashland Theological Journal* 29 (1997): 7–22.

Baker, Don. *Beyond Forgiveness: The Healing Touch of Church Discipline*. Portland, OR: Multnomah, 1984.

Baker, J. Wayne. "Calvin's Discipline and the Early Reformed Tradition: Bullinger and Calvin." In *Calviniana: Ideas and Influence of Jean Calvin*. Vol. 10, Sixteenth Century Essays and Studies, ed. Robert V. Schnucker, 107–19. Kirksville, MO: Sixteenth Century Journal Publishers, 1988.

Baldwin, Joyce G. *1 and 2 Samuel: An Introduction and Commentary*. Tyndale Old Testament Commentaries. Downers Grove, IL: InterVarsity, 1988.

Barr, James. "'Abba, Father,' and the Familiarity of Jesus' Speech." *Theology* 91 (1988): 173–9.

Barrett, C. K. *The Second Epistle to the Corinthians*. Black's New Testament Commentary. Peabody, MA: Hendrickson, 1973.

Barth, Karl. *The Theology of Schleiermacher*. Lectures at Göttingen, Winter Semester of 1923/24. Translated by Geoffrey W. Bromiley, ed. Dietrich Ritschl. Grand Rapids, MI: Eerdmans, 1982.

Beentjes, Pancratius C. "They Saw That His Forehead Was Leprous (2 Chr 26:20): The Chronicle Narrative of Uzziah's Leprosy." In *Purity and Holiness: The Heritage of Leviticus*, ed. M. J. H. M. Poorthuis and J. Schwartz, 61–72. Leiden, Netherlands: Brill, 2000.

Bender, Harold. S. "The Mennonite Conception of the Church and Its Relation to Community Building." *Concern* 18 (July 1971): 25–35.

Best, Thomas F., and Martin Robra, eds. *Ecclesiology and Ethics: Ecumenical Ethical Engagement, Moral Formation, and the Nature of the Church*. Geneva, Switzerland: World Council of Churches, 1997.

Betz, Otto. "Jesus and Isaiah 53." In *Jesus and the Suffering Servant: Isaiah 53 and Christian Origins*, ed. William Bellinger Jr. and William R. Farmer, 70–87. Harrisburg, PA: Trinity Press, 1998.

Blocher, Henri. "The Sacrifice of Jesus Christ: The Current Theological Situation." *European Journal of Theology* 8, no. 1 (1999): 23–36.

Block, Daniel I. *The Gods of the Nations*. 2d ed. Studies in Near Eastern National Theology. Grand Rapids, MI: Baker Academic, 2000.

Blomberg, Craig L. *Matthew*. The New American Commentary. Nashville: Broadman, 1992.

———. *1 Corinthians*. The NIV Application Commentary. Grand Rapids, MI: Zondervan, 1994.

Bonhoeffer, Dietrich. *Life Together*. San Francisco, CA: Harper & Row, 1954.

Bray, Gerald. "Evangelicals Losing Their Way: The Doctrine of the Trinity." In *The Compromised Church*, ed. John H. Armstrong, 53–65. Wheaton, IL: Crossway, 1998.

Brock, Rita Nakashima. "And a Little Child Will Lead Us: Christology and Abuse." In *Christianity, Patriarchy, and Abuse: A Feminist Critique*, ed. Joanne Carlson Brown and Carol R. Bihn, 42–61. New York: Pilgrim, 1989.

Brown, Harold O. J. "The Role of Discipline in the Church." *Covenant Quarterly* 41, no.3 (1983): 51–2.

Brown, Joanne Carlson, and Carole R. Bohn, eds. *Christianity, Patriarchy, and Abuse: A Feminist Critique*. New York: Pilgrim, 1989.

Brown, Peter. *Augustine of Hippo: A Biography*, 2d ed. Berkeley, CA: University of California, 2000.

Bruce, F. F. *The Epistle to the Hebrews*, rev. ed. The New International Commentary on the New Testament. Grand Rapids, MI: Eerdmans, 1990.

Brueggemann, Walter. *David's Truth in Israel's Imagination and Memory*. Minneapolis, MN: Fortress, 1985.

———. *Theology of the Old Testament: Testimony, Dispute, Advocacy*. Minneapolis, MN: Fortress, 1997.

Buckley, James J., and David S. Yeago, eds. *Knowing the Triune God: The Work of the Spirit in the Practices of the Church*. Grand Rapids, MI: Eerdmans, 2001.

Burnett, Amy Nelson. *The Yoke of Christ: Martin Bucer and Christian Discipline*. Sixteenth Century Essays and Studies, vol. 26. Kirksville, MO: Sixteenth Century Journal Publishers, 1994.

Caird, George B. *The Language and Imagery of the Bible*. London: Gerald Duckworth & Co., 1980. Reprint, Grand Rapids, MI: Eerdmans, 1997.

Calderone, Philip J. *Dynastic Oracle and Suzerainty Treaty: 2 Samuel 7, 8-16*. Manila, Phillipines: Loyal House of Studies, 1966.

Calvin, John. *Institutes of the Christian Religion*. The Library of Christian Classics. 2 vols. Translated by Ford Lewis Battles, ed. John T. McNeIL Philadelphia, PA: Westminster, 1960.

———. *On the Doctrine and Worship of the Church*. Vol. 2, *Tracts and Treatises*. Translated by Henry Beveridge. Grand Rapids, MI: Eerdmans, 1958.

———. *In Defense of the Reformed Faith*. Vol. 3, *Tracts and Treatises*. Translated by Henry Beveridge. Grand Rapids, MI: Eerdmans, 1958.

———. vol. 2." In *Calvin's Commentaries*, Vol. 16. Translated by William Pringle. Reprint, Grand Rapids, MI: Baker 1999.

Carson, D. A. *The Gospel According to John*. Pillar New Testament Commentary. Grand Rapids, MI: Eerdmans, 1991.

———. *The Expositor's Bible Commentary, Matthew 13-28*. Grand Rapids, MI: Zondervan, 1995.

———. *The Difficult Doctrine of the Love of God*. Wheaton, IL: Crossway, 2000.

Childs, Brevard. *Isaiah*. Old Testament Library. Louisville, KY: Westminster John Knox, 2001.

Christian, C. W. *Friedrich Schleiermacher*. Makers of the Modern Mind, ed. Bob E. Patterson. Waco, TX: Word, 1979.

Clark, Mary T. *Augustine*. Washington DC: Georgetown University, 1994.

Clements, Keith. *Friedrich Schleiermacher: Pioneer of Modern Theology*. The Making of Modern Theology 1, ed. John de Gruchy. London: Collins, 1987.

Consedine, Jim, and Helen Bowen, eds. *Restorative Justice: Contemporary Themes and Practice*. Lyttelton, New Zealand: Ploughshares, 1999.

Cooper John W. *Our Father in Heaven: Christian Faith and Inclusive Language for God*. Grand Rapids, MI: Baker, 1998.

Coppedge, Allan. *Portraits of God: A Biblical Theology of Holiness*. Downers Grove, IL: InterVarsity, 2001.

Corcoran, John Anthony. *Augustinus Contra Donatistas*. Dissertation Monograph Series. Donaldson, IN: Graduate Theological Foundation, 1997.

Cox, Dan R. "Church Discipline in Growing Churches." *Strategies for Today's Leader* 33, no. 2 (1996): 5-7.

———. "The Forgotten Side of Church Discipline." *The Southern Baptist Journal of Theology* 4, no. 4 (2000): 44-58.

Craig, Hugh. "The Word and Discipline in the Church." *Churchman* 103, no. 2 (1989): 150-65.

Craig, Kenneth M. Jr. "The Character(ization) of God in 2 Samuel 7:1-17." *Semeia* 63 (1993): 159-76.

Craigie, Peter C. *The Book of Deuteronomy*. The New International Commentary on the Old Testament. Grand Rapids, MI: Eerdmans, 1976.

Crespin, Rémi. *Ministère et Sainteté: Pastorale du Clergé et Solution de la Crise Donatiste dans la Vie et la Doctrine de Saint Augustin.* Paris: Études Augustiniennes, 1965.

Cross, Frank Moore. *Canaanite Myth and Hebrew Epic: Essays in the History of the Religion of Israel.* Cambridge, MA: Harvard University, 1979.

Croy, N. Clayton. *Endurance in Suffering: Hebrews 12:1–13 in Its Rhetorical, Religious, and Philosophical Context.* Cambridge, UK: Cambridge University, 1998.

D' Angelo, Mary Rose. "Abba and 'Father': Imperial Theology and the Jesus Traditions." *Journal of Biblical Literature* 111 (1992): 611–30.

Daane, James. "Father." In *The International Standard Bible Encyclopedia.* Vol. 2, ed. Geoffrey Bromiley, 284–6. Grand Rapids, MI: Eerdmans, 1982.

Daly, Mary. *Beyond God the Father.* Boston, MA: Beacon, 1973.

Danker, Frederick William, ed. *A Greek-English Lexicon of the New Testament and other Early Christian Literature (BGAD),* 3d ed. Chicago: University of Chicago, 2000.

Davis, George B. "Whatever Happened to Church Discipline?" *Criswell Theological Review* 1 (1987): 345–61.

Davis, Kenneth R. "No Discipline, No Church: An Anabaptist Contribution to the Reformed Tradition." *The Sixteenth Century Journal* 13, no. 4 (1982): 43–58.

De Ridder, Richard R. "John Calvin's Views on Discipline: A Comparison of the *Institution* of 1536 and the *Institutes* of 1559." *Calvin Theological Journal* 21, no. 2 (1986): 223–30.

Delitzsch, F. *Proverbs, Ecclesiastes, Song of Solomon.* Translated by M. G. Easton. Vol. 6, *Commentary on the Old Testament,* by C. F. Keil and F. Delitzsch. Edinburgh: T&T Clark, 1866–1891. Reprint, Peabody, MA: Hendrickson, 1966.

Demarest, Bruce. *The Cross and Salvation: The Doctrine of Salvation.* Wheaton: Crossway, 1997.

DeSilva, David A. *Perseverance in Gratitude: A Socio-Rhetorical Commentary on the Epistle "to the Hebrews."* Grand Rapids, MI: Eerdmans, 2000.

Dever, Mark. *Nine Marks of a Healthy Church.* Wheaton, IL: Crossway, 2000.

————. "Biblical Church Discipline." *The Southern Baptist Journal of Theology* 4, no. 4 (2000): 28–43.

Driver, John. *Understanding the Atonement for the Mission of the Church.* Scottsdale: Herald, 1986.

Domeris, W. R. "ירה." In *New International Dictionary of Old Testament Theology and Exegesis.* Vol. 1, ed. Willem A. VanGemeren, 1055–7. Grand Rapids, MI: Zondervan, 1997.

Du Veer, A. C. "L'exploitation du schisme maximianiste par Saint Augustin dans la lutte contre Donatisme." *RechAug* 3 (1965): 219–37.

Edwards, Jonathan. *The Works of Jonathan Edwards.* 2 Vols. Great Britain, 1834. Reprint, Peabody, MA: Hendrickson, 2000.

Ellingworth, Paul. *The Epistle to the Hebrews.* The New International Greek Testament Commentary. Grand Rapids, MI: Eerdmans, 1993.

Erickson, Millard. *Where Is Theology Going?* Grand Rapids, MI: Baker, 1994.

Estep, William R. *The Anabaptist Story,* rev. ed. Grand Rapids, MI: Eerdmans, 1975.

Estes, Daniel J. *Hear, My Son: Teaching and Learning in Proverbs 1–9.* Grand Rapids, MI: Eerdmans, 1997.

Evans, G. R. *Problems of Authority in the Reformation Debates.* Cambridge, UK: Cambridge University, 1992.

Fee, Gordon. *1 Corinthians*. New International Commentary on the New Testament. Grand Rapids, MI: Eerdmans, 1987.

Feinberg, John S. *No One Like Him: The Doctrine of God*. Wheaton, IL: Crossway, 2001.

Ferguson, Everett. *Christian Life: Ethics, Morality, and Discipline in the Early Church*. Studies in Early Christianity. New York: Garland, 1993.

Ferguson, Sinclair B. *Children of the Living God*. Colorado Springs, CO: NavPress, 1987.

Fitzgerald, Allan D. *Augustine Through the Ages: An Encyclopedia*. Grand Rapids, MI: Eerdmans, 1999.

Forkman, Göran. *The Limits of the Religious Community*. Coniectanea Biblica. New Testament Series 5. Translated by Pearl Sjölander. Lund, Sweden: CWK Gleerup, 1972.

Foucault, Michel. *Discipline and Punish: The Birth of the Prison*, 2d ed. Translated by Alan Sheridan. New York: Vintage, 1995.

Frame, John. *The Doctrine of God*. Phillipsburg, NJ: Presbyterian and Reformed, 2002.

Frend, W. H. C. *The Donatist Church: A Movement of Protest in Roman North Africa*. New York: Oxford University, 1952. Reprint, New York: Oxford University, 1985.

Fulop, Timothy E. "The Third Mark of the Church? Church Discipline in the Reformed and Anabaptist Reformations." *The Journal of Religious History* 19, no. 1 (1995): 26–42.

Gage, Ken, and Joy Gage. *Restoring Fellowship: Judgment and Church Discipline*. Chicago: Moody, 1984.

Gammie, John G. "The Theology of Retribution in the Book of Deuteronomy." *Catholic Biblical Quarterly* 32 (1970): 1–12.

Garland, David E. *2 Corinthians*. The New American Commentary. Nashville, TN: Broadman & Holman, 1999.

Garrett, Duane A. *Proverbs, Ecclesiastes, Song of Songs*. The New American Commentary, no. 14. Nashville, TN: Broadman, 1993.

Geffré, Claude. "Father as the Proper Name of God." In *God as Father?* ed. Johannes-Baptist Metz and Edward Schillebeeckx, 43–50. New York: Seabury, 1981.

Gelander, Shamai. *David and His God*. Translated by Ruth Debel. Jerusalem Biblical Studies, no. 5. Jerusalem, Israel: Simor Ltd., 1991.

George, Timothy. *Galatians*. The New American Commentary, no. 30. Nashville, TN: Broadman & Holman, 1994.

Gibson, J. C. L. *Language and Imagery in the Old Testament*. Peabody, MA: Hendrickson, 1998.

Girard, Rene. *Violence and the Sacred*. Translated by Patrick Gregory. Baltimore, MD: John Hopkins University Press, 1977.

———. *The Scapegoat*. Baltimore, MD: John Hopkins University Press, 1986.

Girolimon, Michael Thomas. "John Calvin and Menno Simons on Religious Discipline: A Difference in Degree and Kind." *Fides et Historia* 27 (1995): 5–29.

Goldingay, John, ed. *Atonement Today*. London: SPCK, 1995.

Gorringe, Timothy. *God's Just Vengeance*. Cambridge, UK: Cambridge University Press, 1996.

Grebel, Conrad. *The Sources of Swiss Anabaptism, The Grebel Letters and Related Documents*. Classics of the Radical Reformation, no. 4, ed. Leland Harder. Scottsdale, AZ: Herald, 1985.

Green, Joel B., and Mark D. Baker. *Recovering the Scandal of the Cross: Atonement in New Testament and Contemporary Contexts*. Downers Grove, IL: InterVarsity, 2000.

Grudem, Wayne. *Systematic Theology: An Introduction to Biblical Doctrine.* Grand Rapids, MI: Zondervan, 1994.

Gunton, Colin E. *The Actuality of the Atonement.* Edinburg, Scotland: T&T Clark, 1988.

Gunton, Colin E., and Daniel W. Hardy, eds. *On Being The Church: Essays on Christian Community.* Edinburg, Scotland: T&T Clark, 1989.

Hahn, Scott. *A Father Who Keeps His Promises: God's Covenant Love in Scripture.* Ann Arbor, MI: Servant, 1998.

Hamerton-Kelly, Robert. *God the Father: Theology and Patriarchy in the Teaching of Jesus.* Philadelphia, PA: Fortress, 1979.

Hanson, R. P. C. *God: Creator, Saviour, Spirit.* London: S. C. M., 1960.

Harris, Gerald. "The Beginnings of Church Discipline: 1 Corinthians 5." *New Testament Studies* 37 (1991): 1–21.

Hartley, John E. *The Book of Job.* The New International Commentary on the Old Testament. Grand Rapids, MI: Eerdmans, 1988.

———. "גער." In *New International Dictionary of Old Testament Theology and Exegesis.* Vol. 1, ed. Willem A. VanGemeren, 884–887. Grand Rapids, MI: Zondervan, 1997.

———. "יכח." In *New International Dictionary of Old Testament Theology and Exegesis.* Vol. 2, ed. Willem A. VanGemeren, 441–445. Grand Rapids, MI: Zondervan, 1997.

Hauerwas, Stanley. "Discipline as a Craft, Church as a Disciplined Community." *Christian Century* 108 (1991): 881–884.

Hays, Richard B. *The Moral Vision of the New Testament: A Contemporary Introduction to New Testament Ethics.* New York: HarperCollins, 1996.

———. *First Corinthians.* Interpretation. Louisville, KY: John Knox, 1997.

Heschel, Abraham J. *The Prophets.* New York: HarperCollins, 1969. Reprint, Peabody, MA: Prince, 2000.

Hoffecker, W. A. "Friedrich Daniel Ernst Schleiermacher." In *Evangelical Dictionary of Theology,* 2d ed., ed. Walter A. Elwell, 1064–5. Grand Rapids, MI: Baker, 2001.

Horton, Michael S. *Covenant and Eschatology: The Divine Drama.* Louisville, KY: Westminster John Knox, 2002.

House, H. Wayne. *Charts of Christian Theology and Doctrine.* Grand Rapids, MI: Zondervan, 1992.

Hoyles, J. Arthur. *Punishment in the Bible.* London: Epworth, 1986.

Hubmaier, Balthasar. *Balthasar Hubmaier: Theologian of Anabaptism.* Classics of the Radical Reformation, no. 5. Translated and edited by H. Wayne Pipkin and John H. Yoder. Scottsdale, AZ: Herald, 1989.

———. "On Brotherly Discipline (1527)." In *Every Need Supplied: Mutual Aid and Christian Community in the Free Churches, 1525–1675,* trans. and ed. by Donald F. Durnbaugh, 27–37. Philadelphia, PA: Temple University, 1974.

Hulse, E. V. "The Nature of Biblical Leprosy." *Palestine Exploration Quarterly* 107 (1975): 87–105.

Hurowitz, Avigdor. *I Have Built You an Exalted House: Temple Building in the Bible in Light of Mesopotamian and Northwest Semitic Writings.* Journal for the Study of the Old Testament, Supplement, no. 115. Sheffield: JSOT Press, 1992.

Hütter, Reinhard. "The Church, the Knowledge of the Triune God: Practices, Doctrine and Theology." In *Knowing the Triune God: The Work of the Spirit in the Practices of the Church,* ed. James J. Buckley and David S. Yeago, 23–47. Grand Rapids, MI: Eerdmans, 2001.

Isom, Steven W. "The Concept of *Mûsār* in the Old Testament." M.Div. thesis, Emmanuel School of Religion, 1980.

Japhet, Sara. *1 and 2 Chronicles.* Old Testament Library. Louisville, KY: Westminster John Knox, 1993.

Jenkins, Gary. *In My Place: The Spirituality of Substitution.* Cambridge, UK: Grove Books, 1999.

Jeremias, Joachim. *New Testament Theology.* New York: Charles Scribner's Sons, 1971.

———. *The Prayers of Jesus.* London: S. C. M., 1976.

Jeschke, Martin. *Discipling in the Church.* Scottsdale, PA: Herald, 1988.

Jones, L. Gregory. *Embodying Forgiveness: A Theological Analysis.* Grand Rapids, MI: Eerdmans, 1995.

Josephus, Flavius. *The New Complete Works of Josephus,* rev. and exp. Translated by William Whiston. Grand Rapids, MI: Kregel, 1999.

Keating, Geoffrey I. *The Moral Problems of Fraternal, Paternal, and Judicial Correction According to Saint Augustine.* Rome: Pontificia Universitas Gregoriana, 1958.

Keleher, James P. *Saint Augustine's Notion of Schism in the Donatist Controversy.* Dissertationes ad Lauream. Mundelein, IL: Saint Mary of the Lake Seminary, 1961.

Keys, Gillian. *The Wages of Sin: A Reappraisal of the "Succession Narrative."* Journal for the Study of the Old Testament, Supplement, no. 221. Sheffield, UK: Sheffield Academic Press, 1996.

Kimel, Alvin F. Jr., ed. *Speaking the Christian God: The Holy Trinity and the Challenge of Feminism.* Grand Rapids, MI: Eerdmans, 1992.

———. *This Is My Name Forever: The Trinity and Gender Language for God.* Downers Grove, IL: InterVarsity, 2001.

Kingdon, D. P. "Discipline." In *New Dictionary of Biblical Theology,* ed. T. Desmond Alexander, Brian S. Rosner, D. A. Carson, and Graeme Goldsworthy, 448–50. Downers Grove, IL: InterVarsity, 2000.

Kirk, J. Andrew, and Kevin J. Vanhoozer, eds. *To Stake a Claim: Mission and the Western Crisis of Knowledge.* Maryknoll, NY: Orbis, 1999.

Klaasen, Walter, ed. *Anabaptism in Outline.* Scottsdale, AZ: Herald, 1981.

Knight, George W. III. *The Pastoral Epistles.* The New International Greek Testament Commentary. Grand Rapids, MI: Eerdmans, 1992.

Knuteson. Roy E. *Calling the Church to Discipline.* Nashville, TN: Action, 1977.

Krašovec's, Jože. "Is There a Doctrine of 'Collective Retribution' in the Hebrew Bible?" *Hebrew Union College Annual* 65 (1994): 25–89.

Kruse, Colin. "The Offender and the Offense in 2 Corinthians 2:5 and 7:12." *Evangelical Quarterly* 88, no. 2 (1988): 129–39.

Ladd, George E. *A Theology of the New Testament,* rev. ed. Grand Rapids, MI: Eerdmans, 1993.

Lampe, G. W. H. "Church Discipline and the Interpretation of the Epistles to the Corinthians." In *Christian History and Interpretation: Studies Presented to John Knox,* ed. W. R. Farmer, C. F. D. Moule, and R. R. Niebuhr. London: Cambridge University Press, 1967.

Lane, Anthony N. S. *John Calvin: Student of the Church Fathers.* Grand Rapids, MI: Baker, 1999.

Lane, Tony. "The Wrath of God as an Aspect of the Love of God." In *Nothing Greater, Nothing Better: Theological Essays on the Love of God,* ed. Kevin J. Vanhoozer, 138–67. Grand Rapids, MI: Eerdmans, 2001.

Lane, William L. *Hebrews 9–13*. Word Biblical Commentary, no. 47. Dallas, TX: Word, 1991.

Laney, J. Carl. *A Guide to Church Discipline*. Minneapolis, MN: Bethany House, 1985.

Lang, Bernhard. *The Hebrew God: Portrait of an Ancient Deity*. New Haven, CT: Yale University, 2002.

Larson, Knute. *1 and 2 Thessalonians, 1 and 2 Timothy, Titus, and Philemon*. Holman New Testament Commentary. Nashville, TN: Broadman & Holman, 2000.

Lauterbach, Mark. *The Transforming Community: The Practice of the Gospel in Church Discipline*. Carol Stream, IL: Reformation and Revival Ministries, 2003.

Letham, Robert. *The Work of Christ*. Downers Grove, IL: InterVarsity, 1993.

Lidgett, J. S. *The Fatherhood of God*. Edinburgh, Scotland: T&T Clark, 1902. Reprint, Minneapolis, MN: Bethany House, 1987.

Lincoln, Andrew T. *Ephesians*. Word Biblical Commentary, no. 42. Dallas, TX: Word, 1990.

Littell, Franklin Hamlin. *The Anabaptist View of the Church*, 2d ed. Beacon Hill, MA: Starr King, 1958.

Loetscher, Frederick. W. "St. Augustine's Conception of the State." In *Studies in Early Christianity: Church and State in the Early Church*. Vol. 7, ed. Everett Ferguson. New York: Garland, 1993.

Luck, Donald G. "Reaffirming the Image of God as 'Father.'" *Trinity Seminary Review* 16 (1994): 91–100.

Ludwig, Josef J. "The Relationship Between Sanctification and Church Discipline in Early Anabaptism." *Evangelical Journal* 14 (1996): 77–85.

Luther, Martin. "The Keys." In *Luther's Works*. Church and Ministry II. Vol. 40, ed. Conrad Bergendoff. Philadelphia, PA: Muhlenberg, 1958.

MacArthur. John Jr. *2 Corinthians*. The MacArthur New Testament Commentary. Chicago: Moody, 2003.

Mack, Alexander. *The Complete Works of Alexander Mack*. Translated by Donald Durnbaugh, ed. William R. Eberly. Winona Lake, IN: BMH Books, 1991.

Marchel, Witold. *Abba, Père! La Prière du Christ et des Chrétiens*. Rome: Biblical Institute, 1971.

Markus, Robert A. "Donatus, Donatism." In *Augustine Through the Ages: An Encyclopedia*, ed. Allan D. Fitzgerald, 284–287. Grand Rapids, MI: Eerdmans, 1999.

Marshall, Christopher D. *Beyond Retribution: A New Testament Vision for Justice, Crime, and Punishment*. Grand Rapids, MI: Eerdmans, 2001.

Marshall, Michael. *The Restless Heart: The Life and Influence of St. Augustine*. Grand Rapids, MI: Eerdmans, 1987.

Martin, Francis. *The Feminist Question: Feminist Theology in the Light of Christian Tradition*. Grand Rapids, MI: Eerdmans, 1994.

Martin, Maurice. "The Pure Church: The Burden of Anabaptism." *The Conrad Grebel Review* 1, no. 2 (1983): 29–41.

Mawhinney, Allen. "God as Father: Two Popular Theories Considered." *Journal of the Evangelical Theological Society* 31 (1988): 181–89.

McCarthy, Dennis J. "Notes on the Love of God in Deuteronomy and the Father-Son Relationship between Yahweh and Israel." *The Catholic Biblical Quarterly* 27 (1965): 144–7.

McCasland, Selby Vernon. "Abba, Father." *Journal of Biblical Theology* 72, no. 2 (1953): 79–91.

McClister, David. "Where Two or Three Are Gathered Together: Literary Structure as a Key to Meaning in Matt 17:22–20:19." *Journal of the Evangelical Theological Society* 39, no. 4 (1996): 549–58.

McDonald, H. D. *The Atonement of the Death of Christ*. Downers Grove, IL: InterVarsity, 1986.

———. *New Testament Concept of Atonement: The Gospel of the Calvary Event*. Grand Rapids, MI: Baker, 1994.

McDonnell, Kilian. *John Calvin, the Church, and the Eucharist*. Princeton, NJ: Princeton University, 1967.

McFague, Sallie. *Metaphorical Theology: Models of God in Religious Language*. Philadelphia, PA: Fortress, 1982.

McGrath, Alister. *Christian Theology: An Introduction*, 2d ed. Malden, MA: Blackwell, 1997.

McGrath, William R. *Christian Discipline: How and Why the Anabaptists Made Church Standards*. Carrollton, OH: Amish Mennonite Publications, 1989.

McKay, J. W. "Man's Love for God in Deuteronomy and the Father/Teacher–Son/Pupil Relationship." *Vetus Testamentum* 22, no. 4 (1972): 426–35.

McWilliams, David B. "Book Review: Nonviolent Atonement." *Westminster Theological Journal* 64, no. 2 (2002): 217–20.

Merdinger, J. E. *Rome and the African Church in the Time of Augustine*. New Haven, CT: Yale University, 1997.

Merrill, E. H. "יסר." In *New International Dictionary of Old Testament Theology and Exegesis*. Vol. 2, ed. Willem A. VanGemeren, 479–82. Grand Rapids, MI: Zondervan, 1997.

Milbank, John. *Theology and Social Theory: Beyond Secular Reason*. Cambridge, UK: Basil Blackwell, 1990.

Miller, John W. *Calling God "Father": Essays on the Bible, Fatherhood, and Culture*. New York: Paulist, 1999.

Mitchell, C. Ben. "The *SBTJ* Forum: Perspectives on Church Discipline." *The Southern Baptist Journal of Theology* 4, no. 4 (2000): 84–91.

Mohler, R. Albert. "Church Discipline: The Missing Mark." *The Southern Baptist Journal of Theology* 4, no. 4 (2000): 16–27.

———. "The Glory of Christ as Mediator." In *The Glory of Christ*, ed. John H. Armstrong, 57–75. Wheaton: Crossway, 2002.

Moltmann, Jürgen. "I Believe in God the Father: Patriarchal or Non-Patriarchal Reference." *Drew Gateway* 59 (1990): 3–25.

Monceaux, Paul. *Histoire Littéraire De L'Afrique Chrétienne: Depuis Les Origines Jusqu'à L'Invasion Arabe*. Vols. 6, 7. Paris: Leroux, 1901.

Moo, Douglas. *The Epistle to the Romans*. The New International Commentary on the New Testament. Grand Rapids, MI: Eerdmans, 1996.

Morris, Leon. *The Apostolic Preaching of the Cross*, 3d ed. Grand Rapids, MI: Eerdmans, 1965.

———. "Theories of Atonement." In *Evangelical Dictionary of Theology*, 2d ed., ed. Walter A. Elwell, 116–9. Grand Rapids, MI: Baker, 2001.

Mounce, Robert. *Matthew*. New International Biblical Commentary. Peabody, MA: Hendrickson, 1991.

Muller, Kirk J. "The Concept of Discipline in the Book of Proverbs." Th.M. thesis, Dallas Theological Seminary, 1973.

Murray, Stuart. *Explaining Church Discipline*. Tonbridge, Kent, UK: Sovereign World, 1995.

Mutetei, Philip. "Church Discipline: The Great Omission." *Africa Journal of Evangelical Theology* 18, no. 1 (1999): 3–28.

Naudé, Jackie A. "חרם." In *New International Dictionary of Old Testament Theology and Exegesis*. Vol. 2, ed. Willem A. VanGemeren, 276–77. Grand Rapids, MI: Zondervan, 1997.

Nel, Philip J. "שׁלם." In *New International Dictionary of Old Testament Theology and Exegesis*. Vol. 4, ed. Willem A. VanGemeren, 130–5. Grand Rapids, MI: Zondervan, 1997.

Niebuhr, Richard R. *Schleiermacher on Christ and Religion: A New Introduction*. New York: Charles Scribner's Sons, 1964.

Oden, Thomas C. *Corrective Love: The Power of Communion Discipline*. Saint Louis, MO: Concordia, 1995.

Oswalt, John N. *The Book of Isaiah, Chapters 40–66*. New International Commentary on the Old Testament. Grand Rapids, MI: Eerdmans, 1998.

Overland, Paul. "Did the Sage Draw from the Shema? A Study of Proverbs 3:1–12." *Catholic Biblical Quarterly* 62 (2000): 424–40.

Packer, J. I. "What Did the Cross Achieve?: The Logic of Penal Substitution." *Tyndale Bulletin* 25 (1974): 3–45.

———. "Anger." In *New Dictionary of Biblical Theology*, ed. T. Desmond Alexander, Brian S. Rosner, D. A. Carson, and Graeme Goldsworthy, 381–383. Downers Grove, IL: InterVarsity, 2000.

Packer, J. I. and Mark Dever. *In My Place Condemned He Stood: Celebrating the Glory of the Atonement*. Wheaton, IL: Crossway Books, 2007.

Parmelee, Daniel. "An Exegetical Study of Ecclesiastical Discipline: Comparing Paul's Application with Christ's Principles." Masters thesis., Trinity Evangelical Divinity School, 1969.

Pascuzzi, Maria. *Ethics, Ecclesiology, and Church Discipline: A Rhetorical Analysis of 1 Corinthians 5*. Rome: Gregorian University Press, 1997.

Peterson, David, ed. *Where Wrath and Mercy Meet: Proclaiming the Atonement Today*. Carlisle, UK: Paternoster, 2001.

Philips, Dirk. *The Writings of Dirk Philips, 1504–1568*. Translated and edited by Cornelius J. Dyck, William E. Keeney, and Alvin J. Beachy. Scottsdale, AZ: Herald, 1992.

Pipkin, H. Wayne, and John H. Yoder, eds. *Balthasar Hubmaier: Theologian of Anabaptism*. Classics of the Radical Reformation, no. 5. Scottsdale, AZ: Herald, 1989.

Placher, William C. *Jesus the Savior: The Meaning of Jesus Christ for Christian Faith*. Louisville, KY: Westminster John Knox, 2001.

Pritchard, James B., ed. *Ancient Near Eastern Texts Relating to the Old Testament*, 3d ed., with supplement. Princeton, NJ: Princeton University, 1969.

Ramm, Bernard. *The Evangelical Heritage: A Study in Historical Theology*. Waco, TX: Word, 1973. Reprint, Grand Rapids, MI: Baker, 2000.

Redeker, Martin. *Schleiermacher: Life and Thought*. Translated by John Wallhauser. Philadelphia: Fortress, 1973.

Reed, Esther. "Friedrich Daniel Ernst Schleiermacher." In *The Dictionary of Historical Theology*, ed. Trevor Hart, 507–509. Grand Rapids, MI: Eerdmans, 2000.

Richard, Michael. *The Nature and Necessity of Christ' Church*. New York: Alba House, 1983.

Ricouer, Paul. "Fatherhood: From Phantasm to Symbol." In *The Conflict of Interpretations*, ed. Don Ihde. Evanston, IL: Northwestern University, 1974.

Ringgren, Helmer. "אב." In *The Theological Dictionary of the Old Testament*, rev. ed. Vol. 1, translated by John T. Willis, ed. G. Johannes Botterweck and Helmer Ringgren, 2–19. Grand Rapids, MI: Eerdmans, 1974.

Rosner, Brian. "Corporate Responsibility in 1 Corinthians 5." *New Testament Studies* 38 (1992): 470–73.

———. *Paul, Scripture, and Ethics: A Study of 1 Corinthians 5–7*. Grand Rapids, MI: Baker, 1999.

Ross, Allen P. "שׁם." In *The New International Dictionary of Old Testament Theology and Exegesis*. Vol. 4, ed. Willem A. VanGemeren, 147–51. Grand Rapids, MI: Zondervan, 1997.

Roth, John D. "The Church 'Without Spot or Wrinkle' in Anabaptist Experience." In *Without Spot or Wrinkle: Reflecting Theologically on the Nature of the Church*. Occasional Papers 21, ed. Karl Koop and Mary H. Schertz, 7–25. Elkhart, IN: Institute of Mennonite Studies, 2000.

Ruether, Rosemary Radford. *Sexism and God-Talk: Toward a Feminist Theology*. Boston, MA: Beacon, 1993.

Ryken, Leland, James C. Wilhoit, and Tremper Longman III, eds. *Dictionary of Biblical Imagery*. Downers Grove, IL: InterVarsity, 1998.

Sanders, Jim Alvin. *Suffering as Divine Discipline in the Old Testament and Post-Biblical Judaism*. Colgate-Rochester Divinity School Bulletin, 28. Rochester, NY: Colgate-Rochester Divinity School, 1955.

Schleiermacher, Friedrich. *The Christian Faith*. Edited by H. R. Mackintosh and J. S. Stewart. Edinburgh, Scotland: T&T Clark, 1928. Reprint, New York: Charles Scribner's Sons, 1956.

Schniedewind, William M. *Society and the Promise to David: The Reception History of 2 Samuel 7:1–17*. New York: Oxford University, 1999.

Schrenk, Gottlob. "πατήρ." In *The Theological Dictionary of the New Testament*. Vol. 5, translated by Geoffrey W. Bromiley, ed. Gerhard Friedrich, 945–59. Grand Rapids, MI: Eerdmans, 1967.

Schultz, Richard. "Justice." In the *New International Dictionary of Old Testament Theology and Exegesis*. Vol. 4, ed. Willem A. VanGemeren, 836–46. Grand Rapids, MI: Zondervan, 1997.

———. "Integrating Old Testament Theology and Exegesis: Literary, Thematic, and Canonical Issues." In *A Guide to Old Testament Theology and Exegesis*, ed. Willem A. VanGemeren, 182–202. Grand Rapids, MI: Zondervan, 1999.

Shults, F. Leron, and Steven J. Sandage. *The Faces of Forgiveness*. Grand Rapids, MI: Baker, 2003.

Seitz, Christopher R. *Word Without End: The Old Testament as Abiding Theological Witness*. Grand Rapids, MI: Eerdmans, 1998.

Simons, Menno. *The Complete Writings of Menno Simons, 1496–1591*. Translated by Leonard Verduin, ed. J. C. Wenger. Scottsdale, AZ: Herald, 1984.

Snyder. C. Arnold. *The Life and Thought of Michael Sattler*. Studies in Anabaptist and Mennonite History, no. 26. Scottsdale, AZ: Herald, 1984.

———. *The Swiss Anabaptists: A Brief Summary of Their History and Beliefs*, rev. ed. Ephrata, PA: Eastern Mennonite Publications, 1994.

———. *Anabaptist History and Theology: An Introduction*. Kitchener, ON: Pandora, 1995.

Soskice, Janet M. *Metaphor and Religious Language*. Oxford: Clarendon, 1985.

South, J. T. "A Critique of the Curse/Death Interpretation of 1 Corinthians 5:1-8." *New Testament Studies* 39 (1993): 539-61.

Spalding, James C. "Discipline as a Mark of the True Church in its Sixteenth Century Lutheran Context." In *Piety, Politics, and Ethics*. Vol. 3, Sixteenth Century Essays and Studies, Reformation Studies in Honor of George Wolfgang Forell, ed. Carter Lindberg, 119-38. Kirksville, Mo.: Sixteenth Century Journal Publishers, 1984.

Spinks, Bryan D. "A Seventeenth-Century Reformed Liturgy of Penance and Reconciliation." *Scottish Journal of Theology* 42, no. 2 (1989): 183-97.

Stoney, J. B. *Discipline in the School of God: Its Nature and Effect*. London: Billings & Sons, 1970.

Stott, John R. W. *The Cross of Christ*. Downers Grove, IL: InterVarsity, 1986.

Studer, Basil. "Die Kirche als Schule des Herrn bei Augustinus von Hippo." In *Stimuli: Exegese und Ihre Hermeneutik in Antike und Christentum, Festschrift für Ernst Dassmann*, ed. George Schöllgen and Clemens Scholten, 485-98. Münster: Aschendorff, 1996.

Sunshine, Glenn S. "Discipline as the Third Mark of the Church: Three Views." *Calvin Theological Journal* 33 (1998): 469-80.

Swain, Scott Rupert. "The Fatherly Discipline of God: The Meaning and Significance of a Biblical Metaphor." Unpublished doctoral seminar paper, Trinity International University, Fall 1999.

The Swiss Anabaptists: A Brief Summary of Their History and Beliefs, rev. ed. Ephrata, PA: Eastern Mennonite Publications, 1994.

Tate, Marvin. *Psalms 51-100*. Word Biblical Commentary, no. 20. Dallas, TX: Word, 1990.

ten Doornkaat Koolman, Jacobus. *Dirk Philips: Friend and Colleague of Menno Simons*. Translated by William E. Keeney, ed. C. Arnold Snyder. Kitchener, ON: Pandora, 1998.

Thiselton, Anthony C. *The First Epistle to the Corinthians: A Commentary on the Greek Text*. Grand Rapids, MI: Eerdmans, 2000.

Thompson, J. A. *1, 2 Chronicles*. The New American Commentary, no. 9. Nashville, TN: Broadman & Holman, 1994.

Thompson, Marianne Maye. *The Promise of the Father: Jesus and God in the New Testament*. Louisville, KY: Westminster John Knox, 2000.

Tigay, J. H. "Israelite Religion: The Onomastic and Epigraphic Evidence." In *Ancient Israelite Religion: Essays in Honor of Frank Moore Cross*, ed. P. D. Miller et al., 157-194. Philadelphia, PA: Fortress, 1987.

Tilley, Maureen A. "Anti-Donatist Works." In *Augustine Through the Ages: An Encyclopedia*, ed. Allan D. Fitzgerald, 34-39. Grand Rapids, MI: Eerdmans, 1999.

Travis, Stephen. "Christ as the Bearer of Divine Judgment in Paul's Thought about the Atonement." In *Atonement Today*, ed. John Goldingay, 21-38. London: SPCK, 1995.

Torrance, Thomas F. *The Christian Doctrine of God: One Being, Three Persons*. Edinburgh, Scotland: T&T Clark, 1996.

van Bavel, Tarsicius J. "Discipline." In *Augustine Through the Ages: An Encyclopedia*, ed. Allan D. Fitzgerald, 274-5. Grand Rapids, MI: Eerdmans, 1999.

Van Ypren, Jim. *Making Peace: A Guide to Overcoming Church Discipline*. Chicago: Moody, 2002.

Vander Broek, Lyle. "Discipline and Community: Another Look at 1 Corinthians 5." *Reformed Review* 48 (1994): 5–13.

VanGemeren, Willem A. *"Abba* in the Old Testament?" *Journal of the Evangelical Theological Society* 31, no. 4 (1988): 385–98.

———. *Psalms.* In *The Expositor's Bible Commentary.* Vol. 5, ed. Frank E. Gaebelein, 2–880. Grand Rapids, MI: Zondervan, 1991.

————. "Offerings and Sacrifices in Bible Times." In *Evangelical Dictionary of Theology,* 2d ed., ed. Walter A. Elwell, 854–8. Grand Rapids, MI: Baker, 2001.

Vanhoozer, Kevin J. *Is There a Meaning in This Text?: The Bible, the Reader, and the Morality of Literary Knowledge.* Grand Rapids, MI: Zondervan, 1998.

————. "The Atonement and Postmodernity: Guilt, Goats, and Gifts." In *The Glory of the Atonement,* ed. Charles E. Hill and Frank A. James III, 367–404. Downers Grove, IL: InterVarsity, 2004.

Visser't Hooft, W. A. *The Fatherhood of God in an Age of Emancipation.* Geneva, Switzerland: World Council of Churches, 1982.

Volf, Miroslav. *Exclusions and Embrace: A Theological Exploration of Identity, Otherness, and Reconciliation.* Nashville, TN: Abingdon, 1996.

Warkentin, Marvin L. "Church Discipline in a Pluralistic Society." *Direction* 12, no. 2 (1983): 15–27.

Weaver, J. Denny. *Becoming Anabaptist: The Origin and Significance of Sixteenth Century Anabaptism.* Scottsdale, AZ: Herald, 1987.

———. *The Nonviolent Atonement.* Grand Rapids, MI: Eerdmans, 2001.

Welch, Claude. *Protestant Thought in the Nineteenth Century,* vol. 1. New Haven, CT: Yale University, 1972.

Wendel, François. *Calvin: Origins and Development of His Religious Thought.* Translated by Philip Mairet. Grand Rapids, MI: Baker, 1997.

Wenham, Gordon J. *Genesis 1–15.* Word Biblical Commentary, no. 1. Waco, TX: Word, 1987.

White, John, and Ken Blue. *Church Discipline That Heals: Putting Costly Love into Action.* Downers Grove, IL: InterVarsity, 1985.

———. *Healing the Wounded: The Costly Love of Church Discipline.* Downers Grove, IL: InterVarsity, 1985.

White, Robert. "Oil and Vinegar: Calvin on Church Discipline." *Scottish Journal of Theology* 38 (1986): 25–40.

Widdicombe, Peter. *The Fatherhood of God from Origen to Athanasius.* Oxford: Clarendon, 1994.

Williams, Robert R. *Schleiermacher the Theologian.* Philadelphia, PA: Fortress, 1978.

Williams, Tyler F. "פָּקַד." In *New International Dictionary of Old Testament Theology and Exegesis.* Vol. 3, ed. Willem A. VanGemeren, 657–63. Grand Rapids, MI: Zondervan, 1997.

Willis, Geoffrey Grimshaw. *Saint Augustine and the Donatist Controversy.* London: S.P.C.K., 1950.

Willoughby, William. *Counting the Cost: The Life of Alexander Mack, 1679–1735.* Elgin, IL: Brethren Press, 1979.

Wills, Garry. *Saint Augustine.* New York: Penguin, 1999.

Wilson, Gerald H. "בְּרִית." In *New International Dictionary of Old Testament Theology and Exegesis.* Vol. 1, ed. Willem A. VanGemeren, 655–657. Grand Rapids, MI: Zondervan, 1997.

Winter, Bruce. "The Lord's Supper at Corinth: An Alternative Reconstruction." *Reformed Theological Review* 37 (1978): 73–82.

Witherington, Ben III. *Conflict and Community in Corinth: A Socio-Rhetorical Commentary in 1 and 2 Corinthians*. Grand Rapids, MI: Eerdmans, 1995.

Witherington, Ben III, and Laura M. Rice. *The Shadow of the Almighty: Father, Son, and Holy Spirit in Biblical Perspective*. Grand Rapids, MI: Eerdmans, 2002.

Wright, Christopher J. H. *Knowing Jesus Through the Old Testament*. Downers Grove, IL: InterVarsity, 1992.

———. *Deuteronomy*. New International Biblical Commentary, ed. Robert L. Hubbard Jr. and Robert K. Johnston. Peabody, MA: Hendrickson, 1996.

———. "אָב." In *New International Dictionary of Old Testament Theology and Exegesis*. Vol. 1, ed. Willem A. VanGemeren, 219–23. Grand Rapids, MI: Zondervan, 1997.

Yoder, John Howard. *The Royal Priesthood: Essays Ecclesiological and Ecumenical*. Grand Rapids, MI: Eerdmans, 1994. Reprint, Scottsdale, PA: Herald, 1998.

Younger, K. Lawson. *Judges/Ruth*. The NIV Application Commentary. Grand Rapids, MI: Zondervan, 2002.